SUICIDAL EMPATHY

DYING TO BE KIND

Gad Saad

BROADSIDE BOOKS

HarperCollins books may be purchased for educational, business, or sales promotional use. For information, please email the Special Markets Department at SPsales@harpercollins.com.

Broadside Books™ and the Broadside logo are trademarks of HarperCollins Publishers.

hc.com

FIRST EDITION

Designed by Elina Cohen

Library of Congress Cataloging-in-Publication Data has been applied for.

ISBN 978-0-06-344653-3

Printed in the United States of America

26 27 28 29 30 LBC 5 4 3 2 1

To all those who enrich the world via
their adaptive and well-modulated empathy

To AASLLAN

Suicidal empathy is a tragic manifestation,
at the civilization level, of the well-known proverb
"The road to hell is paved with good intentions."

Gad Saad

CONTENTS

PREFACE

My 2020 book, *The Parasitic Mind: How Infectious Ideas Are Killing Common Sense*, explored what happens to human minds when they become zombified by ideological rapture. It largely addressed how human cognition (thinking) can misfire in ways that cause people to question whether men can menstruate or bear children; whether science is an enterprise of white supremacy; or whether objective truths do indeed exist. Humans, though, rely on both their cognitive as well as emotional systems when navigating the world. Hence, not only can our thought processes go awry but also our emotions and associated virtues can operate suboptimally in several possible ways.

Imagine for a moment that the West's intelligentsia, including its elitist progressive political class, is infected by a mind parasite that causes its empathy module to misfire in every conceivable manner. Many of the policy decisions that have wreaked havoc in the West stem from this poor calibration of empathy, resulting in a society that is galloping rapidly toward the abyss of infinite lunacy. Whether when dealing with immigration, the justice system, the homelessness crisis, or transgender rights in women's sports, outlandish policies are instituted precisely because of suicidal empathy. This results in a wide range of misguided "empathetic" inequalities, including:

The diversity, inclusion, and equity cult > meritocracy

The feelings of marginalized groups > the Truth

My truth > the Truth

Illegal migrants > legal citizens or American veterans

Criminals > victims

Squatters > homeowners

Homeless people > tax-paying park users

Drug addicts > children playing in parks (drug needles everywhere)

Transgender "women" > women

Twerking drag queens during kindergarten reading hour > children's innocence

Saving Mother Earth > having children

Foreign aid with no strings attached > expecting reciprocity

Noble Hamas terrorists > "genocidal" Zionist Israelis

Islam > all other religions

Socialism (the redistribution of wealth is a form of suicidal empathy) > capitalism

Feminist foreign policy (rooted in kindness and empathy) > muscular foreign policy

I begin with an overview of empathy and then lay out the theoretical and evolutionary mechanisms that correspond to its misfiring. I then delve into how the erecting of forbidden knowledge (e.g., race differences in criminality) and the rejection of reality (e.g., transwomen are women too) serve as forms of epistemological empathy. If the truth lacks empathy, reject it! The remainder of the book explores suicidal empathy across a broad range of cases at the domestic and foreign levels (as exemplified by the inequalities shown immediately above). I highlight how the disastrous open-door immigration policies of the West are rooted in a form of suicidal empathy, wherein it is presumed that all potential immigrants are equally likely to assimilate (and even more so if they are from Islamic societies). The West's lack of a cultural theory of mind is destroying our societies. In addition to being infinitely kind to poorly vetted migrants, suicidal empathy can cause people to care more about rapists and other felons than their victims. Viewed from this perspective, the criminals are the real victims of society. They are blank slate felons, born noble and perfect, only to be corrupted by our evil social order. I then posit that many dreadful policies are justified by the suicidally empathetic by invoking the *settled science* canard, as a means of ignoring the inherent trade-offs of such policies, for to otherwise do so is construed as morally repugnant taboos. I then argue that the elevating of the diversity, inclusion, and equity cult over the ethos of meritocracy is a means of exhibiting (misguided) empathy toward so-called marginalized groups, a form of selling indulgences to expatiate one's existential civilizational sins. I then demonstrate that communism, socialism, and the welfare and nanny states are rooted in various forms of suicidal empathy. I conclude by offering a vaccine of sorts to inoculate oneself from the existential threats of suicidal empathy.

In his classic 1995 book *The Vision of the Anointed: Self-Congratulation as a Basis for Social Policy*, Thomas Sowell explained how the intelligentsia espouse policies that make them feel virtuous in their unlimited compassion while being fully decoupled from the negative consequences of said policies, which in many instances are borne by those whom they are supposed to help (e.g., marginalized communities). What Sowell identified more than thirty years ago has been expanded to include the associated concepts of moral licensing, luxury beliefs, and performative allyship.[1] For example, the political class and the intellectual elites empathetically push for open borders, in part by wearing #RefugeesWelcome pins, while protected behind their safe and gated wealthy neighborhoods. This luxury belief grants them the moral license to be suicidally empathetic toward their society. By paying their due indulgences, the Anointed Ones can commit civilizational suicide assured that their moral preening will protect them. Suicidal empathy is the facilitatory lubricant for each of these phenomena, and is the equivalent of necrotizing fasciitis, the flesh-eating bacteria, albeit, in this case, the destructive pathogen constitutes a misfiring of the emotional system resulting in the self-eating of one's culture. Parasitic ideas linked to woke social justice ultimately flourish best when coupled with a narrative of empathy, as exemplified by the following quote: "Within feminist and antiracist theory the achievement of cross-cultural and transnational social justice has been linked in part with the development of empathy."[2] Suicidal empathy serves as a collective psychiatric diagnosis plaguing the West, and in doing so unleashes the Rumpelstiltskin effect, namely the therapeutic benefits of having a named clinical diagnosis for this societal malady.[3]

Many phenomena spread across human populations in a manner akin to a contagion. The political scientist James Fowler and the physician-sociologist Nicholas Christakis have conducted several network studies to demonstrate this precise point.[4] They have shown in separate studies that obesity and happiness spread in a manner akin to a contagion within large-scale networks.[5] If your friends and their friends are thin and happy, you are more likely to be so as well. Beware of whom you choose as a friend! Many other phenomena spread as contagions within social networks, including fashionable psychiatric disorders such as the multiple personality disorder craze of the 1960s and 1970s, the repressed memory epidemic of the 1990s, and more recently, the transgender "epidemic." Epidemic hysteria, which includes mass psychogenic illness (e.g., the Tanganyika laughter epidemic), and mass delusions and collective moral panics (e.g., the Salem witch hunt) have been documented across cultures and time periods, and they, too, spread akin to an infection across a population.[6] I posit that suicidal empathy also spreads akin to an emotional contagion throughout an entire society, and its effects are long-lasting. It need not take an excessively long time for a parasitic idea or poorly calibrated emotion or virtue to wreak havoc on a society. Recall the speed at which critical race theory; diversity, inclusion, and equity initiatives; and transgender activism took over. Their spread was akin to a profoundly infectious contagion or a fast-spreading wildfire. Suicidal empathy is a deadly contagion of one of our most noble virtues. If not properly contained, it will destroy the West.

SUICIDAL
EMPATHY

1

A Good Virtue Gone Bad

. . . the new view of human nature that is emerging in the natural and social sciences and in the humanities, with the discovery of Homo empathicus . . . The Age of Reason is being eclipsed by the Age of Empathy. The most important question facing humanity is this: Can we reach global empathy in time to avoid the collapse of civilization and save the Earth.[1]

Empathy is a noble and evolutionarily selected virtue, a central feature of our humanity given that we are a deeply social species.[2] We are drawn to empathetic people. When asked about the traits that they prefer in their mate, both sexes agree that kindness and intelligence are essential qualities.[3] Kindness is correlated to empathy.[4] All other things equal, most of us prefer to be involved with people who exhibit kindness and, by extension, empathy. The level of satisfaction within a romantic relationship is correlated to dyadic empathy (between the two partners) and the self-perceived congruity of dyadic empathy between the two partners.[5] This is in line with the "Birds of a feather stick together" maxim that I discussed in *The Saad Truth about Happiness*, namely the success of a long-term union depends on the congruity of the two partners across key metrics, including their respective empathy scores. The importance of empathy manifests itself across other key personal relationships, including in forming cross-sex friendships, albeit empathy matters more to teenage girls than it does to their male counterparts.[6] Furthermore, empathetic people have a larger network of friends; namely, your popularity is in part determined by how empathetic you are.[7]

Empathy is crucially important in domains beyond mate choice and friendships. Take, for example, the decision of how to choose a mental health therapist. Not surprisingly, the success of therapy is positively correlated to a therapist's empathy.[8] Perhaps the most obvious therapeutic context where empathy is needed and yet so often sorely lacking is in the physician-patient relationship. Physician empathy yields a wide range of improved healthcare outcomes, including a reduction in malpractice suits.[9] The importance of empathy is perhaps best captured within the field of veterinary medicine, where veterinarians are expected to exhibit empathy to their animal patients as well as their human family members.[10]

While most people understand the meaning of empathy and how it relates to compassion and sympathy, the academic literature draws some fine distinctions that are unnecessary for our current treatment.[11] As such, these terms can be construed here as roughly interchangeable. Empathy itself has up to forty-three distinct definitions within the academic literature and is often separated into a cognitive and affective component (e.g., understanding another person's emotional state versus experiencing it; I get your pain versus I feel your pain).[12] An individual's level of empathy is measurable, and it correlates to several personality traits, including agreeableness and conscientiousness.[13] A recent meta-analysis found that empathy is in part heritable, albeit emotional empathy was more heritable than cognitive empathy (48.3 percent versus 26.9 percent of the variance explained is due to genetic factors).[14] This implies that the ability to empathize can be developed, using a wide range of creative tools, including via the use of art, movies, and literature.[15] Professional schools recognize the importance of empathy and accordingly seek to educate their graduates on its value, including in medicine, law, education, and business.[16]

While the capacity for empathy is a human universal, there are features of empathy that are culturally inscribed.[17] Individuals stemming from collectivist societies tend to score higher on empathy than their counterparts from individualistic ones. Incredibly, a person's level of empathy is correlated to their likelihood of exhibiting contagious yawning. To the extent that contagious yawning constitutes a form of mirroring, people who are more empathetic are more likely to exhibit this physiological contagion.[18] Additionally, contagious yawning is more likely to occur between close individuals (e.g., kin or close friends versus strangers), and the yawn contagion has even been documented between humans and dogs, suggesting that our canine companions, also a social species, exhibit the aptitude for empathy.[19]

Are there any contexts where being empathetic does not pay? Well, the fact that individuals with greater empathy are more likely to choose lower-paying helping professions might explain the negative correlation between the salaries of recent university graduates and their empathy scores.[20] All things considered, nurses are more likely to be empathetic than hedge fund managers and regrettably are typically paid much smaller salaries. Of interest, business school students ranked empathy as the least important quality that a leader should possess.[21] In many business settings, too great a focus on empathy can become problematic.[22] This should not be taken to mean that empathy has no place in business. In *The Saad Truth about Happiness*, I argued that a key universal law of maximal flourishing is the "everything in moderation" maxim, which Aristotle made famous in his *Nicomachean Ethics* treatise. I demonstrate that the inverted-U curve, namely that too little or too much of something is often much worse than some middle sweet spot, applies across innumerable human contexts. For example, the relationship between empathy and creativity follows an inverted-U, as does that of chief executive officers' empathy scores and their abilities to lead through organizational turbulence.[23] Our emotional system is thus calibrated according to this universal law. If you are insufficiently empathetic, you might be a callous psychopath. But if you are indiscriminately hyper-empathetic across all possible targets, this can stunt your ability to navigate through the trials and tribulations of life.

Empathy-Related Disorders

Empathy is associated with a wide range of other-oriented behaviors, ranging from the positive (e.g., altruism) to the negative (e.g., aggression).[24] Not surprisingly, criminality is linked to a lack of empathy. A meta-analysis of thirty-eight studies found that offenders score lower than nonoffenders on empathy.[25] Interestingly, psychopathic offenders are able to fake a sense of empathy (e.g., exhibiting remorse during a parole hearing).[26] Dr. Park Dietz is one of the foremost forensic psychiatrists in the United States who first came to prominence over forty years ago when he testified at the trial of John Hinckley Jr., the individual who sought to assassinate President Reagan to impress the actress Jodie Foster. Dietz was subsequently involved with numerous other high-profile cases of murderers and serial killers, including Richard Kuklinski, aka the Iceman. Kuklinski was serving a multiple-life sentence in a New Jersey prison when he agreed to be interviewed by Dietz. The chilling exchange exemplifies the lack of empathy and remorse that is typical of an actual psychopath. Dietz asked Kuklinski whether he had ever harmed animals in his youth. Kuklinski proceeded to explain how he tortured animals, to which Dietz asked him how this made him feel. Kuklinski did not seem to understand Dietz's question, and he explained that he did not feel anything. This caused Dietz to slowly explain to Kuklinski that for most people, such a description of animal torture would trigger a deeply aversive reaction.

The Silence of the Lambs stars Jodie Foster as an FBI agent in training who solicits the help of an imprisoned psychiatrist and serial killer Dr. Hannibal Lecter (played by Anthony Hopkins) to track Buffalo Bill (played by Ted Levine), another serial killer on the loose. In one of many memorable scenes, Buffalo Bill kidnaps a woman by pretending that he is disabled, due to an arm cast, and hence requires help to lift a sofa into his van. He does so by triggering the prospective victim's empathy, even though her survival instinct was alerting her that something was off. The real serial killer Ted Bundy used this empathy ruse to lure women into his car; psychopaths understand they can use a misfiring of the empathy module to their advantage. Hence, rather than "to kill with kindness," sadistic psychopaths "kill through kindness." They use our natural proclivity to be empathetic to their advantage. The Danish anthropologists Nils Bubandt and Rane Willerslev recognize that empathy has a darker and more sinister side: "The dominant trend in the academic study of empathy across the disciplines has been, and remains, to see it not only as a human capacity, but also as a human virtue. As a result, it has been conceptualized as a universal good associated with care, altruism, and social bonding; the antithesis of deceit, aggression, and conflict. But this assumption leaves unquestioned those instances of social life where empathy is entangled with or even the basis for deception and violence."[27] Incidentally, humans are not the sole species to be lured into dangerous situations via an appeal to their empathy. When protecting an injured member of their pod, sperm whales adopt a defensive Marguerite formation, which makes it easier for whale hunters to kill off the entire pod. The whales' empathy is used against them.[28]

While most people typically associate empathy-related disorders with a lack of empathy (e.g., psychopathy), there are numerous psychiatric disorders that involve hyper-empathy.[29] Our empathy system can effectively misfire in several ways. Since humans are endowed with both cognitive and emotional empathy (in line with the fact that we are a thinking and feeling species), things can go awry in four possible ways. An individual might possess: (1) high cognitive but low emotional empathy, (2) low cognitive but high emotional empathy, (3) low cognitive and low emotional empathy, (4) high cognitive and high emotional empathy.[30] Each of these four options is hypothesized to map onto specific disorders (e.g., option 1 is evident in autism, whereas option 4 occurs with sufferers of Williams syndrome). That said, the empathy system could be hijacked in suboptimal ways without necessarily being concomitant with a diagnosed psychological disorder. Take, for example, compassion fatigue, which afflicts many people who work in the helping professions (e.g., nurses and physicians).[31] In such instances, notwithstanding that an individual might have an empathetic disposition, their compassion tank hits the empty gauge, metaphorically speaking. When it is an inherent feature of your profession to be empathetic and compassionate, you might end up facing an emotional burnout. This can often happen to people who suffer from "helper syndrome," a term that was introduced in 1977 by German psychoanalyst Wolfgang Schmidbauer,[32] and even more so to those who might be classified as being super-helpers.[33] A related concept within the psychological literature is the savior (messianic) complex, wherein an individual feels compelled to help/save others.

Several books have recently warned about the dangers of empathy and associated phenomena. In *Against Empathy: The Case for Rational Compassion*, Paul Bloom argues that empathy can lead us astray when it comes to making moral decisions.[34] While he recognizes the importance of our emotions in making us human, he warns against the misapplication of empathy in domains best served by a rational cognitive calculus. A behavioral outcome of empathy is the human capacity to be altruistic toward others. But this noble reflex can itself behaviorally misfire, as Barbara Oakley and her coeditors highlight in *Pathological Altruism*.[35] In *The Dark Sides of Empathy*, Fritz Breithaupt posits that there are ugly manifestations of this otherwise noble virtue, including empathetic sadism and vampiristic empathy (e.g., helicopter parenting).[36] In other words, empathy could misfire in ways that yield negative outcomes to the target of the dysregulated empathy. Empathy can also be gamed by taking advantage of Christian doctrines that promote compassion and kindness, a phenomenon that Allie Beth Stuckey refers to as "toxic empathy."[37] Even Buddhists recognize that this laudable virtue can misfire, as evidenced by master Tibetan Buddhist Trungpa Rinpoche's "idiot compassion."[38] Suicidal empathy, though, is a uniquely distinct phenomenon to which I turn next.

Suicidal Empathy

Prior to delving into the mechanisms and causes of suicidal empathy, I offer a brief cross-cultural and historical perspective of various forms of suicide. Two of the most difficult questions to address from an evolutionary perspective are suicide and homosexuality. Whereas the latter denies a person's capacity to reproduce, the former is contrary to our most fundamental instinct: survival. And yet, scholars have offered evolutionary explanations for each of these two phenomena.[39] The Jewish historian Josephus recounts how nearly a thousand Jewish men, women, and children, fleeing the Romans nearly two thousand years ago, took a last stand at the Masada fortress (overlooking the Dead Sea) but decided to commit a mass suicide rather than fall captive to their pursuers.[40] Notwithstanding the challenge to this account by recent scholars, Masada remains an important story within Jewish lore because it captures the resilient spirit of Jews even when facing imminent doom. The practices of Jauhar and Saka are two elements of a ritual of mass suicide that Hindus in Rajput would engage in when it was clear that they were facing an imminent military conquest at the hands of Islamic armies. The women and children would kill themselves via self-immolation (in part, in order to avoid a life of sexual slavery), whereas the men would subsequently walk toward the enemy expecting to be assuredly killed, albeit with their honor intact.[41] These two practices were meant to precisely avoid what recently happened to the Yazidi at the hands of ISIS fighters, wherein the men and elderly women were summarily killed off while the younger women and children were taken as sexual slaves.[42] The archaeological site of Chichén Itzá in the Yucatan Peninsula (Mexico) was the location of a violent Mesoamerican ball game, wherein the winning players had the honor of being sacrificed to the gods. Notwithstanding the controversy as to whether the sacrificial player(s) was chosen from the winning or losing team, the bottom line is that someone's head was coming off![43] In any case, there is an argument to be made that the links between suicide and human sacrifice are evolutionarily linked.[44]

In some honor cultures where the reputational and existential costs of being shamed are catastrophic, one can redeem their honor and dignity via suicide. Take, for example, the practice of seppuku, suicide by disembowelment, practiced by the samurai, the Japanese warrior class. In his 1899 book *Bushido: The Soul of Japan*, Inazō Nitobe offers the following explanation of this gruesome act: "Now my readers will understand that *seppuku* was not a mere suicidal process. It was an institution, legal and ceremonial. An invention of the middle ages, it was a process by which warriors could expiate their crimes, apologize for errors, escape from disgrace, redeem their friends, or prove their sincerity."[45] Two other culture-specific suicides, albeit carried out in the pursuit of military and/or political gain, are Islamic suicide terrorism and Japanese kamikaze pilots during World War II. Both of these forms of suicide can be understood via the evolutionary lens.[46] Suicide in this context could be construed as the activation of evolutionary-based forms of altruism. Furthermore, some of the reaped rewards are rooted in Darwinian impulses: "Commit Jihad and have all of your desires met, including access to seventy-two beautiful virgins, in the afterlife."

In other cases, collective suicides take place within smaller cult groups. In 1997, thirty-nine members of Heaven's Gate committed mass suicide. They believed that they could ascend to eternal life by "leaving" Earth. In this sense, by committing suicide, one is not dying but rather ensuring that they will be immortal in some higher plane. The Peoples Temple headed by Jim Jones (Jonestown) met their demise in Guyana in 1978 when more than nine hundred of its members died in a murder-suicide pact. Jones referred to the looming tragedy as a "revolutionary suicide." The collective suicide served as an honest signal of the group's commitment to their belief system. Smaller suicide pacts have also been studied, albeit they constitute around 1 percent of all suicides.[47] One of the most famous of all Shakespearean plays is *Romeo and Juliet*, wherein both young lovers end up committing suicide. Of note, "The word *shinju* in Japanese originally meant a mutual suicide agreement by lovers in order to prove the genuineness of their love to each other."[48] This motif of ultimate devotion is captured by the sentence "I would die for you," which is depicted in countless songs, including Prince's "I Would Die 4 U" and the Weeknd's "Die for You." Finally, and notwithstanding the position of the Catholic Church that suicide is an unforgivable sin against God, many theologians have debated whether Jesus committed suicide as a form of "death by cop" as an ultimate expression of His love for mankind.[49]

To recap, while individual and group suicides have been documented across cultures and eras for many reasons, there is something unique about the West's feverish desire to commit collective suicide by misguided empathy. Interestingly, in his mammoth twelve-volume *A Study of History*, the British historian Arnold J. Toynbee explained why civilizations die. This has since been summarized by the following maxim:

"Civilizations die from suicide, not by murder."[50] The general argument is that societies decay because of the self-inflicted failures of their elites in a myriad of ways.[51] The American philosopher James Burnham echoed that sentiment in his 1964 book *Suicide of the West,* wherein he proclaimed: "It may be added that suicide is probably more frequent than murder as the end phase of a civilization" and added that "[L]iberalism is the ideology of Western suicide."[52] I posit that in the current zeitgeist, the collective suicide of the West is occurring via the orgiastic misfiring of one of our most noble virtues, empathy, which of course is deeply anchored within the ethos of progressive liberals.

Empathy misfires akin to how a wide range of human emotions can also malfunction. Take, for example, anger. It can be a useful emotion when deployed at the right moment and in the right amount. If someone attacks you in an alley, you will experience an autonomic affective response, including fear and anger, which will permit you to mount an appropriate defensive behavioral pattern. However, if you become insanely angry in otherwise innocuous situations, you might need to enroll in an anger management class. A key precept of Stoicism is that oftentimes what harms us is not an actual event but the adverse reaction to said event. Hence, the Stoics would propose that when facing a situation that might trigger our ire, remain calm and composed. I recently held a chat with Donald J. Robertson on his podcast, in which we discussed the difference between how the Stoics viewed anger and how anger might be analyzed from an evolutionary lens.[53] I disagreed with the view that anger is a useless and irrational emotion, or, as the ancient Roman Stoic Seneca referred to it, a "temporary madness." Anger is clearly within our emotional repertoire, and it can lead to one of the seven deadly sins if it is poorly regulated (wrath). That said, it cannot be true that humans have somehow outgrown their need ever to be angry, as this would be akin to positing that anger is a vestigial emotion. Vestigial traits or behaviors are those that were once selected by evolution but no longer confer any adaptive benefits (e.g., wisdom teeth).[54] Clearly though, the potential for anger has many functional and adaptive purposes. One of the main reasons that person A does not attack person B to steal their coveted resources is the recognition that such an attack might be met with anger-fueled retalia-tory violence. A society wherein all its members adhere to deontological pacifism (an inviolable absolute principle) would quickly be overrun by other tribes that do not share this penchant for kumbaya. It is rather triv-ial to demonstrate the game theoretic outcomes of such an interaction. Absolute pacifists will always be victimized. Hence, human aggression, anger, physical formidability, revenge (and forgiveness) all possess clear adaptive benefits.[55] Deontological pacifists suffer from suicidal empathy in that they shut off adaptive mechanisms meant to ensure their survival, in the service of a maladaptive worldview.

To reiterate, emotions exist because they help us solve evolutionarily important problems.[56] This holds true whether we are dealing with pos-itive emotions (empathy, kindness, contentment, love) or negative ones (anger, disgust, guilt, envy). That said, our emotional system can go awry in several ways, resulting in suboptimal outcomes, be it at the individual or societal levels. First, our emotions can lead us astray when they are deployed in contexts when it would serve us best to invoke our reason-ing faculty. Humans have evolved cognitive and emotional systems to address key challenges that arose in our ancestral past. As I explain in *The Parasitic Mind*, the feeling-versus-thinking dichotomy is a false one. The problem arises when we invoke the wrong system in a particular situa-tion. When voting for a political candidate, people end up being largely driven by their emotions ("Donald Trump disgusts me") rather than by a coherent set of cognitive justifications ("I disagree with Donald Trump's immigration and fiscal policies for reasons X, Y, and Z"). Kamala Harris's 2024 campaign strategy was to precisely invoke people's affective system (joy and fun) rather than their cognitive one, knowing full well that she did not stack well on substantive matters. The electorate did not fall prey to the affective ruse, leading to a decisive victory for Donald Trump. Suicidal empathy is a manifestation of such a systems failure whereby a noble virtue is hijacked and used to make policy decisions that are best tackled via a sober analysis rooted in our reasoning faculty.

Emotional dysregulation is a feature of many psychiatric disorders. Too much anxiety and sadness can lead to a clinical bout of depression.

Emotional dysregulation, though, is not solely reserved for the hyperactivation of negative emotions (sadness, anger, anxiety). It can also stem from the dysregulation of positive emotions. Laughter is medically therapeutic, as I briefly explained in *The Saad Truth about Happiness*. It is wonderful to adopt a playful mindset in life. But there are times when laughter is activated in wrong situations and in the wrong amounts. Emotional incontinence (pseudobulbar affect) is one such disorder where patients can laugh hysterically in profoundly inappropriate manners. If you have seen *The Joker* starring Joaquin Phoenix, you know exactly what I am referring to. There are several haunting scenes where his character laughs uncontrollably, the condition ostensibly arising from the severe childhood abuse that he had suffered. Of course, inappropriate laughter is not restricted to infamous villains in the movies. The cackler Kamala Harris can go toe-to-toe with the Joker when it comes to cringey laughter.

Suicidal empathy is a manifestation of a similar dysregulation of an otherwise noble virtue. More specifically, it is maladaptively hyperactive. There are many instances of such a misfiring, namely an adaptive process becomes hyperactive. Take, for example, obsessive-compulsive disorder (OCD), which is often rooted in a targeted fear. It makes perfect evolutionary sense that humans have evolved an assiduous scanning of environmental threats (e.g., washing our hands to avoid germ contamination; checking that the front door is locked).[57] The problem with OCD is that the checking is stuck in an infinite loop. Hence, rather than washing one's hands once and moving on with the day, an OCD sufferer will spend several hours washing their hands in scalding-hot water. An adaptive process (checking for threats) becomes maladaptive when it misfires. I used this argument in *The Evolutionary Bases of Consumption* and *The Consuming Instinct* to explain dark side consumption (e.g., pathological gambling, pornography addiction, compulsive buying, eating disorders). For example, women constitute the great majority of compulsive buyers, albeit their product hoarding largely occurs within the beautification domain. An adaptive process (beautifying oneself) becomes hyperactive, leading to many downstream negative consequences (financial ruin, divorce).

The misfiring of an otherwise adaptive emotional response is a common feature of the human condition. Take, for example, crying along with the production of tears. As far back as Charles Darwin in his 1872 book, *The Expression of Emotions in Man and Animals*, scientists have explored the evolutionary roots of this response, its equivalent counterpart in other animals, along with its universality notwithstanding culture-specific norms regarding its expression.[58] Generally speaking, crying serves as an honest signal of distress that activates parental or social support from the receiver of the signal (e.g., parent tending to an infant, offering succor to one's best friend post a romantic heartbreak). Crying is such an important feature of the human condition that there are countless idioms that reference it, including "cry me a river," "for crying out loud," "a voice crying in the wilderness," and "it's a crying shame." Two idioms, though, refer to how people engage in either fake crying ("crocodile tears") or hyperactive alarmism ("cry wolf"). In a classic *Seinfeld* episode titled "The Understudy" (season 6, episode 24), Jerry is annoyed by his girlfriend who has a habit of easily crying for minor issues that should otherwise not trigger such a response. He is forced to repeatedly console her. In other words, even an otherwise honest signal of our emotional state (happy or sad) can be coopted deceptively or in a dysregulated manner. The same occurs with suicidal empathy.

The insight that humans can laugh or cry in inappropriate ways also applies to our empathy impulse. In the summer of 2016, my family and I were in Newport Beach lounging at one of our favorite beaches. I taught our children early in life the importance of the "Leave the world better than you found it" maxim, as applied to cleaning up beach litter.[59] As we settled into the warm sand, I noticed a woman sitting at the beach with a plastic container filled with cupcakes. The local birds descended on the woman, hoping to pick up some rather unhealthy morsels of these sugary treats. To my abject horror, as the woman got up to leave, I saw that she left the plastic container and its contents on the beach. As beachgoers walk away from the beach, there are numerous garbage cans available to throw away one's trash. I politely engaged the woman about her abhorrent behavior, to which she retorted by denigrating my then five-year-old son (for having long hair, and apparently this makes him a girl) and insulting me (for being overweight at the time). After a moment of frozen astonishment, I responded by calling her a "human pig," which frankly is offensive to pigs.[60]

After that incident but during that same trip, I had lunch with two colleagues who were keen on hiring me for a professorship at a Southern California university. One of my hosts explained that she had recently watched the clip in question and was very concerned by my use of the term "human pig." This university, which had tried on two previous occasions to hire me and yet had repeatedly strung me along, was not focusing on my academic dossier or the fact that the human pig had been less than empathetic toward Mother Earth. The colleague was not concerned that the human pig had insulted a five-year-old boy or that she had fat-shamed me. Her empathy alarm bell was activated solely by my use of the "mean" appellation. This reminds me of my university dean who unfollowed me on then Twitter because, as she explained to me, I use very "nasty" words such as "imbecile" when interacting with someone who has otherwise been insulting me for days on end.

Another means by which our emotional system might misfire is when it is deployed on the wrong target. We have evolved the ability to judiciously discriminate between people in terms of how much emotional investment we grant these. A good person might wish for all children to live safe and fulfilled lives, and yet they are clearly more concerned about their own biological children than those of a stranger. Even among our kin, we tend to love our children more than we do our first cousins, as the former are genetically closer to us than the latter. Now imagine if our emotional system were to misfire such that we wrongly discriminate across targets in ways that are inconsistent with reason and biology. We end up with a situation such as that exhibited by Karsten Nordal Hauken, a Norwegian man who was raped by a Somali immigrant. When the Norwegian judicial system decided that the rapist was to be deported back to Somalia, Hauken was wracked with guilt and worry that his rapist might lead a difficult life in his homeland.[61] Human beings have not evolved to exhibit such "virtuous" empathy toward one's rapist, as further discussed in chapter four.

The ability to recognize clear demarcations between kin and nonkin, friends and foes, and in-group and out-group members is a fundamental feature of our innate coalitional psychology. The us-versus-them mindset manifests itself in innumerable settings, be it when deciding how much to spend on a gift for someone, or in extraordinarily darker contexts such as genocide. It is no surprise that a common feature of large-scale collective brutality requires the dehumanization of those you wish to eradicate.[62] I have seen this firsthand in the dehumanizing names that I have been called by a large swath of Jew-haters since the October 7 massacre of more than twelve hundred innocent people in Israel. Apparently, I am a parasite, a rat, a genocidal baby killer, and Satan, among many other insults. A milder form of this in-group-out-group dynamic applies to empathy. We do not mete out our sympathy, compassion, and empathy equally to all. This is why parents are more likely to jump in front of a bus to save their biological children than some random stranger. We have evolved the cognitive, emotional, and behavioral systems to discriminate between people. Our empathy does not apply to all people equally.[63] This in-group favoritism applies to our willingness to cooperate with others or how we respond to the pain of others.[64] Suicidal empathy eradicates this evolutionary-based calculus.

Randy Nesse is a pioneer in the field of evolutionary medicine. Physicians are trained to understand the proximate causes of diseases, whereas there are unique insights that can be gleaned from appreciating the ultimate (Darwinian) mechanisms that yielded the unique designs of our bodies.[65] A woman experiencing severe pregnancy sickness symptoms might obtain a prescription from her gynecologist to quell the discomfort, but from an evolutionary perspective, these symptoms protect the fetus from exposure to foodborne pathogens during organogenesis.[66] A subdiscipline within evolutionary medicine is the field of Darwinian psychiatry, which incorporates the evolutionary lens in treating mental health conditions.[67] Viewed from this perspective, many psychological ailments are a misfiring of otherwise adaptive processes (as explained earlier). Nesse has argued that many negative emotions are ultimately rooted in an evolutionary calculus. On occasions, it pays off to be sad or anxious. The problem though arises when the emotional system misfires. He states, "Excesses and deficiencies are only the most obvious kinds of emotional abnormalities. Responses can also be too quick, too slow, too enduring, or in response to the wrong cues." He offers the following six means by which our emotional system might falter:

1. Baseline is too low.
2. Baseline is too high.
3. Response is deficient.
4. Response is excessive.
5. Response is aroused by inappropriate cues.
6. Response is independent of cues.[68]

While Nesse is arguing that there are good reasons for bad feelings, in this book, I am positing that there are bad reasons for good feelings. But to Nesse's six-item list, suicidal empathy is a manifestation of items 2, 4, and 5 (too high, too excessive, and the response is at times to inappropriate cues, in this case empathy focuses on the wrong targets).

Given that empathy has deep evolutionary roots and since we are a sexually dimorphic species, should we expect any sex differences in terms of our capacity to be empathetic, let alone suicidally empathetic? Sex differences in empathy have indeed been documented across the lifespan and across cultural settings.[69] Specifically, women/girls tend to be more empathetic than men/boys, and this is due both to cultural as well as biological forces, highlighting the fact that patterns of socialization are congruent with biological imperatives. To the extent that the parasitic ideas that define wokeism are driven by misguided empathy, one would expect that women are much more likely to succumb to such emotional and ideological capture. This is precisely what the research has found, namely women are much more likely to support woke ideas, including the censorship of free speech in the service of supposed empathetic harm reduction, emotional safety, kindness, and inclusivity (among many other forms of wokeism and social justice activism).[70] In other words, women are more likely than men to violate the deontological principles that define academic freedom, freedom of speech, and the pursuit and defense of truth, in the service of a consequentialist ethos rooted in misguided empathy. The rapid feminization of academia has been astonishing to watch.[71] I have recently attended departmental meetings where it was unclear to me that it was not a kindergarten classroom in terms of the incessant focus on emotional safety and empathetic understanding. Of note, the Social Empathy Index scale, which was developed by three women, contains items firmly rooted within an ethos of empathetic woke social justice (e.g., "I think the government needs to be a part of leveling the playing field for people from different racial groups").[72]

Pathways to Suicidal Empathy—Nature versus Nurture and Internal versus External Locus of Control

The nature versus nurture debate has been a defining one across the social sciences. Most social scientists adhere to the social constructivist view, namely that most human phenomena are largely shaped by nurture. Of course, they seldom if ever attribute a biological genesis to such socialization forces, as they suffer from biophobia (the fear of using biology to explain human behavior). Why do men prefer women who possess the hourglass figure? They must have learned it by watching videos of Beyoncé. Why do women prefer high-status men? They must have learned of this preference by reading romance novels. The supposed experts never question at the outset what drives the commercial success of such products. The reality is that cultural products exist in these universal forms because they cater to biological imperatives.[73] How does the nature-nurture debate lead to suicidal empathy? Most progressive and liberal professors reject evolutionary psychology for a broad range of reasons, and they prefer to subscribe to the tabula rasa view of the human mind. Viewed from this perspective, criminals are never born but always made. In other words, since all humans are born with equal potentiality, it is solely the environment that shapes people's future life trajectories.

Psychologist Julian B. Rotter developed arguably one of the most important concepts of how people attribute causality in their lives.[74] Rotter's internal-versus-external locus of control scale captures the extent to which an individual believes that things happen in a person's life due to their own doing or due to external forces. Did you fail to get admitted to your preferred Ivy League school because of the shortcomings of your academic dossier or was it due to "systemic racism"? The former is an internal attribution whereas the latter is an external one. Progressive people prefer to attribute all failures to external forces rooted in the evils of the West. Viewed from this lens, Kamala Harris lost the 2024 presidential election in a humiliating manner not because she was a lobotomized cackler but because Americans are sexist and racist, albeit they were insufficiently racist when they elected Barack Obama twice to office. The internal-versus-external locus of control issue is relevant in innumerable settings. How do people become wealthy? What causes homelessness? What drives people into a life of criminality? The reader hopefully sees how the nature-nurture debate can be reframed within the context of Rotter's dichotomy. Nature is an internal attribution, whereas nurture is an external one. Hence, if you are poor or rich, living in a mansion or homeless, or a law-abiding citizen or a criminal, it is the vagaries of the environment that led to these outcomes. You can begin to see how suicidal empathy can form if all life outcomes are due to external forces. Why close the borders to El Salvadoran gang members? They did not choose to be born in Central America. Why punish criminals when it is society that led them to a life of crime? Why protect the rights of homeowners from the squatters who have taken over their homes? The squatters did not choose to become homeless. How about showing illegal migrants, criminals, and homeless people their due empathy? A 2019 Cato Institute report provides empirical support for these causal attributions. It concludes that "[l]iberals and conservatives emphasize the impact of personal agency on outcomes differently. Conservatives are more likely to believe that people are responsible for their situations and use their agency to direct their lives, and liberals are more likely to believe that people's situations are shaped by their environment and other external factors. These differences in perception and emphasis likely lead liberals and conservatives to reach different conclusions about how public policy should approach poverty, welfare, work, and wealth."[75]

The self-serving bias is a well-known psychological phenomenon that explains how people attribute successes and failures in their lives.[76] For most people, successes are attributed internally (e.g., my new venture has been a smashing success because I am a talented entrepreneur), whereas failures are attributed externally (e.g., my new venture failed because customers are too dumb to understand my vision). Given the challenges that life throws at us, one could argue that this rose-colored prism serves a valuable ego-protective function, but of course it also leads to an inability to learn from one's mistakes. If every one of my business endeavors fails, and I always find an external cause to blame, I will never exhibit the necessary introspection to learn from my errors. The reader will note that Democrats are violating the self-serving bias in a most peculiar manner. They attribute the failures of others, especially those of so-called marginalized groups, to their own societal doings, and as such they seek to remedy these "injustices" via policies rooted in suicidal empathy.

Narcissism and Existential Guilt Drive Suicidal Empathy

In Greek mythology, Narcissus represents the ultimate form of self-absorption. He is so enamored with his own beauty that he dies transfixed by his reflected image in a pool of water. The dangers of excessive self-love are also captured by the seven deadly sins, of which pride is the apex transgression from which all others flow. Now imagine that instead of admiring your own reflection as did Narcissus, you come up with the ultimate form of narcissistic moral grandstanding: You will be the epitome of kindness, compassion, sympathy, and empathy. As you admire yourself in the "mirror of progressive moral purity and piety," you see the reflection of the best of human beings: You never judge others; you never criticize other religions; you are welcoming to all illegal immigrants; you realize that Islamophobia is the real scourge; you fight for the rights of criminals as they deserve a second chance (ergo seventy-fifth chance); you cry every time that you fill up your car with gas (the juice extracted from the rape of Mother Earth); you march for Free Palestine and note that Hamas terrorists were engaging in a noble defense of their human rights. You are a good person. Keep stroking your hair as you admire your moral purity. While I am hardly a fan of Freudian psychoanalysis, one can perhaps apply his death drive here, which includes the two stages of sadomasochism and suicidal ideation.[77] Rather than the impulse for destruction to be directed outward, what could be more "pleasurable" than to destroy one's own society? Turn the destruction inward and commit "Civilizational Seppuku." The political scientist William Voegeli argues that so-called liberal compassion is nothing short of "pious preening," as instantiated by "empathy crusaders."[78] He is spot-on.

Suicidal empathy is driven by misplaced existential guilt, not unlike how survivors of a plane crash might suffer from survivor guilt. The suicidally empathetic person feels guilty that they were born in the West, whereas others were not as fortunate. They feel guilty that they were born with white skin and hence they suffer from "Dermatological Original Sin." By committing Civilizational Seppuku, they can demonstrate their noble virtues as a form of pious self-hatred. By recognizing their supposed existential privilege and thus destroying it from within, they can seek penance for their "unearned" advantages. Confessing to one's privilege guilt has become a common reflex among Western intelligentsia.[79] I also believe that suicidal empathy is in part shaped by what I call "collective impostor syndrome." At the individual level, impostor syndrome is a gnawing feeling that some successful people experience, namely that they are somehow not deserving of their accolades and as such they are fake impostors.[80] Well, imagine if this ruminative self-defeating pattern were to spread to the societal level. The West suffers from this collective malady, namely it has become a definitional "truth" that this civilization has achieved its greatness in a fraudulent manner (e.g., colonialism and slavery), which can only be remedied via suicidal empathy.

Is suicidal empathy linked to Stockholm syndrome, which describes a favorable affiliation that a captive person feels toward their kidnappers?[81]

This is very different from suicidal empathy in several ways. First, to exhibit sympathy and empathy toward one's captor can on many occasions be an effective survival strategy.[82] A serial sexual predator might refrain from killing his victim if he views her as an actual human being rather than a sexual object to eventually be discarded. Second, even if the positive feelings toward one's kidnappers are genuine, the outcome is likely to protect the victim from possible harm. Suicidal empathy is the proactive will to be victimized for a supposed higher noble goal. Psychiatrist and historian Kenneth Levin has offered another "Scandinavian" disorder, which he coined the Oslo syndrome.[83] It refers to the wishful thinking of Israel during the 1992 Oslo Accords, wherein it was wrongly perceived that if they were to acquiesce a bit more, perhaps the Palestinians would agree to coexist peacefully. On a related note, Yahya Sinwar, the Hamas leader and mastermind of the October 7 massacre, was serving a life sentence in an Israeli prison when he was diagnosed with a brain tumor.[84] Staying true to the Hippocratic oath, which applies to one's avowed enemies as well, an Israeli surgeon saved Sinwar's life by performing the necessary surgery. In 2011, as part of a swap of prisoners, Israel released Sinwar. One might think that Sinwar would subsequently soften his genocidal hatred of Jews. Regrettably, the Israeli victims on that tragic day found out that no amount of empathy and kindness that was offered to Sinwar could eradicate the other untreated and more malignant cancer that had long ago ravaged his entire body, mind, and soul: the cancer of Jew-hatred, which consumes all in its wake. While the Oslo syndrome can result in a manifestation of suicidal empathy, it is distinct in that the latter is much more proactive in actively seeking to destroy one's existence as the ultimate act of virtue.

The Firebugs is a 1953 play that captures the absurdity of ignoring profoundly obvious realities that otherwise pose an existential threat.[85] The protagonist welcomes two individuals into his home that are exhibiting astoundingly clear signals that they are the arsonists that have been setting fires in town. The West's civilizational self-immolation via suicidal empathy is the tragic real-life manifestation of this absurdist play. It is never a good idea to ignore the warning signs of reality, a topic to which I turn next.

2

Forbidden Knowledge

Knowledge forbidden?
Suspicious, reasonless. Why should their Lord
Envy them that? Can it be a sin to know?
Can it be death?[1]

He [man] is free to evade reality, he is free to unfocus his mind and stumble blindly down any road he pleases, but not free to avoid the abyss he refuses to see. Knowledge, for any conscious organism is the means of survival . . . Man is free to choose not to be conscious, but not free to escape the penalty of unconsciousness: destruction.[2]

The American literary critic Roger Shattuck delineated six categories of forbidden knowledge, including "[i]naccessible, unattainable knowledge"; "[k]nowledge prohibited by divine, religious, moral, or secular authority"; and "[d]angerous, destructive, or unwelcome knowledge."[3] In many instances, the refusal to explore forbidden knowledge lies in a calculus of misguided empathy. Suppose that you saw your best friend's wife cheating on him; should this knowledge be shared with him? This is the driving theme of the 2011 movie *The Dilemma*, starring Vince Vaughn and Kevin James. If you believe that it is always best to be truthful (deontological ethics), then you must have that difficult conversation with your friend. If, on the other hand, you feel that it is important to weigh the costs and benefits of doing so, you are abiding to a consequentialist ethos (e.g., the likely divorce might have severe negative consequences on the children). Bite your tongue or share the truth? Should you be empathetic by omission or does the maxim "The truth hurts" apply here, in which case you are obligated to share this unwelcomed knowledge?

In academia, forbidden knowledge is often justified as a form of epistemological empathy. Roland G. Fryer Jr. was the youngest black professor to be granted tenure at Harvard University. He exemplified the ultimate dream of the white progressive class in that in addition to his skin color, he came from a difficult upbringing. He epitomized the uplifting redemptive narrative that the Harvard faculty club members can feast on. Then he did something unthinkable. He pursued forbidden knowledge. He authored papers that were contrary to the accepted politically correct narrative regarding the ubiquitous evils of white supremacy. He allowed data and facts to destroy a perfectly fine false narrative. This could not be tolerated, and hence a witch hunt began to oust him, led by none other than serial plagiarist Claudine Gay, who at the time was the dean handling his case.[4] Suicidal empathy is the common thread across this tragic situation. First, his work highlighted the fact that blacks are not perpetual victims of white supremacist institutions, be it in education or policing. Suicidal empathy, though, requires that blacks be forevermore perceived as victims in need of saving. Second, Claudine Gay, who eventually ascended to become the first black female president of Harvard, epitomized the suicidal empathy of the diversity, inclusion, and equity cult. It seems unlikely that she could have ascended to such administrative heights had Harvard been committed to a meritocratic ethos. Subsequently, when she was found to have engaged in innumerable cases of plagiarism (which would be grounds to have a student expelled), she retained her $900,000 annual salary.[5] Plagiarism does not apparently apply to noble administrators of color. She is engaging in justified reparations of other people's words and ideas. Incidentally, Gay claimed that the plagiarism charges were driven by racism. In supporting a serial plagiarist, Harvard was willing to damage its reputation, a clear form of institutional suicidal empathy. Beyond the serial plagiarism, Gay had appeared in front of a House panel to discuss the astounding Jew-hatred on Harvard's campus, and during the exchange with Congresswoman Elise Stefanik, she explained that whether the calls for the genocide of Jews violated Harvard's code of conduct "depended on context."[6] Apparently, #BlackLivesMatter but #JewishLivesDoNot.

In August 1996, I spoke at the XXVI International Congress of Psychology held that year in my hometown of Montreal. My talk was neither controversial nor politically charged, and yet when I entered the venue where my session was being held, I detected palpable tension. The room was packed with perhaps fifteen hundred people, a rare audience size for a session at an academic conference. The audience members were certainly not there to see me, as I was a young academic without much of a reputation. I had failed to check who the other participants were in my session, as this might have perhaps explained the atmosphere in the room. One of the speakers who preceded my talk turned out to be the reason why the room was brimming with electric hostility. Philippe Rushton, a controversial psychologist who for several decades conducted research at the University of Western Ontario (since rebranded as Western University) on the relationship between race and intelligence, spoke prior to me in the order of presenters.[7] As he discussed the size of the craniums of white and black men and women, audience members seated next to me were shaking their heads with great disapproval, and I felt a sudden dread at the prospect of being lynched by proxy! Once Rushton finished his lecture and walked out of the room without fielding any questions, nearly the entire room cleared out, and there must have been perhaps no more than seventy-five individuals left when I was summoned for my talk. This was arguably the only time in my career where I was thankful that I had a small audience.

I share this story because it speaks to the notion of forbidden knowledge, namely, some research topics should not be pursued lest they lead to negative consequences.[8] By that logic, we should have canceled physics because it led to the dropping of two atomic bombs on Japan at the end of World War II. Returning to Rushton, I once asked a colleague who knew him well whether he thought that Rushton's research was inspired by racist considerations or whether he was merely pursuing this research topic unencumbered by any politically correct constraints. He did not think that Rushton was racist. My own position is that if your research adheres to the epistemological rigor of the scientific method and does not violate any ethical precepts, everything is allowed. Otherwise, this is precisely how you end up with an inability to speak about the links between race and criminality in the United States, or immigration and criminality across the West. The empathetic argument is that such research, to the extent that it will yield findings that are contrary to the accepted politically correct narrative, will cause harm to "marginalized" communities. Hence, it is best to refrain from conducting such research, or if the research has been carried out, to report it only if the findings are "progressively palpable." Take, for example, research on sex differences. If the findings demonstrate women as superior on a given task, then publish the research with great progressive pride. If, heaven forbid, men are shown to be better on said task, make sure to file the study in your proverbial file drawer.

Faulty Consequentialism as Misguided Empathy

In March 2023, I spoke at the ten-year anniversary of the University of Southern California's Center for Economic and Social Research. The title of the one-day event was The End of Enlightenment? The title of my talk was "The Deontological Pursuit of Truth—The Slippery Slope of Forbidden Knowledge."[9] I picked up on a theme that I first covered in *The Parasitic Mind*, namely that some principles are deontological, whereas others can be evaluated according to their consequences. I covered four recent examples of what I refer to as faulty consequentialism: (1) Many people who supposedly support freedom of speech were in full agreement when Donald Trump was banned from his then Twitter account while he was the sitting president of the United States. The argument was that while freedom of speech is a great idea, it did not apply to Trump, as he was an existential threat to civilization, democracy, and our way of life, albeit the official position of Twitter was that he was banned "due to the risk of further incitement to violence."[10] (2) Presumption of innocence is apparently a wonderful idea (to be contrasted, say, with ancient legal codes, which required that the accused prove their innocence[11]) but it did not apply to Brett Kavanaugh when he was being confirmed as a US Supreme Court justice. Hence, despite the paucity of evidence supporting the accusation that he was a serial rapist, his detractors argued that serving on the Supreme Court was simply too consequential a position to require the evidentiary threshold expected in a court of law. Apparently, if it is simply a "job interview," presumption of innocence is not as important a principle, especially when there are other viable candidates for the position. (3) Many progressive people are quick to argue that in order for a democracy to properly function requires that governmental power be kept in check by an impartial press that is fully committed to reporting truths. However, when social media platforms colluded with various governmental entities to suppress the Hunter Biden laptop story ahead of the 2020 presidential elections, this was viewed as perfectly reasonable because the alternative, namely to adhere to strict journalistic integrity, might have led to a Trump victory, and this could not be tolerated, given that he was an "existential threat." (4) The same progressives, many of whom inhabit the world of academia, are in full support of freedom of inquiry as long as it is in line with the empathetic ethos of social justice. If a research question is antithetical to social justice, well, forget about freedom of inquiry.

Note that from the perspective of a progressive mindset, shutting down Trump's ability to communicate in the digital marketplace of ideas is the epitome of being a caring and empathetic person. After all, who wants to listen to a mean and petty tyrant tweeting hurtful content? Shutting him down in the service of creating a kinder society is the highest virtue. Similarly, what could be more empathetic than believing Christine Blasey Ford? Remember, #IBelieveHer. Women never lie. They are inherently honorable creatures except if they are Jewish (and even worse Israeli) in which case, their harrowing testimony of the depraved rapes that they suffered are mere Zionist lies. When Blasey Ford proclaims without any proof that Kavanaugh had sexually assaulted her—somewhere, at some point—believe her. If there are several hours of recorded footage of Jewish women being raped on October 7, 2023, those are Zionist fabrications. Empathy is important but only when applied to non-Zionist women. As

Sam Harris infamously stated in his appearance on the *Triggernometry* podcast, "At that point, Hunter Biden literally could have had the corpses of children in his basement. I would not have cared."[12] In other words, in an orgiastic and grotesquely immoral manifestation of the ends justify the means, Harris is condoning the suppression of truth if the sharing of such information results in a political outcome that he deems undesirable. Of note, Harris authored a book (a long essay, really) titled *Lying,* wherein he extols the virtue of being truthful. Apparently, honesty as a moral virtue applies only when Sam Harris deems it so. Suicidal empathy requires the murder of truth at times.

The reader might recall the open letter released by fifty-one so-called intelligence professionals, wherein they proclaimed that the Hunter Biden laptop story had the hallmark of Russian disinformation.[13] Of course, this astounding gaslighting, rooted in hyper-political tribalism, was proven wrong, but apparently disinformation applies only to veridical information that is otherwise deemed too dangerous by the ruling party. When the ruling party willfully spreads falsehoods, then it is undoubtedly Plato's Noble Lie.

Hate Speech, Misinformation, and Disinformation—Be Empathetic!

In 2022, Joe Biden's administration appointed Nina Jankowicz as the executive director of the Disinformation Governance Board. The more I live, the more I appreciate George Orwell. Imagine that in the twenty-first century, the United States created a government board to establish in a top-down manner what constitutes misinformation (the inadvertent spread of incorrect information) or disinformation (the willful spread of incorrect information). It is difficult to imagine that such a reflex could exist in a free society. Nearly all societies that have ever existed had a top-down approach to what is considered true and, hence, permissible to believe or promulgate. Early in Islam's history, there was a theological battle between the Mu'tazila and the Ash'ariyya camps. The former sought to apply reason in the interpretation of Islamic concepts, whereas the latter rejected such earthly interpretations.[14] According to the Ash'ariyya, you needed to jump into the pool of faith precisely by modulating your capacity to reason against the backdrop of faith-based revelation. Guess which camp won? The Mihnah (a form of Islamic Inquisition) resulted in the persecution of those who did not adhere to the accepted perspective of Islam, or, to use the current parlance, those who spread doctrinal disinformation were punished.

In terms of the monitoring of religious-based "disinformation," perhaps no historical movement is as prolific as the Catholic Church's Inquisition. It led to more than 1.5 million accusations and 300,000 trials.[15] Receiving a knock on the door in the middle of the night during the Middle Ages might be a prelude to your being burned at the stake for heretical disinformation. Two of the most infamous cases involving the Inquisition were those in which Giordano Bruno was burned at the stake for his theological and possible cosmological views, and when Galileo Galilei was placed under house arrest for his cosmological positions.[16] In both instances, the Catholic Church was the purveyor of what is true, and those who held heretical views (a form of disinformation) had to pay the price for believing if not spreading "falsehoods." The philosopher Baruch Spinoza was excommunicated from the Jewish community ("herem" is the Hebrew word) for his "abominable heresies" and "monstrous deeds."[17] In the context of today's parlance, he held views that were contrary to Jewish teachings, and as such his "disinformation" could not be tolerated. The examples stemming from the three Abrahamic faiths demonstrate that there is no monopoly when it comes to the reflex to silence those who hold "incorrect" and unorthodox views. Human history is defined by the penchant to shut down any speech that is not accepted by the rulers of the day whether they be political leaders, religious clergy, or scientific experts.

John Kerry, who served as secretary of state under Barack Obama, and more recently was the special presidential envoy on climate under Joe Biden, spoke in September 2024 at an event organized by the World Economic Forum. He bemoaned the fact that the First Amendment was an impediment to addressing so-called misinformation and disinformation on climate issues.[18] This is the same John Kerry who justified why he had to travel by private jet to a climate conference in Iceland.[19] He is doing the necessary empathetic work to save Mother Earth, so he must use private jets. Taylor Swift and Leonardo DiCaprio are also empathetic protectors of Mother Earth. Sure, they might gallivant around the globe on private jets,[20] but they are important people, unlike all of you selfish degenerates. To all the plebs reading this, please eat tofu and use homing pigeons for your communication needs. If you cared about Mother Earth, you would understand this.

Hillary Clinton, another former secretary of state under Barack Obama, is of the same opinion as Kerry when it comes to the indignities of allowing unfettered free speech. In a conversation with CNN's Michael Smerconish in October 2024, she explained that if information is not properly vetted and regulated online, "we lose total control."[21] A few weeks earlier, Clinton had appeared on Rachel Maddow's show on MSNBC, and there she pontificated about the need to hold people who spread Russian-type political propaganda liable, potentially both criminally and civilly.[22] There are several problems with this position. First, anything with which the Empathetic Democrats disagree magically becomes "Russian disinformation," as per the fact that fifty-one intelligence officers had proclaimed the Hunter Biden laptop story to be. An ugly truth can magically become "Russian disinformation" when it does not suit one's political aims. Second, when many Trump-hating public figures apparently stated that Donald Trump will end democracy, that he will institute martial law, that he will be a literal dictator indistinguishable from Hitler, such hysteria is not disinformation. It is a Noble and Empathetic Lie because the truth is too important to worry about when seeking to eradicate the Trumpian "existential threat."

The Europeans have sought to regulate free speech, a contradiction of terms, with equal if not greater alacrity. That all the social media platforms have been historically owned by billionaires who supported the Democrats was apparently a laudable testament to free enterprise. But when Elon Musk, who himself had previously been a Democrat, bought

Twitter (now X), and removed all the grotesque censorship of "problematic voices" that had taken place under the previous owner Jack Dorsey's reign (with whom I had a nice chat on my show back in 2019[23]), well this was simply unacceptable. On August 12, 2024, Thierry Breton, who served as a member of the European Commission, sent Elon Musk a letter that is breathtakingly Orwellian.[24] Breton warned that should Musk host a chat with then US presidential candidate Donald Trump on X, he "will not hesitate to make full use of our toolbox, including by adopting interim measures, should it be warranted to protect EU citizens from serious harm." Of course, the reason is always the same with tyrants. They are empathetic protectors who are looking out for your best interest. Breton states in the same letter "that all proportionate and effective mitigation measures are put in place regarding the amplification of harmful content in connection with relevant events, including live streaming, which, if unaddressed, might increase the risk profile of X and generate detrimental effects on civic discourse and public security." Hence, while Breton "supports" free speech, to hold a live stream chat with a US presidential candidate is simply too corrosive to allow. Incidentally, Musk's response to the letter in question was quite succinct: "Bonjour!"

Katherine Maher, the CEO and president of NPR since March 2024, speaking remotely at the Atlantic Council 360/Open Summit, stated: "The number one challenge here that we see is, of course, the First Amendment in the United States . . . is a fairly robust protection of rights, and that is a protection of rights, both for platforms, which I actually think is very important that platforms have those rights to be able to regulate what kind of content they want on their sites, but it also means that it is a little bit tricky to really address some of the real challenges of 'where does bad information come from?' and sort out the influence peddlers who have made a real market economy around it."[25] It is incontestable that Maher views freedom of speech via a consequentialist lens and does so by invoking a variant of misguided empathy (e.g., shutting down those who disagree with the "settled science" regarding climate change; otherwise, Mother Earth will suffer). A litany of progressive American politicians has espoused deeply worrisome views regarding free speech, including

Kamala Harris's 2024 vice presidential running mate, Tim Walz, who proclaimed that there is "no guarantee to free speech on misinformation or hate speech, and especially around our democracy" and Alexandria Ocasio-Cortez who explained, "We're going to have to figure out how we reign in our media environment so that you can't just spew disinformation and misinformation. It's one thing to have differing opinions but it's another thing entirely to just say things that are false."[26] Let us suppress speech that promulgates non-empathetic truths.

Say No to Fat Phobia—Your Fat Folds Are Healthy!

Medical students have historically taken the Hippocratic oath, which includes the famous "primum non nocere" or "first, do no harm." This may seem like an easy deontological rule to follow, but oftentimes it leads to gray areas rooted in consequentialist ethics. In the past, physicians would often lie to their patients to spare them some bad news. In a sense, they were being empathetic. Should medical information be withheld from a patient if it is nonactionable and can lead only to despair, or does one always deserve to hear the truth as a central element of ethical healthcare? This is where the fat acceptance and fat liberation movements come in with their objective to protect the feelings and self-esteem of what I satirically refer to as the differently weighted. An empathetic form of Ostrich Parasitic Syndrome (denial of reality) drives much of the discourse, namely the desire is to elevate the sense of self-worth of overweight people, even if it means espousing pure fiction. This results in imbecilic arguments such as "healthy at any size" and "the patriarchy teaches arbitrary standards of beauty." Pointing to your healthy and overweight aunt who lived to be ninety years old does not invalidate the fact that obesity reduces one's lifespan. This is akin to arguing that since your uncle Bob smoked his entire life and lived to be ninety, this "proves" that smoking does not cause cancer. Ceteris paribus, being overweight is not good for your health. The empathetic celebration of your fatness does not protect you against the ravages of diabetes, heart disease, and high blood pressure, along with many other health complications. In 2015, the reality series *My Big Fat Fabulous Life* premiered. It stars Whitney Way Thore fighting against the stigma of obesity one episode at a time. No kind and compassionate person wants to see an overweight person discriminated against because of their weight. This does not mean, though, that in the service of such a noble reflex, we reject reality.

As I explained earlier, one of the ways that people engage in faux empathy is by shifting the blame from personal responsibility to external forces. Hence, you weigh as much as a California sea lion not because you eat 25,000 calories a day without ever getting off the couch but because "obesity is a disease." It is not your fault! Let us hug it out and celebrate with a few dozen doughnuts. Or better yet, the negative health consequences of being overweight are apparently a form of white supremacy. I am not being satirical. Sabrina Strings, a professor of Black Studies at the University of California, Santa Barbara, espouses this position among many other "fat liberation" activists. In 2023, she authored a paper titled "How the Use of BMI [body mass index] Fetishizes White Embodiment and Racializes Fat Phobia."[27] The article was a natural follow-up to her 2019 book titled *Fearing the Black Body: The Racial Origins of Fat Phobia*. Not only is the actuarial BMI table a manifestation of white supremacy, but if you were to try and reduce your BMI to healthy levels via dieting, this, too, is a form of white supremacy. Specifically, "Toxic diet culture is a pervasive and insidious influence on our lives. Many people may recognize its connection to fatphobia and its harmful consequences on body image, mental health, and eating patterns. But they may be less aware of its racist and White supremacist history and how diet culture continues to uphold White supremacy and perpetuate systemic racism to this day."[28] The desire to exercise is itself a form of white supremacy, as explained by historian Natalia Mehlman Petrzela.[29] I recently lost eighty-six pounds via a regimen of strenuous physical activity and caloric counting. Imagine my surprise when I realized that this places me among the leading contenders of becoming the next Grand Wizard of the KKK. If I were to be appointed to the role, it might be problematic, given that I am a Lebanese Jew. Hopefully, though, via my excessive weight loss through diet and exercise, I can highlight my commitment to white supremacy and hence compensate for being Jewish.

Part of being suicidally empathetic is to incorporate an intersectionality in your victimhood narrative. Hence, it is insufficient that overweight people are discriminated against by being told that they must lose weight to be healthy. Imagine if you are queer and fat, or Indigenous and fat, or better yet, queer, Indigenous, and fat. Rest assured, there is an academic discipline that tackles such sizable and weighty matters. Recently, the journal *Fat Studies* released a call for papers for a special issue titled *Indigenous(ly) Fat, Fat(ly) Indigenous*. The two guest editors state in the call for papers: "We seek to explore the space of Indigenous fat studies, posing the question: What does Indigenous fat studies look like? Fatness is intersectionally experienced and, for those of us who occupy multiple identities that are minoritised, our experiences of navigating fatness are complex."[30] They then proceed to list possible topics for the special issue, including "Indigenous experiences of fatness," "The intersections of fatness, Indigeneity, queerness, disability, age, sexuality," "Shifts in fat social justice related to Indigenous sovereignty," "Being socially assigned as Indigenous and fat," and "Building and promoting solidarity for fat Indigeneity."

This captures the extraordinary rot within some "academic" disciplines. The point is never to advance human knowledge through science, reason, and logic but to create narratives of empathy and care rooted in a never-ending recursive web of intersectional victimhood. The scientific method, namely the epistemology for seeking truth, becomes secondary to an epistemology of care: "It seems important to demonstrate how caring across disciplines, and other borders can work, for instance, by showing how methods (other than the obligatory research methods and their ethical approval) and other research practices, and teaching can be made accessible through open discussion, open syllabuses and increased demands for space to allow 'care' in the academy."[31] Academia should not be about the celebration, elevation, and care of "marginalized" voices. It should always be about the pursuit of truth.

The empathetic call to combat the scourge of fat shaming has reached the mecca of progressivism, the city of San Francisco. The city's public health department hired Virgie Tovar as the city's weight stigma czar.[32] Tovar has the necessary gravitational gravitas (she is fat) to assume this sizable role, a position that is funded by the taxpayers. Undoubtedly, the residents of San Francisco are less concerned with their children walking by the endless drug-infested homeless encampments than ensuring that differently weighted people are free of stigmatization. Diabetes, heart disease, and high blood pressure are surely less important health concerns than managing the self-esteem of people of girth.

Journalistic and Linguistic Empathy

In a well-functioning democracy, journalists are bound to share the news in a truthful and unbiased manner. The Society of Professional Journalists, founded in 1909, states that "public enlightenment is the forerunner of justice and the foundation of democracy. Ethical journalism strives to ensure the free exchange of information that is accurate, fair and thorough."[33] The society offers four key principles that are necessary for an ethical journalist, including "Seek Truth and Report It" and "Minimize Harm." The former deals with a deontological principle (truth) whereas the latter is rooted in a consequentialist ethic. Therein lies the problem. If the truth "harms" a particular group, should you refrain from sharing it or perhaps obfuscate key features to "minimize harm"? Under the "Minimize Harm" principle, one finds the following prescription: "Show compassion for those who may be affected by news coverage." It is such a consequentialist bent to journalistic integrity that yields a much greater likelihood of an American newspaper article reporting the race of a murderer if they are white as opposed to when they are black. In the same way that our calendars are marked by two eras, namely prior to and after the birth of Jesus Christ (BC and AD), the racial bias in the reporting of murders has two apparent eras as well. In this case, His Eminence George Floyd, the patron saint of the Church of Black Lives Matters, serves as the crucial temporal marker. Prior to Floyd's death, white murderers were approximately twice as likely to have their races mentioned as compared to their black counterparts; after Saint Floyd's death, this skyrocketed to seven times more likely.[34] In other words, journalists felt the need to show compassion to murderers of color, given that the death of Floyd had served as a watershed moment in American race relations. I should add that in my previous few sentences, I engaged in non-empathetic capitalization of the two races. The heroic Associated Press established new standards in 2020, namely "Black people" would be capitalized moving forward but not "white people."[35] Move aside, Steve Biko and Nelson Mandela (legendary anti-apartheid activists), Frederick Douglass, and Martin Luther King Jr. The pathway to eradicating racism must pass through empathetic race-based capitalization.

In *The Parasitic Mind*, I explained that of all parasitic idea pathogens, postmodernism is the worst, in that it provides the framework for the rejection of reality. If there are no objective truths, then all bets are off. Deconstructionism is an offshoot of postmodernism popularized by the French scholar Jacques Derrida. It purports that reality is shaped by language; hence, it is important to "deconstruct" texts to extract the proper meaning. If language creates reality, then this offers an opportunity to reshape the world into a better place. If only we could sufficiently sanitize language, we will eradicate all forms of bigotry and associated injustices. The problem, though, is that this forces us to abide to the arbitrary whims of the language police as they seek to identify ever-shrinking cases of actual linguistic malfeasance. In 2014, I delivered a lecture at Wellesley College titled "How Thought Police Regulate the Free Exchange of Ideas." On one of the slides, I listed a series of changes that the Empathetic Language Police has requested that we implement (suggested change in parentheses): secretary (administrative assistant), stewardess (flight attendant), janitor (custodial engineer), garbage collector (sanitation engineer), waiter (server), prostitute (sex worker), chairman (chairperson), mankind (humankind), the Founding Fathers of the United States (the Founders), birth defect (congenital disability), mentally ill (person with mental illness; this is known as people-first language), handicapped (differently abled), healthy/normal (able-bodied), older student (non-traditional student), and illegal immigrant (undocumented immigrant).

Some teachers and professors are so kind and empathetic that they refuse to correct poor grammar, as this would apparently amount to linguistic racism.[36] Let us celebrate grammatical and spelling diversity instead! Case in point, a $60,000 yearly tuition at a posh private school will hopefully ensure that the teacher will not marginalize your kids if they misspell "machine" as "macien."[37] Whatever you do, never penalize a student on their grade if they are writing in Ebonics. To do so would undoubtedly perpetuate white supremacy. The 2023 critically acclaimed film *American Fiction* satirizes the race-specific expectations of black authors. In the quest to be empathetic toward so-called authors of color, one ends up perpetuating racist stereotypes. The absurdity of wokeism has yielded a real exemplar of this phenomenon. A poet who suffered from the dreadful disease of being a heterosexual white man finally experienced publishing success once he came out as a gender queer Nigerian.[38]

Laken Riley was killed while jogging by a Venezuelan man who was in the United States illegally. The murderer had also tried to rape her. He was eventually convicted of ten felonies and was handed a life sentence with no chance of parole. A key reason that the death penalty was not sought is because of a suicidally empathetic progressive district attorney named Deborah Gonzalez who does not believe in the death penalty.[39] If there ever was a case necessitating the death penalty, this would be a good exemplar, but Ms. Gonzalez is more enlightened than all of you bloodthirsty degenerates. This is hardly, though, the most galling element of this tragedy. In describing the murderer, then-President Joe Biden stated that he regretted the fact that he had referred to the murderer as an "illegal" during his State of the Union address; instead, he should have used the more inclusive and empathetic term "undocumented."[40] You read that correctly. No society can withstand such a broken moral compass. Not to be outdone by the misguided empathy of her boss, Vice President Kamala Harris shared her displeasure with the national intelligence community, as they were insufficiently using gender inclusive language in their reports.[41] Perhaps she was inspired by the feminist foreign policy that Canada and Sweden have sought to pursue.[42] Finally, in the original draft of the continuing resolution spending bill that was to be passed under the tutelage of House Speaker Mike Johnson in December 2024, there were some suggested linguistic changes meant to be more empathetic toward various groups, including a change from "criminal offender" to "justice-involved individual" and "homeless individuals" to "individuals experiencing homelessness."[43]

In my quest to be a progressive and empathetic speaker of the English language, I have suggested that we stop using the hurtful term "rapist" as this might marginalize the Rapist Community. I propose "undocumented lovemaker" or perhaps "altruistic sperm donor." Notwithstanding my satire, there is an actual academic movement that has sought to change the term "pedophile" to "minor attracted people."[44] Here are the first two sentences of the abstract of a paper titled "Humanizing Pedophilia as Stigma Reduction: A Large-Scale Intervention Study": "The stigmatization of people with pedophilic sexual interests is a topic of growing academic and professional consideration, owing to its potential role in moderating pedophiles' emotional well-being, and motivation and engagement in child abuse prevention schemes. Thus, improving attitudes and reducing stigmatization toward this group is of paramount importance."[45]

Not only should the feelings of pedophiles be spared, but also let us make sure to be kind to cannibals. To most people, cannibalism is one of the most repugnant acts, certain to trigger the evolved disgust response. It turns out, though, that you are a racist bigot for having that reflex. In doing so, you are "othering" the ways of non-Western cultures that have long engaged in this practice for compassionate and empathetic reasons. You see, it is very important not to marginalize the cannibal community, as addressed in a *New Scientist* article titled "Is It Time for a More Subtle View on the Ultimate Taboo: Cannibalism."[46] Perhaps this is a channeling of political philosopher Leo Strauss who stated back in 1953, "If principles are sufficiently justified by the fact that they are accepted by a society, the principles of cannibalism are as defensible or sound as those of civilized life."[47]

Be Empathetic to the Homeless (Unhoused) and to Home Invaders (Surprise Guests)

In May 2018, I was speaking in San Francisco at the 30th Annual Association for Psychological Science Convention. As I arrived at my hotel in downtown San Francisco, an apparently homeless woman had pulled down her pants to defecate on the sidewalk while barely crouched. Welcome to the new San Francisco, which now resembled a dystopian *Mad Max* movie set. The transformation of the city has been breathtaking. Similar patterns of homelessness were documented across many cities of utopian progressivism. For example, in 2022, the top fourteen cities registering the greatest number of homeless people were all run by Democrat mayors (Los Angeles, New York, Seattle, San Jose, Oakland, Sacramento, Phoenix, San Diego, San Francisco, Denver, Las Vegas, Portland, Philadelphia, and Boston).[48] This is largely due to how one's political orientation ascribes causes for homelessness. Democrats are much more likely than Republicans to offer external attributions for homelessness.[49] If homelessness does not arise from one's personal actions and choices, this provides the right conduit for infinitely compassionate and empathetic policies. To remove homeless encampments from public spaces becomes a mean endeavor lacking in compassion. To compel mentally ill homeless individuals to check into psychiatric treatment centers becomes an infringement on their rights. Longitudinally speaking, Americans are exhibiting greater compassion and an increase in liberal attitudes toward the homeless, leading to "The largest changes in attitudes we observed were related to greater support for the rights of homeless individuals to sleep, set up shelter, and panhandle in public areas."[50] Progressive policies presume that it is compassionate to ignore the fact that homelessness is in large part due to mental disease and substance addiction.[51] It is perhaps more empathetic, albeit incorrect, to blame greedy capitalist landlords for the lack of affordable housing, as this would serve to protect the homeless from being further marginalized. It is mean and hurtful to point to a homeless person's paranoid schizophrenia and/or their addiction to crystal meth. Empathetic policy makers in Los Angeles have solved the housing problem: build luxury towers for the homeless at a cost of roughly $600,000 per dwelling to be paid by the compassionate tax-payers.[52] As poignantly explained by activist Michael Shellenberger: "The homelessness groups really believe it's more cruel to mandate care than to let people die on the streets. But there is an ideology behind this, too. It's the idea that people suffering from addiction and mental illness are victims of society or the system, which is fundamentally evil. And, according to their logic, to restore justice in the world, we must give victims whatever they want, including the right to camp anywhere and use hard drugs, even if it results in their death. You might call this pathological altruism."[53] And for heaven's sake, please do not call them homeless; use the more empathetic term, "unhoused."

Suicidal empathy extends not only to the homeless but also to home invaders, which in my quest to be linguistically empathetic, I refer to as surprise house guests. Homeowners are at times criminally charged if they shoot home invaders.[54] When you see a masked intruder in your bedroom, it is perhaps best that you deescalate the situation via Socratic dialogue. If you end up shooting him, ensure that your gun ownership papers are up to date lest you might face a felony charge. In any case, he was only trying to steal your property or possibly rape your daughter. It is unjust that you would kill him. Canadian police have suggested to sim-ply call 911 when confronted with a home intruder, and to avoid fighting back.[55] The misguided empathy is also operative when one seeks to evict squatters, problematic renters, or unwelcomed guests.[56] In France, a left-ist theater overflowing with empathetic hospitality toward 250 African migrants invited them in for a free show. Five weeks later, the Africans were still on site, having refused to vacate the premises, forcing the the-ater to contemplate bankruptcy.[57] It is best to be bankrupt and empathetic than to be "racist," I suppose. On a related note, a homeless man who had been given refuge in a woman's apartment but eventually was asked to vacate the premises repaid her empathy and kindness by murdering her.[58] This was apparently not the first time that the victim had offered refuge to the homeless in her apartment. The victim's moral virtue is eternally intact, as her life was terminated by an unhoused man of color. She is dead but at least she is not an elitist racist.

Unicornia—The Enchanted Land of No Risks

Fables are enduring because they communicate universal moral lessons that transcend time and place. Two of my favorites are "The Scorpion and the Frog" and "The Farmer and the Viper," each of which teach a slightly different lesson. In the former, a scorpion asks a frog if it can hitch a ride on its back across the river. The frog is hesitant to do so, given that it fears the scorpion's sting. The frog's fear is assuaged by the scorpion who confirms that it would be irrational to sting it, as it would seal their demise. This convinces the frog, and they proceed across the river. On their journey, and to the frog's utter dismay, it feels the scorpion's sting. The frog asks the scorpion why it broke its promise, thus ensuring that they would both perish, to which the scorpion quips that it could not help but do so because it is in its nature. The lesson here is that we cannot live in a utopian world decoupled from reality. It would be nice to ascribe noble qualities to the scorpion, but ultimately it is going to behave in ways consistent with its evolved dispositional behaviors. In the second fable (attributed to the ancient Greek fabulist Aesop), a farmer sees a viper freezing to death. In his bountiful kindness, and feeling great pity toward the dying reptile, he places it in his coat to allow it to warm up. Once the snake recovers, it bites the farmer. His beneficence did not save him from the snake's nature. Kindness, generosity, compassion, and empathy must be strategically offered. In a contemporary manifestation of this fable, a South African farmer named Marius Els had rescued a young hippopotamus and raised it on his farm. Els dismissed the safety concerns of having a personal relationship with such a dangerous animal. Instead, he argued that the young hippo was akin to a son to him. Well, the "son" ended up killing his adoptive dad.[59]

An important feature when navigating one's life is to possess an accurate calculus of the risks and rewards inherent in any activity. Being an animal lover, when I see a beautiful male lion with a majestic mane, I imagine cuddling with him in the African savannah. But then I am slapped back into reality via the recognition that the lion might not be as keen for a cuddle session, and instead I might end up as a juicy snack. In other words, human beings must navigate the world as it exists and not according to the Unicornia that they would like it to be. This brings me to the tragic story of Jay Austin and Lauren Geoghegan, who set out to cycle around the world in part to demonstrate global human kindness. On their blog, Jay wrote the following passage:

> You watch the news and you read the papers and you're led to believe that the world is a big, scary place. People, the narrative goes, are not to be trusted. People are bad. People are evil. People are axe murderers and monsters and worse.
>
> I don't buy it. Evil is a make-believe concept we've invented to deal with the complexities of fellow humans holding values and beliefs and perspectives different than our own—it's easier to dismiss an opinion as abhorrent than strive to understand it. Badness exists, sure, but even that's quite rare. By and large, humans are kind. Self-interested sometimes, myopic sometimes, but kind. Generous and wonderful and kind. No greater revelation has come from our journey than this.[60]

Well, apparently evil does exist, as Jay and Lauren were executed by ISIS members in Tajikistan along with two other foreigners.[61] My point in sharing this story is not to appear gleeful about their tragic demise but to highlight the fact that the world does not abide to one's erroneous view of human nature. Yes, there are endless nice and decent people in the world, but equally there are those who are willing to cause you great harm. Understanding how to navigate this reality allows you to hopefully avoid unnecessary dangers.

At times, people place themselves in harm's way in their noble desire to help others. In 2017, Michael Sharp and Zaida Catalán, two human rights researchers from the United States and Sweden, respectively, were killed by a Congolese militia group while on a United Nations mission to examine a broad range of crimes, including human rights violations.[62] This is part of the Western Savior complex, namely Westerners deciding to take extraordinary risks in exceptionally dangerous zones as a result of their infinite empathy to help others. Along the same lines, an enormously empathetic female journalist wanted to document the difficulties that illegal immigrants, many of whom stemmed from Islamic countries, faced in their journeys from France to Britain. She foolishly decided to mingle with the undocumented lovemakers in Calais, in a notoriously dangerous area known as "the jungle." Regrettably, her kindness was "reciprocated" with a gang rape.[63] Humans have evolved the calculus to evaluate risks. It is never a good idea to shut off that module in the service of suicidal empathy. There are ways to serve others without putting your life in danger. I have been invited back to Lebanon, my homeland, and my safety was supposedly assured. I politely refused, knowing full well that it would not be safe for me to visit the region.

As a father, it is my responsibility to ensure that my children are safe in every possible way. This is why I have never allowed sleepovers—precisely because I recognize that this would place my children at risk of being sexually molested. I despise when people say things such as "But we know the family. They are good people." No! People who prey on children do not have horns; they do not have a face tattoo that advertises their degeneracy. Child molesters are your uncle, brother, stepfather, friendly neighbor, priest, football coach, or camp counselor. Hence, my approach has always been that since I cannot know with absolute certainty who is a prospective danger to my children, I assume that all men are potential predators. In so doing, I ensure that my children are safe. During the Q&A period following an invited lecture that I had delivered in Iceland in June 2025, I made the point that when choosing a babysitter, it would be statistically wiser to choose a seventeen-year-old girl than a thirty-seven-year-old man. Two very empathetic audience members were deeply triggered by my position because not all thirty-seven-year-old men are sexual abusers.[64] Statistical realities can be so mean. Contrast my approach with that of the Colorado man who housed in his home a twenty-year-old employee who was a Venezuelan illegal migrant, undoubtedly in part because of a sense of misguided empathy. The boss likely thought that it might be racist to presume that the migrant would pose a danger. It is best to be empathetic, even if your fourteen-year-old daughter lives in that home. The man learned an expensive lesson, namely that his hospitality has nefarious consequences, as the undocumented lovemaker was arrested for raping the daughter.[65] It is inconceivable to imagine how a father would place his daughter in such a dangerous situation unless he were parasitized by suicidal empathy.

Reality does not abide by your feelings. Knowledge is either true or false, irrespective of your level of offense. Well-adjusted individuals in free and dignified societies navigate through the world armed with an accurate understanding of reality (and not wishful Unicornia), propelled by the power of the motto that "knowledge is power." Be empathetic to the truth.

3

Cultural Theory of Mind

For the Romans did in this case what all wise princes should do, who look not only at present dangers but also at future ones and diligently guard against them; for being foreseen they can easily be remedied, but if one waits till they are at hand, the medicine is no longer in time as the malady has become incurable.[1]

An ounce of prevention is worth a pound of cure.[2]

Whenever I critique the West's suicidally empathetic open-border policy, I often face the following rebuttal: "Well, have you forgotten that you and your buddy Elon Musk are immigrants? You are such a hypocrite." This reminds me of the brilliant quote attributed to Albert Einstein: "Two things are infinite, the universe and human stupidity, and I am not yet completely sure about the universe."[3] Every day, as I interact with people on social media, I am reminded how accurate Einstein's quote truly is. The inability to recognize that all immigrants are not equally likely to be a net benefit to a host society defies the realm of human imbecility. This is akin to arguing that since both a hummingbird and a cassowary are exemplars of birds, there is no real reason to worry about how dangerous a cassowary is since hummingbirds are harmless. Cassowaries are reputed to be the world's most dangerous bird and can kill a human being by disemboweling it with its large claw.[4] Similarly, since your two-year-old daughter and serial killer John Wayne Gacy are both human beings, there is really no reason for you to worry about inviting Gacy for a sleepover with your children.

An important cognitive skill when navigating the world is to know how to categorize a given stimulus because this allows you to respond in evolutionarily optimal ways.[5] If you see a wild lion in the African savannah, should you categorize it as a cat in the same category as your house cat because they are both members of the feline family? The cognitive scientists who study these processes often use three levels to categorize items, namely the superordinate, basic, and subordinate levels.[6] Hence, animals might be the superordinate level; felines might be the basic level; and lions and house cats would constitute the subordinate level. When deciding whether the lion and the house cat are equally dangerous to your survival, you need to ensure that the comparison is taking place at the proper level in the categorization taxonomy. Or let us suppose that we are discussing an increase in knife attacks in a country. Kitchen tools might be the superordinate category; cutlery might be the basic category; and spoons, knives, and forks would be in the subordinate category. It would be silly to implement a restriction of all cutleries, wherein we fail to recognize that spoons and knives are inherently different from one another (at the basic level). This is the exact categorization error made by the folks who view all immigrants as equal. Elon Musk is an immigrant, as is Mohammad the Jihadist. That they are both male immigrants does not make them indistinguishable in their ability to positively contribute to or harm the host society. Better yet, since cancer cells and healthy cells replicate, they are indistinguishable from one another in their capacity to kill, #CancerLivesMatter. Stop with your cancer-o-phobia. An amoeba has the capacity to not succumb to this categorization error, let alone human beings. But such is the destructive nature of suicidal empathy. It turns the reasoning ability of human beings into that of unicellular organisms.

Lack of Cultural Theory of Mind Leads to Cultural Blindness

A fundamental feature of human sociality is to place ourselves in the mind of the other, thus recognizing that our interlocutors have thoughts, beliefs, knowledge, intentions, desires, and emotions that might be relevant to our interaction. If two people are communicating with each other, each must be able to infer the inner state of mind of the other to maximize the effectiveness of the interaction. This is known as "theory of mind," an ability that many autistic children lack.[7] It is perhaps not surprising then that a feature of being an empathetic person is to possess theory of mind.[8] While theory of mind is an ability at the individual level, I have extended this concept to the cultural level and referred to it as "cultural theory of mind."[9] Are members of one culture capable of accurately inferring the thoughts and feelings of members of a distinct other culture to arrive at meaningful cross-cultural interactions? While cultures possess many shared universal values, they also greatly vary on others.[10] Being able to understand that a given cultural value might be interpreted differently across two cultural settings is an extraordinarily important ability, which is precisely what cultural theory of mind is. Take, for example, virtues such as empathy, generosity, compassion, kindness, and beneficence. The West presumes that if these virtues are extended to members of other cultures, they will be accepted with deep gratitude and reciprocated accordingly. Therein lies the problem. The West lacks cultural theory of mind when it comes to the infinite largesse it offers to members stemming from Islamic societies. The positive virtues that I listed above are interpreted as various manifestation of feminized weakness. This feminization of the West has progressed at an alarming rate. Many of the stereotypically male virtues of boldness, courage, risk-taking, competition, and excellence have been replaced by an ethos of caring, kindness, compassion, and empathy. It is perhaps not surprising then that many Arabic-speaking men have told me in Arabic, "The West is a woman to be mounted." They view the West as a helpless paper tiger ready to be f**ked. The West's suicidal empathy is an aphrodisiac to those stemming from cultures with a supremacist and domineering ethos. While some Western foreign policy and military strategists have encouraged the incorporation of strategic empathy as a means of better understanding our adversaries,[11] the West's suicidal empathy suggests that this imperative is seldom implemented.

Many Islamists have openly explained how they shall conquer the West. They understand that they are incapable of achieving their global Islamization goals via the sword, so instead they have opted for a three-pronged approach:[12] (1) Given that, on average, the fertility rates of Western nations fall below replacement rates and are certainly lesser than those of Muslim women,[13] Islam will conquer the West through the wombs of their women; (2) Using the suicidally empathetic largesse of the welcoming West, Islam will dominate through *hijrah* (the Arabic word for immigration); (3) Using the "miserable" freedoms and liberties afforded by the West, Muslims will subvert the system from within. This is one instance where the Islamists are not employing the religiously sanctioned *taqiyya* to deceive the gullible Westerners.[14] It would be well advised to pay attention to their articulated plans. In a now infamous 1991 Muslim Brotherhood memorandum, one finds the following exhortation: "The Ikhwan [Muslim Brotherhood] must understand that their work in America is a kind of grand Jihad in eliminating and destroying the Western civilization from within and 'sabotaging' its miserable house by their hands and the hands of the believers so that it is eliminated and Allah's religion is made victorious over all other religions."[15] Islam is a binary religion in that it separates the world into two camps: Dar el-harb (the house of war) and Dar el-Islam (the house of Islam). Any nation that is not yet under Islamic dominion is part of Dar el-harb. Any land that was ever under Islamic dominion but was subsequently lost must be regained, as it is forevermore "owned" by Islam. This is precisely why Jihadists proclaim that Al-Andalus (in current Spain) will be reconquered, inshallah. And why Israel cannot exist as a Jewish state. It is an existential affront to Allah's will.

The West is perfectly fine with the following setup: When Westerners are in Islamic societies, make sure to abide to their customs and sensibilities. When Muslims are in the West, make sure to abide to their customs and sensibilities. No need to reciprocate. We are indeed f**ked. The West is tantamount to the psychiatrically damaged young girl engaging in virtuous self-harm.[16]

Cultures Are Not Equal

Cultural relativism, one of the idea pathogens that I discuss in *The Parasitic Mind*, purports that each culture needs to be examined according to its own idiosyncratic reality. Supposedly, it is incorrect to judge the beliefs and practices of one culture using the moral prism of another. While this may be true for some cultural phenomena, it is untrue for a set of human universals shaped by deontological moral principles. In June 2025, I spoke at the Rotary Club's chapter in Midland, Michigan. The Rotary spirit is firmly rooted in empathetic tolerance, as exemplified by this statement: "Rotarians in all countries should recognize these facts (differences), and there should be a thoughtful avoidance of criticism of the laws and customs of one country by the Rotarians of another country."[17] Really? Should the West tolerate child brides, honor killings, and female genital mutilations? Should we be empathetic to the barbarism of other cultures? The West has apparently responded with a resounding yes! Suicidal empathy requires orgiastic tolerance. Cultures that accept gay people as equal citizens are superior to those that throw gays off rooftops as a form of gravity-based conversion therapy. Cultures that do not cut off the clitorises of five-year-old girls are superior to those that do. Cultures that would allow sexual relationships between a mother and her son are inferior to those that do not (this is why we have the universal incest taboo). In the same way that individuals vary greatly in terms of their personality traits, cultures vary in how much importance they place on specific values. Cross-cultural coexistence cannot occur if this goes unrecognized via utter cultural blindness stemming from an abject lack of cultural theory of mind.

Two former Canadian prime ministers, Pierre Elliott Trudeau along with his son Justin Trudeau, are perfect exemplars of Western political leaders who have destroyed their nation's cultural fabric via their empathetic commitment to cultural relativism. Justin Trudeau has stated that Canada was becoming the "first postnational state," wherein "[t]here is no core identity, no mainstream in Canada."[18] He has also stated, "There are shared values—openness, respect, compassion, willingness to work hard, to be there for each other, to search for equality and justice."[19] The current Canadian prime minister, Mark Carney, has proudly proclaimed that Islamic and Canadian values are the same.[20] The lack of cultural theory of mind is breathtaking. The astounding increase of Jew-hatred in Canada following the October 7, 2023, massacres in Israel is a recognition that "openness, respect, compassion . . . and the search for equality of justice" is viewed very differently by traditional Canadians as compared to the recent wave of Islamic immigrants to Canada. Speaking of October 7, a few days prior to its one-year anniversary, the mayor of Toronto, Olivia Chow, issued the following statement: "When hate and darkness surround us, we must continue to be a welcoming, kind and compassionate city. We must keep hearing each other and never lose sight of our common humanity."[21] Fair enough. The problem, though, is that she made sure to repeatedly mention Islamophobia as part of her remarks because it would otherwise be too bigoted to strictly reserve one's empathy to the Jews. Suicidal empathy requires that whenever Jews are attacked, killed, harassed, demeaned, and insulted, Western leaders should remind us that we must redouble our collective efforts to defeat Islamophobia.

When a host society welcomes immigrants with full compassion and generosity, the very least that it should expect in return is due gratitude. Alas, this is not always the case. On June 10, 2020, the then cabinet secretary of justice of Scotland, Humza Yousaf, who is a Muslim of Pakistani origin, spoke in front of the Scottish parliament to lament the fact that all the key governmental positions were held by white people.

Some people have been surprised or taken aback by my mention on my social media that at 99 per cent of the meetings that I go to, I'm the only non-white person in the room. Why are we so surprised when the most senior positions in Scotland are filled almost exclusively by those who are white? Take my portfolio, for example. The Lord President is white, the Lord Justice Clerk is white, every High Court judge is white, the Lord Advocate is white, the Solicitor General is white, the chief constable is white, every deputy chief constable is white, every assistant chief constable is white, the head of the Law Society is white, the head of the Faculty of Advocates is white and every prison governor is white. That is not the case only in justice. The chief medical officer is white, the chief nursing officer is white, the chief veterinary officer is white, the chief social work adviser is white and almost every trade union in this country is headed by white people. In the Scottish Government, every director general is white. Every chair of every public body is white. That is not good enough.[22]

Let us put this into perspective. The 2011 Scottish census established that 96 percent of Scotland was comprised of white people. Hence, the entire country is almost exclusively white, and yet it was sufficiently non-racist to eventually elect Yousaf to be its first minister. Imagine the entitled chutzpah. Scotland has historically been almost exclusively a Christian nation, and yet Yousaf ascended to the highest office of the land. Rather than being thankful that Scotland is such a welcoming country, he whines about the supposed implicit racism of the country that welcomed his grandparents from Pakistan. Perhaps Hamza was channeling his inner Longshanks (Edward I, King of England) in expressing antipathy toward the Scots. In a gripping scene in the 1995 Oscar-winning movie *Braveheart*, Longshanks famously states: "The trouble with Scotland is that it's full of Scots. Perhaps the time has come to reinstitute an old custom. Grant them prima nocta. First night, when any common girl inhabiting their lands is married, our nobles shall have sexual rights to her on the night of her wedding. If we can't get them out, we breed them out."

Islamophilic Immigration—Be Kind to Child Rapists and Terrorists

Over the past several decades, Britain has witnessed the organized sexual exploitation of young white girls by "Asian" grooming gangs across countless cities on an industrial-scale level.[23] There are innumerable bewildering stories of how police declined to intervene, and government officials refused to highlight the problem lest they might be accused of bigotry and, worse, Islamophobia. To the invertebrate castrati who compose our leaders, nothing could be worse than being accused of Islamophobia. The ability of Westerners to come up with euphemisms to hide the real commonality across these groups of perpetrators is downright Orwellian. In the context of the British grooming gangs, one should refer to them as "Asian" and not as British Pakistani Muslims. In France, the Muslims who engage in criminality across the suburbs are referred to as *les jeunes* (the youth). Well, the youth are not Vietnamese Buddhists; they are not Hasidic Jews; they are not Nigerian Christians. They constitute young Muslim criminals, but heaven forbid that one links this criminality to Islamic immigration. This would marginalize the Islamic community. In the calculus of progressive empathy, protecting white British girls from gang rapes is worth a lot less than protecting the perpetrators' Islamic heritage. Sorry, girls, toughen up. Take one for the team or, perhaps more accurately, take it from the entire team.

Here are the names of the twenty convicted child rapists and abusers in the Huddersfield (England) grooming case: Amere Singh Dhaliwal, Irfan Ahmed, Zahid Hassan, Mohammed Kammer, Mohammed Rizwan Aslam, Abdul Rehman, Raj Singh Barsran, Nahman Mohammed, Mansoor Akhtar, Wiqas Mahmud, Nasarat Hussain, Sajid Hussain, Mohammed Irfraz, Faisal Nadeem, Mohammed Azeem, Manzoor Hassan, Mohammed Akram, Niaz Ahmed, Asif Bashir, and Mohammed Imran Ibrar.[24] When I sarcastically asked people to identify any commonalities across the perpetrators, it might not surprise you to know that many blamed the Jews. How is it that when multiple guys named Mohammed gang-rape your daughter, you ended up blaming Mordechai? Clearly, you are not well versed in the popular game that I coined a while ago: Six Degrees of Jew. For any calamity, you have up to six causal steps to blame Jews. Returning to the Muslim grooming gangs in Britain, apparently it is the Jews who control the immigration policies across the West, including Britain. Hence, to the extent that these child rapists were in Britain, it is ultimately the fault of the Jews.

Why did the British authorities fail to act on these monstrous crimes against children for so many decades?[25] Well, to reiterate, they were being empathetic in ensuring that the Muslim communities of Britain would not be marginalized. Sure, protecting white children from endless sexual torture is important, but it is not nearly as important as ensuring community cohesion and refraining from stoking the fire of division and hate. This is what happens when your empathy moral compass is broken. Upon finding out about the Muslim grooming gang in another British city, Newcastle, the Muslim community was quick to point out that they feared a backlash of Islamophobia.[26] Sure, it is bad when thousands of young girls are raped and sodomized, but Islamophobia cannot be allowed to spread. Incidentally, when these Muslim men engaged in the wide-scale organized rape of young white British children, it was because of a "wider failure of British society to integrate these men into their adoptive culture."[27] Speaking of the rape of children, a twenty-eight-year-old Bangladeshi asylum seeker impregnated a ten-year-old child in a small Italian village, at a migrant reception center, forcing the child to have an abortion (the mother of the child was also an asylum seeker).[28] The local population, though, was very quick to point out that they had no problems with the migrants. It might perhaps seem misguided for the local population to rally around the asylum seekers and redouble their efforts to be maximally hospitable as a response to a child's rape.

The West's reflex is always to protect Islam irrespective of the unfolding realities. After the Boston Marathon bombs were exploded by two Muslim brothers in the name of their faith, Justin Trudeau who at the time was the leader of the Liberal Party but had not yet become prime minister, sat down with Peter Mansbridge of the CBC. Here is what Trudeau said when questioned about the horrific terrorist attack:

But there is no question that this happened because there is someone who feels completely excluded, completely at war with innocents, at war with a society. And our approach has to be, okay, where do those tensions come from? I mean yes, we need to make sure that we're promoting security and we're you know keeping our borders safe, and you know monitoring the kinds of, you know, violent subgroups that happen around. But we also have to monitor and encourage people to not point fingers at each other and lay blame for personal ills or societal ills on a specific group, whether it be the West or the government or Bostonians or whatever it is. Because it's that idea of dividing humans against ourselves, of pointing out that they're not like us, and you know in order to achieve our political goals we can kill innocents here.[29]

Canada truly suffers from Stage 4 suicidal empathy. When ISIS fighters were returning to Canada, they were neither tried for treason nor for crimes against humanity. This would be too mean and judgmental. Instead, former prime minister Justin Trudeau reassured us: "We know that actually someone who has engaged and turned away from that hateful ideology can be an extraordinarily powerful voice for preventing radicalization in future generations and younger people within the community."[30] The path forward for ISIS fighters is apparently not punishment but empathetic reintegration and compassionate rehabilitation. On a related note, Omar Khadr, who had grown up in Canada and whose father was a close colleague of Osama bin Laden, was convicted by a US military tribunal of having murdered an American soldier during an armed conflict in Afghanistan between US soldiers and the Taliban. He was handed a forty-year sentence but was eventually turned over to Canadian authorities after having spent ten years at Guantánamo Bay. Khadr eventually filed a lawsuit against the Canadian government (for actions taken by the US military), and Trudeau's government granted him $10.5 million in taxpayer funds and an apology on behalf of Canadians.[31] A teenager who was associated with bin Laden, who fought with the Taliban, and who killed an American soldier was rewarded by the Canadian government using my tax dollars. It would be difficult to come up with a greater case of suicidal empathy.

Following the New Orleans terror attack on January 1, 2025, wherein a Muslim convert killed fourteen people who were simply out celebrating the new year, Tom Wilson, the chairman, president, and chief executive officer of the Allstate Corporation offered the following message: "Welcome to the Allstate Sugar Bowl. Wednesday, tragedy struck the New

Orleans community. Our prayers are with the victims and their families. We also need to be stronger together by overcoming an addiction to divisiveness and negativity. Join Allstate working in local communities all across America to amplify the positive, increase trust, and accept people's imperfections and differences. Together we win."[32] Wilson felt it optimal to lecture Americans about being divisive rather than speaking out forcefully against Islamic terrorism. Such is the pull of suicidal empathy.

But Gad, You're Not a Jew-Jew

I joined the PhD program at Cornell University in 1990 and quickly became friends with a group of Lebanese students with whom I often played soccer. A few weeks into that first semester, one of the group's members invited me out for a coffee. As we settled into a conversation, he pensively paused and said: "You know, Gad, you are a very smart guy. Why have you not yet converted to Islam?" I quickly advised him that if his goal was to proselytize his faith, this would not be a productive get-together. Realizing that this was a fruitless pursuit, he paused again and uttered with a sense of consternation: "You know, Gad, I really like you." I then looked at him with a wry smile and said in return: "You say this with some internal conflict. Oh, I know. Is it because I'm Jewish?" He then quickly retorted, "Come on, Gad. You're not a Jew-Jew." In a reply that has become part of my personal lore, I responded "Well, actually, I am a Jew-Jew-Jew-Jew."

Why am I recounting this story here? The individual in question could not reconcile the exemplar of the diabolical Jew, which had been seared into his mind straight out of his mother's womb, with the feelings of affection and admiration that he felt for me. I was fun, warm, and friendly; Arabic was my mother tongue; and I played soccer better than all the Arabic guys in the group combined. Surely this cannot be a Jew! Leon Festinger, the pioneer of the theory of cognitive dissonance, explained how people will use a broad array of strategies to assuage internal conflict. In this case, by saying that I was not a "real Jew," he was hoping to make sense of his inner emotive struggle. If he could only remove the "Jew" tag from me, his warmth toward me could make sense again.

On October 7, 2023, Hamas attacked Israeli civilians in a manner that harkened to an era of barbarity that the modern world had seldom seen. It was the single greatest number of Jews killed in a day since the Holocaust. How did the world respond to this event in terms of their expressed empathy (or lack thereof) toward Jews? After seeing how more than twelve hundred human beings, the great majority of which were civilians, were butchered and raped in an orgiastic depravity of hate, should this have resulted in an increase of empathy toward Jews, an unchanged level of empathy, or a decrease of empathy? Most rational people armed with a functioning moral compass would quickly state that empathy toward the Jews should have greatly increased. The exact opposite happened around the world. There has been an exponential growth of Jew-hatred across the West, most notably on university campuses throughout North America. "Jew-Jews" are not deserving of empathy.

Prior to the Israel Defense Forces (IDF) engaging in any retaliation, global protests had earnestly begun as a preemptive measure. Hence, it was certainly not the case that the protesters were angered by a so-called disproportionate response since that had yet to occur. Since October 7, the world has witnessed an astounding amount of gaslighting meant to ensure that the Jewish people are never the recipient of any well-deserved empathy.[33] These include the following positions: October 7 never happened; it did happen but was greatly exaggerated in terms of the number of victims, and in any case it was fully justified in light of the occupation; it did happen but most (all) of the victims were killed by the Israelis in order to garner faux empathy from the world (not unlike the Jews' promulgation of the "false" Holocaust narrative). But perhaps one of the most pervasive lies meant to eradicate any empathy toward the Jews is what I refer to as the "amnesia of causality." Many Jew-hating narratives no longer mention October 7 as the catalyst of the Israeli retaliation. Apparently, the "genocidal" Jews decided on October 8 to eradicate Gaza void of any triggering event. And the coup de grâce when it comes to the battle for people's empathy stems from the inflated death toll figures that Hamas-related agencies had been "reporting,"[34] and yet the world remained oblivious to these falsehoods. Truth should not be used to garner empathy toward the Jews. Only the people of Gaza are deserving of empathy, and if falsified death tolls must be generated, so be it. After all, in a hadith attributed to Muhammad, he supposedly stated "war is deceit." Apparently, all bets are off when it comes to discouraging empathy for Jews in the global informational war.

To contrast the global lack of empathy toward the Jews, I would like to describe my reaction to a deeply disturbing ISIS video that captured the summary execution of roughly fifteen hundred unarmed Muslim Iraqi air force cadets as they were being killed off methodically and with a psychopathic detachment. This crime against humanity is known as the Camp Speicher massacre.[35] I saw these young men being led to their death knowing that in the next few seconds, they would cease to exist. I was angry, frustrated, horrified, and filled with a sense of vengefulness for these young men. Recall that I am Jewish, and my family had to flee from guaranteed death at the start of the Lebanese civil war. My parents were kidnapped by Fatah and severely mistreated. I have often criticized foundational tenets of Islam, and yet at that moment as I watched these young souls being massacred, I ached for them. My empathy did not shut off because they were Muslim. I was able to place myself in their shoes and in those of their loved ones, and accordingly, I rightly concluded that such depravity was unbearable. My morality, compassion, and empathy are not reserved for in-group members, as this would make me an immoral person. Regrettably, though, Jews were not granted that courtesy. They are "Jew-Jews" worthy of righteous hatred.

Accommodations to Islam as a Form of Suicidal Empathy

In spring 2011, I was asked to sit on a university-wide ad hoc committee regarding our university's religious accommodation policy. I joined Concordia University in 1994, and we had never previously had to discuss this policy. What had changed? Concordia has always prided itself on its multi-cultural vibrancy, and in all the years that I had been there, no difficulties that I am aware of had ever arisen. But apparently, something had changed that required that we address the issue in an "empathetic" manner. Of course, we all knew what it was all about but only one person at that meet-ing (me) was willing to speak openly and truthfully. The number of Muslim students had increased past some tipping point, resulting in their requests for religious accommodations becoming more forceful. I recall raising sev-eral issues during the meeting, including the fact that it was a contradiction of terms to say that we were a secular university that nonetheless adheres to religious requests. I inquired about how we might handle specific instances, such as if a student were to state that they were feeling weak throughout the entire month of Ramadan (due to the daily fasting), and as such they could not properly perform any evaluative exercises during that time frame. Would we accommodate them? What if a student were to proclaim that he was obligated to perform hajj during a specific semester, a pilgrimage to Mecca that is expected of Muslims once during their lifetimes? Would we accommodate that request? You should have seen the committee members look down at their papers as they shuffled these nervously. My questions and concerns were largely ignored or dismissed.

Now let us contrast such religious accommodation requests to my own approach to such matters. Yom Kippur is the holiest day in Judaism, and it involves a twenty-five-hour full fast that is meant to serve as a day of atonement. Many years ago, I had an important soccer match on the eve of Yom Kippur, meaning that I would have to play the game and not hydrate nor eat until the following evening. This is no easy task, and yet I did not seek to alter the schedule of the soccer match to suit my religious obligations. I had to operate within the confines of a society that did not need to abide by my religious schedule. Returning to my duties as a pro-fessor, I have never canceled a class nor an exam due to my own religious obligations. If I live in a secular society and I work at a secular university, in my view it is morally and ethically wrong of me to impose my religious schedule on my students, even though the university would permit for such an option.

There are countless other examples of religious tolerance that are repeatedly granted to a singular religion (Islam) at the cost of other people's freedoms. Take, for example, the growth of public prayers throughout the West. We never see Seventh-Day Adventists, Buddhists, Jains, or Hasidic Jews taking over public spaces for their prayers. And yet, throughout Europe and increasingly so in Canada and in the United States, sidewalks, parks, and actual streets are shut down by a massive influx of Muslims praying in those spaces. Whenever I have weighed in on the astounding violation of people's rights to be free from another's religious impositions, I am drowned by a cacophony of suicidally empathetic Westerners, utterly oblivious to the underlying dynamics at play. "Why do you care if they pray? How does it harm you? What's the big deal in having to cross to the other side of the street because the sidewalk has been turned into an outdoor mosque? Why can't you be kind?" These empathetic responses were typical of my fellow Quebeckers, albeit the Quebec government has apparently finally woken up by seeking to ban this practice.[36] It is my contention that these mass public prayers are a signal of dominance. "We are here. We are growing in number, and you will eventually have to submit." Again, these prayers start to occur and with increased frequency only when the number of Muslims in a society passes a tipping point. The Islamization of a society follows a well-established historical template and is largely dependent on the percentage of Muslims in the host society. When they are a very small minority, they are construed as an exotic and peaceful community that adds cultural richness to the host society. As their numbers grow, increasingly more forceful demands are made, increased violence and intolerance is exhibited toward non-Muslims, until one day "peace" is achieved in the host society via the erasure of all non-Muslims.[37] Some cultures are so imperialist that they will destroy the historical heritage of a conquered society. This is the case with Islam, which views anything pre-Islamic as part of existential darkness. This is why the Taliban destroyed the magnificent Buddhist statues in Afghanistan. It is why the Hagia Sofia church in Istanbul is now a mosque. It is also why the Dome of the Rock Mosque sits atop the Jewish Second Temple.

The chutzpah of some of these accommodation demands is truly breathtaking. In 2011, Muslim students enrolled at Catholic University, located in Washington, DC, filed a discrimination complaint with the Office of Human Rights because they were offended that they could not have prayer rooms void of Christian symbols.[38] You read that correctly. What allows all of these "peaceful" demands to take place is the West's reflex to be suicidally empathetic. The need to be infinitely tolerant, immeasurably kind, and orgiastically welcoming permits for these entitled demands to flourish. It follows a tried-and-tested strategy beginning with the founder of Islam. When Muhammad began his proselytizing in Mecca, his message was quite peaceful and welcoming. However, it failed to attract many adherents. Later, when he moved to Medina, his message became a lot less tolerant, and this resulted in an exponential growth of followers. With increased numbers so did the intolerance toward those who refused to submit to Allah's will. When in the minority, play the victim. When in the majority, show no mercy. Muslim leaders are very keen on interfaith dialogue in the West while they are a small minority. However, they seem to pursue interfaith dialogue with much lesser alacrity when Islam rules, in part because most non-Muslims cease to exist in those societies. It is tough to dialogue with nonexistent individuals. There is no interfaith dialogue with Jewish community leaders in Algeria, Tunisia, Libya, Syria, Lebanon, Iraq, Yemen, Egypt, Pakistan, Afghanistan, Saudi Arabia, Oman, and Somalia, to name but a few of the members of the Organization of Islamic Cooperation. The status of Christians in the Middle East is following the way of the Jews in the region. Their numbers are precipitously dwindling. I raised this point during my tenth appearance on Joe Rogan's podcast in May 2024: "Egypt used to be completely Coptic Christian 100% many hundreds of years ago. Today there are 10% Copts. There used to be tons of Christians in Syria. What happened to those Syrians? There used to be tons of Christians in Lebanon. There still are some, about 30–35% but Lebanon used to be a majority Christian country."[39] I could have referenced the plight of Christians in Algeria, Tunisia, Iraq, Yemen, Afghanistan, Iran, and Pakistan, to name but a few of the Islamic-majority countries, where Christians are rapidly vanishing, if not fully so. This reality is well captured by the Middle Eastern saying

"First the Saturday people, then the Sunday people," meaning that once we get rid of the Jews, the Christians are next.[40]

The West's Islamophilic suicidal empathy does not impose on Muslims any expectations of reciprocal acceptance. A comparison of the number of mosques in the West versus the number of non-Islamic houses of worship in Islamic countries yields a very clear pattern. Islamic public prayers are permitted in the West, but you would be hard pressed to witness non-Islamic public prayers in Islamic countries. The number of Muslims who have been allowed to emigrate to the West is astronomically high, and yet very few (if any) non-Muslims can obtain citizenship in Islamic countries. Islamic clerics are permitted to spew astoundingly hateful rhetoric from their religious pulpits while in the West. Try to criticize Islam in an Islamic country. Ironically, many such extremist Islamic clerics are banned from Islamic countries but are welcomed with open arms in the West! The tolerance is always one way. A heavily proselytizing and supremacist religion coupled with host nations that are suicidally empathetic in their welcoming nature can yield only one outcome. The death of the West at the Altar of Infinite Tolerance and Orgiastic Empathy.

I recently watched the film *Conclave* starring Ralph Fiennes (as the dean of the college of cardinals), John Lithgow, Stanley Tucci, and Isabella Rossellini. The film was gripping until the ending when a crusade of parasitic wokeism took over. Following an Islamic terror attack committed outside of the walls of the conclave, one of the cardinals stands up and offers a very empathetic and Islamophilic message (the terrorists were apparently deluded) as a counterpoint to one "extreme" cardinal who was exhibiting "Islamophobic" tendencies. This same cardinal who ends up being chosen as the next pope turns out to be intersex (i.e., he was born with a uterus).[41] Jackpot! It takes a uniquely gifted intersex individual to recognize this empathetic reality about True Islam. Art imitates real life, and so the real pope is just as empathetic. Following an Islamic terror attack in Brussels in 2016, Pope Francis, in his infinite empathy and kindness, was quick to point out that we should not hold any ill will toward Islam. During a Holy Thursday mass, he washed and kissed the feet of Muslim migrants and reminded the world that we are "[a]ll brothers and children of the same God" and added that "We want to live together in peace."[42] The near complete erasure of Christianity in the Middle East at the hands of Islam would suggest otherwise. It is best, though, not to let pesky facts get in the way of one's suicidal empathy. Perhaps the injunction from the New Testament to love your enemy is at the root of his earthly suicidal empathy, notwithstanding that it was meant as a prescriptive canonical strategy for entry into heaven. In his infinite largesse, Pope Francis has often criticized the reflex to enact stricter immigration policies,[43] even when such illegal migrants stem from societies that are existentially hostile to Christianity. The pope "unequivocally expresses a preferential option for, and commitment to, accompanying migrants in *empathy* [italics added for emphasis] and solidarity."[44] It helps to be able to pontificate about his divine empathy behind the tall walls of the Vatican. The pope's empathy was apparently not shared by a "bigoted" spiritual colleague who stated that "Europe belongs to the Europeans" and added that refugees should be repatriated to their home nations.[45] The "bigot" in question is the Dalai Lama. The Dalai Lama apparently recognizes that "idiot compassion," the Buddhist notion mentioned earlier, is not laudable.

Eva Brunne has broken an important theological glass ceiling. She is reported to be the first openly gay bishop and is a member of the Lutheran Church in Sweden, a country that has perfected suicidal empathy to an art form. Bishop Brunne, in her infinite munificence, suggested an intriguing theological option to make the innumerable Muslims that had been welcomed by Sweden in the recent past feel even more welcomed. Christian crosses can be so triggering to Muslims, even if within a church, so why not remove them and build an Islamic prayer room instead?[46] It is a win-win situation, namely Bishop Brunne can lean into her suicidal empathy, and the Noble Muslims do not have to be insulted by signs of Christianity in a church. Everyone wins! The Reverend Karen Oliveto is equally kind and empathetic. In 2016, she was elected as the first openly gay bishop in the United Methodist Church, notwithstanding the church's less-than-tolerant position on homosexuality.[47] Perhaps because of her queer identity, which allows her access to Queer Empathy, she had previously fought against Islamophobia by holding a very loving sign "We are all Muslims." These examples are of course well in line with the Queers for Palestine movement that has come out in full force in support of Gaza and against Israel's retaliation to Hamas's October 7 genocidal massacre of more than twelve hundred innocent people. Tel Aviv is one of the most queer-friendly cities in the world. Gaza, on the other hand, has perfected a 100 percent effective gravity-based conversion therapy program for queers (throwing them off rooftops). When you are suicidally empathetic, though, facts should never interfere with your self-loathing delusions. Geese for Foie Gras! This recorded dialogue perfectly captures this suicidal reflex. It was conducted by a street interviewer named Hermes as he interacted with a pink-haired gay woman (recall my explanation in *The Parasitic Mind* of why parasitized people disproportionately seem to have aposematic hair coloring):

HERMES: Are you Pro Palestine?

WOMAN: Yeah, of course. Free Palestine.

HERMES: Are you pro the LGBTQ community?

WOMAN: I am gay.

HERMES: Do you know what would happen to LGBT people in Palestine?

WOMAN: Yeah, but I don't care.

HERMES: Really?

WOMAN: Because something bad is happening to them. It does not matter if they would support me or not. I'm still going to respect them as human beings.

HERMES: So you don't care if they would kill you if you went over there?

WOMAN: No.

HERMES: You're still going to support them?

WOMAN: Yeah. Because it's the right thing to do.

HERMES: What if that, like, ends up killing you in the future?

WOMAN: Then that's the way I was meant to go.[48]

In Franz Kafka's classic novella *The Metamorphosis*, a family man wakes up one day to find that he has been transformed into a loathsome insect. Kafka must have been prescient about realities to unfold more than one hundred years later, as both the woman in the dialogue above and pro-Palestine Jews are part of a new form of human-to-insect metamorphosis, the transformation from a human being endowed with reason to a wood cricket hell-bent on committing self-righteous suicide.

Self-Loathing as a Form of Suicidal Empathy–Human Wood Crickets

There is a chilling Arabic proverb that captures the internalized submissive stance of women in some of these societies. The French translation is as follows: *"Bats ta femme tous les matins; si tu ne sais pas pourquoi, elle le sait."*[49] (Beat your wife every morning. If you don't know why, she knows.) This captures the sinister power dynamic between men and women in such cultures. If the man beats you, surely it must have been your fault for having provoked him. Regrettably, many female victims of domestic violence internalize this attributional style and exist in a precarious world where they constantly walk on eggshells lest they might trigger a "deserved" beating. This is precisely the suicidally empathetic reflex of the West when it comes to the lack of assimilation of some of its immigrants. With that in mind, if Noble Immigrants commit depraved crimes, surely it is the fault of the host societies for having been less than welcoming.

In his work within the Danish juvenile penal system, Nicolai Sennels has stated that 70 percent of offenders were of a Muslim background. I had the chance to invite Sennels on my show many years ago, and we discussed the mindset that yields such outlandishly high rates of criminality.[50] Incidentally, these patterns replicate across Europe and for a wide range of crimes. There are three ways by which the suicidally empathetic respond to such data: (1) They reject the value of collecting such data under the pretext that some knowledge should be forbidden, given that it can lead to harm. As I have previously explained, the pursuit of truth is a deontological principle that should not be shackled by consequentialist concerns. (2) They attack the source of the data as being part of a "Far-Right" movement meant to demonize Noble Immigrants. (3) They blame the host societies for the criminality of the recently arrived immigrants. This is precisely what happened when I last visited Norway in 2013. A Norwegian colleague had picked me up at the airport, where I had noticed many Muslim women donning the freedom veils of sartorial emancipation. Many of the women looked as though they were Somali, which is not what one might expect when arriving in Norway. As we drove away from the airport, I gingerly asked my colleague how the "diversity is our strength" immigration policy was going. He paused and then, with an air of regret and trepidation, he confirmed that the assimilation had not gone well. He quickly added that this was the fault of the host nation for not having done enough to assimilate the Noble Somalis. The Scandinavians love saunas but especially so following a refreshing swim in the infinity pool of suicidal empathy. In 2021, a Nigerian pirate (yes, they still exist) was involved in a gunfight with sailors from the Danish Navy, during which he was injured and eventually lost his leg. In their orgiastic kindness, the Danish government decided to pay for his prosthetic leg, grant him asylum in Denmark, and develop a comprehensive plan to integrate him within Danish society. Despite his crime, the pirate did not serve any time in prison. Danish taxpayers covered the bill for this orgy of kindness to the tune of $615,000.[51] In a twist of cosmic irony, the pirate's name is

Lucky Frances. It is indeed lucky that this pirate's fate crossed paths with a society hell-bent on committing Civilizational Seppuku.

Speaking of suicidal self-loathing, perhaps the most odious exemplar is Wood Cricket Jews. They seek to ingratiate themselves with their executioners by expressing a deep hatred of their own people. "Look at me. I am the ultimate exemplar of an enlightened person. I don't succumb to a superficial basal survival instinct. I rise above it from the safety of my American campus, where I could be patted on the head as a 'good Jew' by Keffiyeh Karen and Keffiyeh Mohammad." It is a form of parasitic posturing that is akin to the wood cricket being parasitized by the hairworm. Under normal circumstances, the wood cricket abhors water and seeks to avoid it at all costs. But when parasitized by the hairworm, it is perfectly happy to commit suicide by jumping to its aquatic death, as the hairworm needs to complete its reproductive cycle in water.[52] Let me introduce you to Wood Cricket Anna Epstein who was caught tearing down posters at Boston University not long after the October 7 massacre.[53] She was unable to muster any empathy for the kidnapped Jewish babies. Her empathy was restricted to those fighting the "Zionist occupation," and she justified her execrably callous actions by reminding the person filming her that she was Jewish. Or take, for example, Jonathan Glazer's acceptance speech at the 2024 Oscars for Best International Feature *The Zone of Interest*, which included the following sentence: "We stand here as men who refute their Jewishness and the Holocaust being hijacked by an occupation which has led to conflict, for so many innocent people."[54] Or Sarah Friedland, who in her acceptance speech for Best Debut Film *Familiar Touch* at the 2024 Venice Film Festival demonstrated that she was a truly enlightened progressive Jew when she said: "As a Jewish American artist working in a time-based medium, I must note I'm accepting this award on the 336th day of Israel's genocide in Gaza and 76th year of occupation. I believe it is our responsibility as film workers to use the institutional platforms through which we work to redress Israel's impunity on the global stage. I stand in solidarity with the people of Palestine in their struggle for liberation."[55] Had Epstein, Glazer, and Friedland been at the Nova Music Festival on October 7, their enlightened kindness would not have saved them from a bullet to their respective empathetic heads. Case in point, Vivian Silver was a seventy-four-year-old peace activist who had dedicated several decades of her life to fostering harmony between Israelis and Palestinians while living in Be'eri, a Kibbutz close to the border with Gaza.[56] Tragically, on that fateful October 7 massacre, her empathy and kindness did not protect her from becoming a victim of the debauchery of cruelty that befell many Israeli peace activists. A similar fate befell Vittorio Arrigoni in 2011, the Italian man who was a staunchly pro-Palestine activist. His empathy for the Palestinian cause did not protect him from being killed in the Gaza Strip by a group of hard-line Islamic extremists.[57]

Gabor Maté is a Canadian physician who has built a self-help empire on the back of his supposed empathetic and compassionate handling of patients who suffer from addiction. He argues that at the root of addiction is childhood trauma, but he goes much further by purporting that countless diseases are rooted in this singular explanation. It stems from the reflex to create explanatory parsimony but in doing so he is falling prey to the misapplication of Occam's razor. At times, the simplest all-encompassing explanation is perfectly incorrect. This reminds me of Freudian psychoanalytical quackery, wherein all psychological disorders have their ultimate genesis in sexual repression; or the hysteria of the repressed memories movement, wherein therapists help their patients recover a memory of past sexual abuse (oftentimes planted by the therapist), which otherwise explains their current psychological ailment.[58] Whenever a health provider offers a singular universal cause for innumerable and diverse ailments, this is a good sign that they are espousing nonsense. Several psychologists have disputed Maté's claims, which are neither theoretically sound nor supported by the empirical evidence.[59] And yet, he has built a very successful business teaching the healing powers of orgiastic empathy via his Compassionate Inquiry training programs.[60] At the bottom of the website's landing page, one finds the following very empathic acknowledgment:

We acknowledge that we work and gather on lands that have been home to many Indigenous peoples around the world, and offer our respect and gratitude to Elders past, present, and future.

We recognize the interdependence and interconnectedness of all beings, including species of plants and animals, land masses, forests, water bodies, and our shared air and atmosphere. We invite feedback, dialogue, and collaboration as we work together to create a more inclusive, compassionate, and equitable world for all.

Maté's infinite well of intergenerational empathy does not apply to Jews, though. He knows, as a Holocaust "survivor," what true trauma is, and he never fails to remind the world that the Palestinians are suffering a genocide at the hands of the Nazi-like Israelis. I engaged the father-son team of wood crickets on X, a portion of which is as follows:

[T]hey are parasitized useful idiots who would be the first to be exterminated. Their infinite suicidal empathy is not an indulgence that will free them from the firing squad. A strong person with dignity is infinitely kind as a default value but breathtakingly ruthless to those who wish to eradicate his family's existence. There is nothing noble about the Mate [sic] duo. They are uninformed fools engaging in malignant narcissism masquerading as infinite compassion.[61]

Cultures add to the rich tapestry of the human experience via unique attire, foods, music, and languages. In this sense, cultural pluralism can be enriching. However, it is wrong to presume that cultures are equal and interchangeable, or that all immigrants are equally likely to assimilate within the West. We have a tsunami of evidence that points to this obvious reality, but to recognize it would render us "mean" and lacking in compassion, tolerance, and empathy. Hence, it is apparently best to commit Civilizational Seppuku under the protective cloak of suicidal empathy. No! The West should unequivocally proclaim that any immigrant who comes to our shores must provide a net benefit without exhibiting an iota of existential hate for our way of life. To the West, I say, be proud of your heritage, and defend it at all costs from its avowed enemies.

4

Blank Slate Felons

There is a point of diseased mellowness and effeminacy in the history of society, at which society itself takes the part of him who injures it, the part of the *criminal*, and does so, in fact, seriously and honestly. To punish, appears to it to be somehow unfair—it is certain that the idea of "punishment" and "the obligation to punish" are then painful and alarming to people. "Is it not sufficient if the criminal be rendered *harmless*? Why should we still punish? Punishment itself is terrible!"[1]

One of my all-time favorite television shows is *Cheers*, which ran from 1982 to 1993. Recently, I rewatched the episode titled "Homicidal Ham" (season 2, episode 4), which recounts the story of Andy, a former convict who decides to commit an armed robbery at the bar, to be sent back to prison. At first, Diane (the waitress and love interest of Sam, the bar's owner) insists that they must get rid of Andy, as he is a dangerous ex-convict. But then, when Andy proceeds with his armed robbery plans, Diane has a change of heart and asks Sam to refrain from calling the cops and instead states: "When Andy shoved that gun in your face, he was asking for help," and then adds: "He stands here as an embodiment of a failure of our penal system. Yes, this man doesn't belong in prison. Sam, we . . . mostly I . . . can save this man's life." Therein lies the perfect embodiment of the progressive mindset and bleeding-heart liberal who is going to ride into town and save all criminals from the injustices that they have faced. Victims be damned! The "real" victims are the criminals who have been victimized by society, and this has led them to a life of crime. Hence, according to the empathetic liberal, to presume that criminals have personal agency for their actions is to victimize them again. Instead of holding them criminally responsible, rehabilitate them through various programs rooted in empathy, kindness, and acceptance.

In 2002, I spent part of that year as a visiting professor at the Tuck School of Business at Dartmouth College. I recall hearing about the double murder of two Dartmouth professors, Half and Susanne Zantop, the previous year.[2] The perpetrators turned out to be two teenagers, James Parker and Robert Tulloch, who decided that they wanted to rob someone to fund their life of crime and adventure in Australia. Prior to randomly landing on the Zantop home, they had tried to enter another home, but the homeowner in that case had the proper intuition. He came to the door with a gun in his hand, albeit he did not open the door. Once the would-be murderers realized that the homeowner was armed, they left the scene, to attempt their diabolical plan another day.[3] Eventually, they landed on the kind and empathetic Zantops, who were willing to let the teenagers into their home to aid the high schoolers, who were supposedly conducting a survey on the environment. Hence, the ruse that was utilized by the psychopathic teenagers to enter the Zantops' home relied on activating two layers of empathy, one for the plight of the environment and the second for the plight of the teenagers who needed respondents. Incidentally, James Parker was convicted to a sentence of twenty-five years to life, and he was granted parole in 2024, having served less than the requisite minimum number of years.[4] Should someone who committed such a heinous double murder be given a second chance at life at the relatively young age of thirty-nine? To most progressive people, the answer is a resounding yes! Progressive empathy is truly limitless, in that it also applies to recidivist murderers. Reginald Lively had been convicted of two prior homicides in 1986 and 2000, and was released early for both homicides, to eventually commit his third murder in 2021.[5] Or, take Washington Pearson, who was convicted of sexual assault in 2024. His rap sheet had 197 criminal entries going back to 1987.[6] Could we not have granted him the empathetic courtesy to reach a round number such as 200 prior to throwing the book at him? Be kind to felons.

Suicidal empathy seeks to reflexively mitigate the actions of violent criminals by proposing external "root" causes. It is society's fault. It is systemic racism. It is an impoverished childhood. It is an abusive parent. From this perspective, criminals are "blank slate felons." Suicidal empathy requires the removal of a criminal's personal agency: ". . . [O]ur empathy for another person can be stretched very far. We can venture too close and lose our perspective on humanity. Once we understand another life by entering it, by seeing it from inside, we may both pardon and forgive a criminal action. We may not even recognize it as criminal. We are all guilty in some way. How can we ever judge anyone else, punish anyone else?"[7]

Do criminals deserve second chances? Of course it depends on the nature of their crimes. The reality, though, is that most incarcerated prisoners within the state and federal penal system have had many more than second chances. A 2016 report from the US Department of Justice presents some disturbing recidivism rates about the profile of the typical male inmate: 19 percent reported five to nine previous incarcerations, and 12 percent reported ten or more.[8] In other words, nearly one-third of US male prisoners have had many more than second chances. Instead of exhibiting endless misplaced empathy for recidivist monsters, perhaps our empathy should be directed toward Stephen Federico, who recently shared his immeasurable grief in a House Judiciary Subcommittee regarding the killing of his daughter by a man who had been arrested thirty-nine previous times and had committed twenty-five felonies.[9] She was white, though, whereas the recidivist felon was black. #BLM

Not only is the US penal system endlessly empathetic in its desire to grant multiple chances to convicted criminals, but so are countless suicidally empathetic Good Samaritans. When he was sixteen years old, Travis Lewis was convicted of killing seventy-five-year-old Sally Snowden McKay and her nephew fifty-two-year-old Joseph Baker, when he was apprehended during a burglary. He was found guilty and sentenced to a 28.5-year prison sentence. Martha McKay, the daughter of the slain woman, was apparently an infinitely kindhearted Buddhist, who communicated with the double murderer during his incarceration and granted him forgiveness. She petitioned for his early release and offered him a job at the house wherein he had committed the double murder. Lewis repaid her kindness by murdering her as well.[10] One might argue that McKay was using a common healing strategy, namely victims' family members recognize that anger, vengefulness, and rancor can eat away at you in a manner akin to a metastatic cancer, and as such, in order to move on with their lives, they must extend forgiveness. And of course, there are many religious precepts that support the power of forgiveness, such as Luke 6:37: "Do not judge, and you will not be judged. Do not condemn, and you will not be condemned. Forgive, and you will be forgiven."[11] In the Catholic faith, the process of confessing your sins to a priest in a booth is rooted in the recognition that to admit one's transgressions allows for penance and repentance to take place in a believer's relationship with God. Hence, there is a pathway for divine forgiveness, even for profoundly egregious acts. But while God may be infinitely forgiving, humans do not necessarily possess this divine quality. We have evolved a sense of revenge precisely because there are countless situations wherein it would have made evolutionary sense for us to be potentially vengeful. The French proverb *Tout comprendre c'est tout pardoner* (To understand all is to forgive all) perfectly captures this sentiment.

Several movies from my childhood come to mind that were very much rooted in a theme of vengefulness. Perhaps the two most haunting revenge movies of my childhood starred Charles Bronson: *Once Upon a Time in the West* and *Death Wish*. The former recounts the story of Bronson's character Harmonica seeking revenge against an outlaw named Frank (played by Henry Fonda) who had been responsible for the murder of Harmonica's older brother many years earlier. The most disturbing revenge movie for me though was another Bronson classic, *Death Wish*, which recounts the story of architect Paul Kersey (played by Bronson) whose wife is murdered and daughter is raped during a home invasion. Bronson's character sets out to eliminate the criminals who attacked his family. Notwithstanding the moral debates regarding vigilantism, the revenge theme is universally appreciated because it caters to an evolved emotion rooted in a tit-for-tat calculus that the Old Testament codified via the "eye for an eye" principle. Not surprisingly, many classic movies revolve around the revenge theme, including *Unforgiven*, *Memento*, *The Equalizer*, *John Wick*, *Taken*, *Kill Bill*, *Inglourious Basterds*, and *Promising Young Woman*. The West, though, has decided that it is too "civilized" ever to activate our evolved mechanism of righteous vengefulness within its repertoire of moral punishments. Many criminals utilize our broken moral compass to commit crimes unencumbered by the concern that there might be severe consequences for their acts.

Progressive Californians are some of the most suicidally empathetic people on earth. Case in point, in 2023 Jen Angel was a baker who was killed during a robbery in Oakland. Her friends and family members wanted to go on record in establishing that Ms. Angel would have been dead set against her murderers being incarcerated.[12] Californians are infinitely kind toward criminals. Never mind getting rid of the death penalty; never mind attempting to repeal the "three strikes" law for violent offenders; never mind the new classification of thefts that are under $950 as misdemeanors. These are all very empathetic positions toward the criminals, but if you truly wish to highlight how kind you are, speak from the grave about how wrong it is to punish the ones who murdered you. This should get you a sainthood from the Church of the Suicidally Empathetic, of which Nathan Clark is a proud member. Clark, a resident of Springfield, Ohio, tragically lost his eleven-year-old son in a vehicular accident. The culprit, a Haitian man who did not have a legal driver's license, was found guilty of involuntary manslaughter and vehicular homicide. The case reignited the discussion on immigration, and it apparently led to some animus toward the twenty thousand Haitians who had settled in this small city in only three years. Mr. Clark used his son's death to signal his infinite empathy toward Haitians when he stated, "I wish that my son, Aiden Clark, was killed by a 60-year-old white man."[13] Apparently, the death of one's child is not nearly as important as communicating to the world that you are not a racist. Nothing could be more tragic than for the world to think that the grieving father harbors ill will toward immigrants. He is a good person but not nearly as enlightened as the mayor of Boston, Michelle Wu. When an off-duty cop shot and killed a man who was ominously attempting to knife random customers at a restaurant, Mayor Wu was quick to extend her condolences to the family of the would-be murderer.[14]

Civilizational Seppuku requires not only that one empathize with violent criminals more so than their victims, but it also demands a hostility toward those tasked to protect us from such criminals. The Defund the Police movement, which spread following the death of blank slate felon George Floyd, was meant as a repudiation of the existing police forces, which were apparently irredeemably racist (an astoundingly false premise). Apparently, policing had to be "reimagined," a nauseating and meaningless woke word. Of course, the defunding of the police force resulted in what the average three-day-old pigeon could have predicted, namely an increase in crimes in so-called communities of color. Hence, the Floyd-triggered empathy served to harm the communities that were supposedly "targeted" by the police. While Canada does not have a history of slavery, it utilizes other forms of existential intergenerational guilt to implement its own form of suicidal empathy. The Royal Canadian Mounted Police (RCMP) is Canada's national police. Recently, two siblings, aged four and six, disappeared in the province of Nova Scotia. The RCMP officer who had been tasked with providing Canadians with an update of the case began as follows: "First, I acknowledge that we are in Mi'kma'ki the traditional and unceded ancestral territory of the Mi'kmaq people. I also recognize that African Nova Scotians are a distinct people whose histories, legacies, and contributions have enriched that part of Mi'kma'ki, known as Nova Scotia, for over 400 years."[15] When children go missing, it is most important to first empathetically cater to the feelings of the Mi'kma'ki people and African Nova Scotians, for realities that might have taken place centuries ago. The whiny missing children will have to wait their turn at the wheel of empathy. Incidentally, I have confidentially received screenshots of various RCMP communiqués, as sent to me by a current RCMP agent.[16] The parasitic suicidal empathy defies logic and common sense. It included an explanation of how to address white privilege during Black History Month, how to create a work environment where people have menstrual dignity, ensuring that agents adhere to equity concerns when issuing moving violation tickets to people of color, and how to address transgender people when stopped for a traffic violation. Protecting Canadians from terrorists takes an empathetic back seat to the true scourges plaguing Canadian society: racist speeding tickets and a lack of menstrual equity for men.

The Rejection of Heroism and the Faux Empathy of Sneaky F**kers

To understand the male archetype that women fantasize about, simply conduct a content analysis of romance novels. Throughout the world, this literary category is almost solely read by women. Evolutionary-minded scholars have conducted the relevant analysis, and, not surprisingly, the main male protagonist possesses certain recurring features.[17] It is as though all writers of romance novels are plagiarizing off the same male exemplar. The male hero is a muscular, strong, tall, bold, risk-taking hero who can be reined in only by the love and succor of the main female character. I just described for you nearly every single romance novel ever written. On the Goodreads website, there is a list titled "All Time Dominant-Alpha Romance Heroes."[18] I am unaware of a list titled "All Time Sensitive Beta Romance Male Protagonists Who Cry When Watching *Sleepless in Seattle*." The 1980s pop singer Bonnie Tyler released a hit titled "Holding Out for a Hero" and not one titled "I Need a Man Afraid of His Shadow." Women are attracted to heroic male figures and, correspondingly, to uniforms that capture such heroism. This is why I have firefighter, navy, and cop uniforms for Role-Playing Thursday Nights in the Saad household. All right, I am kidding, but you get the gist. Women do not fantasize about pear-shaped men with whining nasal voices and effeminate affectations imbued with the requisite highfalutin progressive lisp. This is precisely why the concept of toxic masculinity, as promulgated by a feminized society, is, well, toxic. Once you pathologize key features of 50 percent of the people who comprise a sexually reproducing species, it does not yield good outcomes.[19] Numerous studies have established the unequivocal fact that male heroism is a sexually selected trait, meaning that it is a universal preference that women exhibit.[20] I am unaware of a culture where women repeatedly state that they are desperately seeking to meet cowardly, meek, and pusillanimous weaklings who are proud members of the International Men's Society of Invertebrate Castrati.

Incidentally, the fact that women are attracted to heroic men with a muscular disposition does not imply that these men are emotional brutes. On the contrary, the fantasy man can be both a protector while exhibiting great sensitivity, empathy, and warmth. Both features constitute key elements of the ideal man. Being attracted to a heroic figure does not imply that women prefer neanderthal thugs bereft of any emotional intelligence. This brings me to a recent legal case that pits heroism against the progressive antipathy of such virtue. Daniel Penny is a veteran who served as a US Marine. On May 1, 2023, while riding in the New York subway, he intervened by subduing Jordan Neely, a young man who was homeless, mentally ill, and had had many run-ins with the law. Neely had entered the subway car, acting erratically, and threatening to kill people. Penny intervened, and in doing so he restrained him via a chokehold that led to his death. Rather than hailing the heroism of Penny, the supremely progressive Manhattan district attorney, Alvin Bragg, brought two charges against Penny, criminally negligent homicide and second-degree manslaughter. The manslaughter charge was eventually dismissed due to jury deadlock, whereas Penny was ultimately found not guilty of the negligent homicide charge.[21] That Penny was charged in the first place speaks to two realities: (1) Penny was white, whereas Neely was black. When a few weeks later, a black man killed another black man who was harassing people on the New York subway, the perpetrator was not charged;[22] (2) the reflex of suicidal empathy toward Neely, who was black, mentally ill, homeless, and a repeat criminal. He must be the victim of an unfair society, and as such his bundle of victimhood places him on equal footing as Saint George Floyd.

Radical feminists are so keen to identify misogyny in every nook and cranny that they redefine desired masculine traits as subtle manifestations of the evil patriarchy. This is precisely the "homeostasis of victimology" that I introduced in *The Parasitic Mind*. Case in point, benevolent sexism is apparently a gentler form of misogyny that instantiates itself via an ethos of heroism, protection, and chivalry. All roads lead to men being misogynistic. Hence, if a man opens the door for women, cherishes women, or intervenes when a woman is being raped in an alley, he is engaging in benevolent sexism. To the utter dismay of the rabid feminists in Women's Studies programs, it turns out that women are very attracted to benevolently sexist men.[23] It is called reality as shaped by evolution. Viewed from this perspective, Penny's heroism becomes a form of benevolent sexism.

Comedic actor Will Ferrell, the epitome of a male feminist, has uncovered the panacea to the world's ills. At the 2023 Women in Entertainment gala, Ferrell proclaimed: "This is such a wonderful event where we honor and support and continue to fight for women in all facets of the entertainment world. But you know what? Forget about the entertainment world. Isn't it just time for women to run the planet? I'm not just trying to placate you, I swear. But I don't know what else to do because we, men, we've been running the show since, what, 10,000 B.C.? Something like that? And we're not doing so good. So please, can you guys just take over? Can you? I think it's time."[24] Ferrell is so kind and enlightened. He knows that if women were ruling the world, all the man-made calamities throughout history would not have taken place. Note that I wrote 'man-made' in support of Ferrell's feminist empathy. Of course, the greatest male feminist of all time is our own Canadian Justin Trudeau. At the recent Equal Voice Foundation event, whose goal is to increase women's participation in the Canadian political ecosystem, Trudeau lamented Kamala Harris's defeat against Donald Trump as follows: "It shouldn't be that way. It wasn't supposed to be that way. We were supposed to be on a steady, if difficult sometimes, march towards progress. And yet, just a few weeks ago, the United States voted for a second time to not elect its first woman president. Everywhere, women's rights and women's progress is [sic] under attack. Overtly, and subtly. And I want you to know that I am and always will be a proud feminist. You will always have an ally in me and in my government." To have elected Harris would have been progress because she has lady parts of color. My disdain for Trudeau has been on record for many years, but after this groveling address, I posted the following on my X feed: "There are no words, no sentiments, no non-verbal cues, no telepathic communications that can capture the extent to which this individual is grotesque." To which Elon Musk responded as follows: "He's such an insufferable tool. Won't be in power for much longer."[25] Trudeau's creepy feminist faux empathy manifests itself in the new terms that he comes up with to signal his supposed allyship to women. Who could forget how he proudly introduced the terms "she-cession" (for recession) and "she-covery" (for economic recovery) into the Canadian lexicon?[26] Linguistic empathy strikes again.

Are women attracted to this archetype of a falsely empathetic sneaky f**ker? In arguably one of the most memorable exchanges ever on my show, Megyn Kelly answered this question in her inimitable style:[27]

KELLY: I object to the loss of manhood in our men in general. I don't like the whole toxic masculinity bs. I really don't like the pumpkin spice latte drinking, you know Brooklyn not just regular Brooklyn, Park Slope Brooklyn guys, who are running around trying to be. It's not that they're trans; it's that they're men who think that evolved men look and act like women. That's not attractive to me and I don't want to be around it, and I don't want to elect it in a leader.

ME: Did we speak on your show about my male social justice warriors as sneaky f**kers. That's an actual zoological term. Did we talk about that?

KELLY: No. How did I miss that gold?

ME: Somebody on your team should be fired for not having raised that on your show so let me mention it here if I may and then you can tell me because it speaks exactly to what you just said about men. So, in the zoological literature this came out probably in the 70s, there was a term which was colloquially referred in the scientific literature as sneaky f**ker but the real term is kleptogamy. This is where you typically have males of a species who come in one of two phenotypes: there's the bulky masculine male; there's another type of male that mimics a female; and so what he'll do is, as he comes by a big male and he wants to get access to the females that are you know behind the protective male, he will send out cues as though he is a female so that the big male will let him through and then he will sneak in the copulations. And hence he's known as a sneaky f**ker and so I argued in *The Parasitic Mind* that what male social justice warriors do is they are engaging in a form of sneaky f**ker mating strategy; and that's exactly what Justin Trudeau is doing he is so empathetic; he is so gentle; he's so hugging of the tree so he thinks that that will make him so non-intimidating and hopefully he can sneak in some surreptitious mating opportunities. What do you think of this theory?

KELLY: I think you know another name might be terrible f**kers because I just have every belief that he's terrible in bed somebody like that so the ladies may be wooed while they're over like a glass of wine with somebody like that he looks at them he listens he's empathetic he feels your pain.

This is not to imply that empathy is not desired by women. But as is true of most things in life, empathy should be applied in the right measure, to the right people, at the right time.

Juliet Watson and Sarah Casey, two academic feminists, recently wrote: "For high profile and often white, cis-gendered, heterosexual, able-bodied men who hold significant and multiple privileges, identifying as a feminist offers opportunities to reap further benefits, such as financial gain and increased brand power through media exposure."[28] Clearly, they are unaware of the sneaky f*cker strategy and its associated faux empathy.

To summarize, a feminized society hell-bent on drowning in the infinity pool of suicidal empathy will: (1) label male heroes who intervene to protect women from being raped as benevolently sexist and sufferers of toxic masculinity; (2) elevate the faux-empath male sneaky f**kers—who cross their legs in an effeminate manner and who have the testosterone levels of Betty White—as the idealized male archetype. Most importantly, though, to truly ascend to the highest and purest form of suicidal empathy, one must be able to simultaneously hate the men who save you from being raped (toxic masculinity) while exhibiting unlimited empathy toward the men who rape you, a topic to which I turn next. #Empathy ForRapists

Be Empathetic Toward (Your) Rapists

During her tenure as chancellor of Germany (2005 to 2021), Angela Merkel instituted a breathtaking open-door immigration policy, especially to Muslim migrants. One could imagine that her compassionate suicidal empathy toward migrants was meant as penance for the crimes against humanity committed only a few generations earlier by Germany. Apparently, one of the best ways to make up for the Holocaust is to allow entry to millions of Muslims, and in doing so ensuring that Jewish life in Germany will become intolerable again. Not surprisingly, and as is true throughout Western Europe, there has been an astounding increase in sexual assaults across Europe, disproportionately stemming from Noble Migrants of Peace. Suicidally empathetic Westerners are quick to point out that nonmigrant men also commit crimes, as though this were a worthy retort. Sexual violence is an ugly universal reality that transcends cultures or eras, but this does not mean that all men, irrespective of their backgrounds, are equally likely to commit violence. How women are viewed and treated in Islamic societies is astoundingly different from that in the West. Hence, if you allow entry of millions of men who stem from such societies, it is not rocket science to explain why the prevalence of sexual assaults in the West has correspondingly increased.

Selin Gören is a German politician and activist who served as the national spokesperson for Solid (left-wing youth organization). In 2016, she was sexually assaulted by three migrants in the city of Mannheim. When she reported the crime to the police, she confabulated a story to protect the identity of her attackers who hailed from the Middle East. She lied and stated that they spoke German rather than tell the truth, which was that they were conversing in Arabic or Farsi. Clearly, when one is raped, it is important to safeguard against any backlash that noble people of the Middle East might experience. Furthermore, in an orgiastic display of suicidal empathy, she wrote on Facebook: "I am really sorry that your sexist and line-crossing treatment of me could help fuel aggressive racism. I'm going to scream . . . I will not stand by and watch, and it can happen that racists and concerned citizens name you as the problem. You're not the problem. You're usually a wonderful human being who deserves as much as any other to be safe and free. I will not stand by and watch and let it happen that racists and concerned citizens name you as the problem."[29] You see dear reader, Ms. Gören is so much more empathetic than you. She does not want her rapists to be marginalized. She is a good person who holds no ill will toward blank slate felons. She ended her Facebook letter with the hashtag #refugeeswelcome.

Maria Ladenburger was a nineteen-year-old medical student at the University of Freiburg. As part of her empathetic activism, she volunteered her time at several migrant shelters. While returning from a party in December 2016, she was raped and subsequently murdered by Afghan asylum seeker Hussein Khavari. Prior to coming to Germany, Khavari had been convicted in 2013 of having robbed a woman and then throwing her off a cliff on the Greek island of Corfu.[30] He received a ten-year sentence but served a small fraction of it prior to being released. Undoubtedly, the Greek authorities must have been extremely empathetic toward Hussein as he was only a "child" when he committed his crime (he lied about his age). Maria's family asked that in lieu of flowers, individuals offer donations to refugee charities.[31] Again, when parents are grieving the rape and murder of their daughter, it is important that they ensure that the ethnicity of the killer does not get further marginalized. Of note, Maria's father (Clemens Ladenburger) is a lawyer who had worked on the refugee and migration crisis as part of his professional responsibilities. Hence, it is very likely that he had been exposed to the cultural enrichment that these noble migrants were bringing to Germany. And yet, this did not dissuade him from being infinitely empathetic and forgiving.

Germany has truly developed suicidal empathy into a performative art form. In 2020, a fifteen-year-old girl was gang-raped by nine men, eight of whom received only suspended sentences. In other words, they would not serve a minute of actual prison time. The one gang rapist who would serve some time would do so in a youth prison; he received a rather "empathetic" sentence of two years and nine months.[32] It gets a lot worse. A woman ran into one of the gang rapists who had been set free, and she insulted him by referring to him as a "disgraceful rapist pig" and a "disgusting freak."[33] Because she had apparently defamed the gang rapist, she received a weekend sentence in jail. Hence, in Germany, a gang rapist walks free while a woman who insults the gang rapist goes to jail. No society can survive such insanely misguided empathy. Collective sexual assaults by Muslim immigrants have been documented in Germany but more generally throughout Europe for many years.[34] It even has a "playful" name in Arabic, "Taharrush."[35] The reaction from Westerners is one fully immersed in suicidal empathy driven by Ostrich Parasitic Syndrome, namely, bury your head in the West and pretend that the problem does not exist. Ayaan Hirsi Ali, who was born into an Islamic family, has repeatedly warned the West what will happen if we continue to ignore these patterns.[36] Incidentally, severe punishments loom large for women in Europe who decide to protect themselves from unwanted sexual groping, as an American woman found out in Germany. She is facing a possible ten-year prison sentence for having accidentally killed an Eritrean man who had just sexually assaulted her.[37] Europe does not tolerate violent women who seek to protect themselves from sexual aggressions. It is important that migrant rapists feel welcomed in their host societies.

Nadia Murad was born in Iraq to a Yazidi family. In 2014, the Islamic State of Iraq and Syria (ISIS) were engaging in a systematic genocide of Yazidis, as well as taking countless Yazidi women as sex slaves. Tragically, Murad was one such woman who endured unimaginable horrors at the hands of ISIS. After her eventual escape, she became a vocal activist against sexual violence, which resulted in her being appointed in 2016 as a United Nations Goodwill Ambassador. In 2017, her harrowing autobiography titled *The Last Girl: My Story of Captivity, and My Fight Against the Islamic State* was published and translated to more than forty languages.

This led to her being coawarded the 2018 Nobel Peace Prize. Her story is one of breathtaking cruelty and improbable resilience. It is unsurprising then that she would be a sought-after public speaker. In 2021, she was invited to speak by the Toronto District School Board (Canada's largest school board) in front of several hundred students. Incredibly, her talk was canceled for fear that this might trigger a rise in Islamophobia.[38] Hence, that thousands of Yazidi women had been tortured into sexual servitude by Islamic men created a zero-sum situation in terms of who would serve as the target of empathy. The progressive mindset is very clear: Women who are repeatedly gang-raped and who wish to share their stories deserve less empathy and compassion than their Muslim rapists. To highlight this group of diabolical rapists would shed a negative light on Islam, and we cannot have such a situation. One is reminded of the presciently satirical tweet by the late Canadian comic Norm Macdonald: "What terrifies me is if ISIS were to detonate a nuclear device and kill 50 million Americans. Imagine the backlash against peaceful Muslims?"[39]

We often hear about the United States meddling in Islamic societies to spread democracy and liberty. This is ostensibly one of the arguments that was repeatedly used to justify the long presence of the US military in Afghanistan. However, when it came to American soldiers intervening to stop the grotesque pederasty of a long-standing Afghan tradition known as "Bacha Bazi," they were instructed to refrain from doing so and were told "to look the other way because it's their culture."[40] This practice, immortalized by a very well-known Afghan saying—"Women are for children; boys are for pleasure"—involves the institutionalized hoarding of very young boys for the sexual pleasure of older powerful men.[41] Hence, in this case, American empathy did not extend to young Afghan boys, along with protecting them from a life of sexual slavery.

Cultural relativism coupled with suicidal empathy yields some astounding realities. Let us begin with Adil Rashid, who had sex with a thirteen-year-old British girl when he was a young adult. The supremely empathetic British judge Michael Stokes decided against sentencing Rashid to any prison time because his Islamic upbringing made him unaware that it was wrong to have sex with children.[42] There you have it.

The judge must have been very proud of his progressive penal outlook in that he ensured to protect himself against the possibility of being construed as Islamophobic. It would be excessively mean to hold blank slate felons responsible for their crimes. The empathy and kindness of British judges is truly limitless. Hamada Salah is an Egyptian man who was sexually harassing two women on a train and was eventually found guilty of having sexually assaulted one of them. He was seeking asylum in the UK, so one might have hoped that he would have been on his best behavior. The infinitely compassionate British judge decided that Salah should not serve any prison time because he was bereft of friends in Britain.[43] You cannot blame the Noble Egyptian for his sexual assault; loneliness is a real scourge. An Iranian man who was convicted of rape in London was granted the right to stay in Britain upon completion of his seven-year sentence, because if deported if he might face harsh consequences in Iran.[44] Please be empathetic to the Iranian rapist! It gets worse. A Pakistani pedophile who had been found guilty of several sexual assaults in Britain was granted the right to stay in Britain, because if he were to be deported to Pakistan, he would face persecution due to his alcoholism (given that alcohol is not permitted in Islam).[45] Putting British children at risk of being sexually assaulted is certainly less important than protecting the right of the Pakistani pedophile to rape children while perhaps intoxicated. The Brits are very kind and particularly keen on protecting migrant pedophiles. The suicidal empathy of the British judiciary is truly infinite; it even extends to a Zimbabwean pedophile. To deport him would apparently lead to hardships in his home country, and hence he was permitted to stay in Britain, by a very empathetic female judge.[46] If the well-being of pedophiles were the metric to optimize, none should ever be sent to prison, as they are nearly guaranteed to face hardships in the prison's general population.

Austrian judges are as empathetic as their British counterparts. An Afghani migrant teenager who had participated in the gang rape of a young girl was given fifteen months of probation and fined £670 of punitive damages.[47] That will surely teach him! He probably did not know that it was illegal to gang-rape a child because he stems from another culture. It is best that the Austrians do not impose their "racist" morals on the Afghan gang rapist. An Iraqi refugee was facing in his own words a "sexual emergency," and so he was unable to control his impulse to rape a ten-year-old boy in the bathroom of a public swimming pool in Vienna. He was originally sentenced to a very "empathetic" six-year prison sentence, which was eventually overturned because it had not been established that the ten-year-old had not consented to the rape.[48] Yes, you read that correctly. Upon retrial, the sentence was increased to seven years but eventually decreased to four years upon further appeal by a very empathetic judge who reasoned that it was a "one-time incident."[49] Of course, various Austrian authorities were deeply concerned that this would lead to a reduction of incoming immigrants given the negative public reaction that the case engendered. Nothing could be more egregious than appearing Islamophobic. Incidentally, to combat the growing number of sexual harassments in German public swimming pools, many of which were committed by Muslim migrants,[50] the city of Büren came up with a foolproof strategy. They designed a public service announcement depicting an overweight red-haired white German woman groping the buttocks of a young swimmer of color who had a prosthetic leg.[51] Even my immeasurably spicy satire cannot compete with such a suicidally empathetic reality. The real threat in German pools stems from overweight red-haired women attacking one-legged boys of color.

The Dutch are also infinitely kind and empathetic but especially toward Afghan migrants who rape disabled young girls. The presiding judge gave the undocumented lovemaker a lighter sentence because he might otherwise be deported to his home country, and this would dampen the ability of the rapist from etching a new life in the Netherlands with his wife.[52] Surely, the disabled girl will forgive his "small transgression" once she realizes that it was probably the rampant Islamophobia in the Netherlands that drove him to commit the act. It is too bad that the victimized disabled Dutch girl did not live in Finland, because supremely empathetic Finnish officials have come up with a solution to stop the increase in migrant rapes. They are leveraging the power of TikTok to engage in a progressive dance wherein they remind noble undocumented lovemakers to refrain from touching a woman's "no-no square."[53] Incidentally, it took the rape of a ten-year-old child by an asylum seeker before the Finnish authorities changed the law to confirm that a child cannot consent to sex![54] Swedish police are equally adept at solving the surge of migrant sexual assaults; they distributed anti-groping bracelets that are certain to stop young migrants, who view women as less valuable than goats, from committing any sexual assaults.[55] Imagine if serial killers Ted Bundy, John Wayne Gacy, and Jeffrey Dahmer had watched the TikTok video in question. This is what happens when you have a fully delusional and yet empathetic view of the world that is perfectly decoupled from reality. Viral TikTok clips and armbands will eradicate migrant sexual assaults. Sweden is so empathetic that even when it recognizes that its open-door immigration policy has been an abject failure, it turns inward to find the culprit. Apparently, it "is facing a national crisis because of its failure to successfully integrate record number of immigrants."[56] Surely, if you are suicidally empathetic, you could not arrive to the "racist" conclusion that some immigrants arrive to host nations with values that are perfectly antithetical to theirs, and as such no amount of integration efforts could ever work.

This next story perfectly highlights the current zeitgeist of the West. Amanda Kijera is a white woman who is an ally to black men. She is better than you because she is implementing the hard work of anti-racism. I will let her words explain what happened to her next and the anti-racist and deeply empathetic conclusions that she reached.[57]

Ever committed to preserving the dignity of Black men in a world which constantly stereotypes them as violent savages, I viewed this writing [editorial about the violence faced by Haitian women] as yet one more opportunity to fight "the man" on behalf of my brothers. That night, before I could finish the piece, I was held on a rooftop in Haiti and raped repeatedly by one of the very men who I had spent the bulk of my life advocating for. . . .

Afraid he would kill me, I pleaded with him to honor my commitment to Haiti, to him as a brother in the mutual struggle for an end to our common oppression, but to no avail. He didn't care that I was a Malcolm X scholar. He told me to shut up, and then slapped me in the face.

It is difficult to imagine that the Haitian man did not stop in his tracks when he found out that she was a Malcom X scholar. Perhaps she should have also done the no-no square dance that the Finns choreographed as a defense against migrant rapes. Haitians appreciate a good dancer. In all seriousness, though, one would hope that this horrific tragedy would have served as an important lesson for the victim. Alas, she concluded that her rape was due to the white patriarchy: "Women are not the source of their oppression; oppressive policies and the as-yet unaddressed white patriarchy which still dominates the global stage are." And she added that when all told, she was "grateful for the experience."

The woman who was raped by the Haitian man was effectively fore-telling what an OXFAM training manual purported is the culprit when it comes to sexual violence: "privileged white women."[58] Take a deep breath and read that again. The genesis of rapes lies square at the feet of whiny and uppity white women. I end this section with a brief overview of the tragic case of Anat Kimchi, a white woman and doctoral student whose research and activism sought to highlight the supposed endemic racism of the American justice system. While walking in a dangerous area in Chicago, she was murdered by a black homeless man who has been linked to other attacks on women.[59] Kimchi would be alive today were it not for the suicidal empathy extended to repeat criminals and the homeless.

No Right to Self-Defense—Empathy for Criminals

The great majority of people who reach out to me have nothing but pos-itive things to say. Of the small number of people who dislike my posi-tions, an even smaller number will express their animus in problematic ways. In the fall of 2017, though, I faced a tsunami of online death threats necessitating that I report these to my university administrators, who then compelled me to file a report with the Montreal police. I held several meetings and exchanges with the university's security team, resulting in the implementation of a security protocol. During one of my meetings with the then head of the university's security department (Jacques Lachance),[60] I asked if I might be able to own and carry a gun (not necessarily on campus but more generally while in public). He informed me that he used to be a general in the Canadian military, tasked with various protective assignments of high-profile dignitaries, and he was not allowed to carry a gun. In other words, if someone with his military profile could not carry a gun, good luck in my getting one!

Notwithstanding the security services' best efforts, it was a very difficult semester for me. I felt under perpetual siege, not knowing where the next threat was coming from. Once I had finished a lecture, I would furtively leave the building and head off to meet my wife in our waiting car. Upon entering the car, I would let out a sigh of relief, knowing that I had made it for another week. This was happening to a professor in Canada in the twenty-first century. I am someone with a strong sense of honor and personal agency, so the idea that I was made to feel afraid did not sit well with me. I did not have the personal agency to defend myself. This was left to my university's security team, none of whom are armed.

The online threats eventually subsided, and by the 2018 winter semester, things had somewhat returned to normal. Fast-forward to late summer 2022 when I faced my first in-person ominous situation. I was walking with my son when I noticed an individual intensely staring at me. As I passed him by, he asked if I were Gad Saad. I turned around, pleased that this was a likely fan. With a big smile on my face, I replied in the affirmative. The next few seconds were quite chilling. He took a deep breath as if to restrain his apparent hatred and stated that he was not going to say or do anything to me out of respect for my son. It took me a second to realize what had just taken place, and then I answered "Thank you" and continued walking. The police tracked down the video clip of our exchange (two detectives reached out to me), but they were unable to clearly identify the individual. When I requested to be shown a list of possible suspects on file, they stated that they could not do so because that would be profiling (ergo racist, as the individual in question was black). The most fundamental tool of policing is now considered racist if the perpetrator is of a protected progressive class. We need to empathize with those who levy threats of color.

In speaking to a policeman at our local precinct, he thought that, given that I had young children, it might be best for me to refrain from enunciating any controversial positions. Oh yes, the old "blame the victim" routine. Hey, ladies, if you do not wish to get raped, please refrain from inflaming a man's passions by dressing provocatively! When I asked the officer about the possibility of acquiring a gun, I was told that even they were not allowed to carry a gun once off duty. That semester again necessitated that various security protocols be implemented at my university. Is this a reality that professors should be experiencing in the twenty-first century in a supposedly free society? Canada is a fully castrated society. Criminals are armed but law-abiding citizens are sitting ducks. It is important to be empathetic to those who wish to victimize us.

Suicidal empathy leads to caring more about the rights of rapists and felons than their victims. It pathologizes heroic masculinity as a form of toxic and destructive energy. It elevates male sneaky f**kers as the epitome of manhood. It calls for the defunding of the police as they are apparently the real problem in high-crime areas. It removes people's innate right to defend themselves by creating evermore strict gun laws. It promotes open-border policies wherein millions of people who do not share the fundamental values of a civil society can brazenly prey on members of the host society. Suicidal empathy stacks all the odds against our inalienable right to feel safe.

5

Settled Science, Taboo Trade-Offs

[T]he great tragedy of Science—the slaying of a beautiful hypothesis by an ugly fact . . .[1]

[T]aboo trade-offs covary strongly with emotional reactions of anger and disgust.[2]

Psychologists Amos Tversky and Daniel Kahneman pioneered the study of human decision-making by identifying myriad ways by which cognitive biases render our decision-making less than fully rational.[3] The number of documented biases is now well over 150, highlighting how the architecture of the human mind is very prone to cognitive frailties.[4] Take, for example, the framing effect.[5] If a prospective date is described as having seven out of ten of his friends state that he is intelligent (positive frame), this is equivalent to stating that three out of ten of his friends do not think so (negative frame), and yet women end up evaluating the same individual differently as a function of how the information is framed.[6] Of relevance to the current chapter, two cognitive errors that often occur involve the unwillingness to navigate through the trade-offs inherent to a given decision, and the failure to recognize the costs, including the opportunity costs, of making a particular decision. In other words, people engage in trade-offs neglect and cost blindness when making decisions.[7] This is prevalent across the three phenomena covered in this chapter, namely the suicidal empathy associated with COVID policies, climate activism, and transgender activism, require the invoking of taboo trade-offs and willful cost neglect via the canard of so-called settled science. Do not discuss the pros and cons of a given policy for the science is settled.

Karl Popper is perhaps the leading philosopher of science of the twentieth century. Popper's Falsification theory posits that scientific theories must be falsifiable; otherwise, they are not within the realm of science. When I explain this principle to my students, I use "destiny" as an example of an unfalsifiable concept. Suppose I wish to test whether it is my destiny to be hit by a train while crossing the train tracks. There are two possible states of the world: (1) I get hit by the train; (2) I do not get hit by the train. In either instance, the event that unfolds is proof that this was my destiny. Hence, there are no data that might falsify the concept, and hence, it is not within the realm of science. Popper's falsification theory is antithetical to the notion of "settled science." Science is never settled. It is always provisional. In other words, it possesses the epistemological humility to recognize that that which is construed as true today might be falsified tomorrow. This is the history of intellectual thought, and to posit otherwise in the name of some misguided calculus of empathy is the epitome of anti-science reasoning. As Popper so poignantly stated, "The game of science is, in principle, without end. He who decides one day that scientific statements do not call for any further test, and that they can be regarded as finally verified, retires from the game."[8] Of note, Popper's "paradox of tolerance" (to tolerate the intolerable), which he famously explained in *The Open Society and Its Enemies*, stems from the reflex of suicidal empathy.

Settled Science Is Anti-Science

One of my favorite books is *Born to Rebel: Birth Order, Family Dynamics, and Creative Lives* by historian of science Frank Sulloway. Sulloway argues that the great majority of radical scientific innovations were espoused by laterborns and resisted by firstborns. Using a compelling evolutionary-based argument, he posits that by virtue of their birth order, laterborns are much more likely to score highly on open-mindedness, which leads them to go against the accepted scientific orthodoxy of the time. Sulloway identified twenty-eight scientific revolutions to test his theory (e.g., the Copernican revolution, Darwin's theory of evolution, the scientific method, germ theory, and Semmelweis's puerperal fever). Each of these radical scientific innovations, by definition, went against the settled science of the day. Imagine if there had been a governmental committee that decided that each of these ideas were a manifestation of misinformation or disinformation. We would be living in a very different world.

In 2023, I was invited by British psychiatrist Dr. Alex Curmi on his show. Toward the end of our chat, he asked me what had surprised me the most about human nature, to which I responded, the difficulty in getting someone to change their minds about an issue, despite the amount of evidence that might suggest that they should.[9] This is known as the "Semmelweis reflex," named after Ignaz Semmelweis, the nineteenth-century Hungarian obstetrician who had a calamitous life trajectory.[10] The death of a mother during or shortly after childbirth is an existential cruelty in that one of the happiest and momentous life events is irrevocably tainted by the untimely dying of the giver of life. The juxtaposition of these two realities is unbearable, but this is precisely what Dr. Semmelweis was dealing with, as innumerable mothers were dying of puerperal fever shortly after giving birth. Between 1840 and 1846 at the Vienna Maternity Hospital, where Semmelweis joined in 1846, nearly 10 percent of mothers in one of the two clinics died, most due to puerperal fever.[11] The second clinic at the hospital in question had more than 2.7 times a lesser likelihood of such deaths. Semmelweis reasoned that this stemmed from the fact that in the former clinic, the attending physicians would perform autopsies prior to delivering babies, and without washing their hands between the procedures.

Semmelweis's insights took place without knowledge of germ theory, which was elucidated by Louis Pasteur and Robert Koch later that century. His colleagues did not appreciate the accusation of being the culprits of these women's tragic demise, and as such his insight was feverishly resisted. Semmelweis was eventually vindicated, and his insight has since saved innumerable women. As one of his biographers stated: "Semmelweis's saga demonstrates that when a given group, and physicians are no exception, learns some set of facts, those facts too often become immutably ingrained in the minds of that group. Then, tragically, when a valid revolutionary scientific discovery comes along, that group is either unable or unwilling to accept it."[12] In his commencement speech at Southampton College in 1981, the American author Kurt Vonnegut offered a powerful ode to Semmelweis's courage to go against the orthodoxy.[13]

To be awarded a Nobel Prize has historically been viewed as the hallmark of scientific excellence, notwithstanding some dubious cases such as the awarding of the prize to António Egas Moniz in 1949 for having developed the surgical procedure known as a lobotomy. The Nobel Prize committee must have been lobotomized to arrive to this conclusion. In any case, a common feature of many Nobel laureates is the extent to which their pioneering ideas were at first rejected by their peers.[14] Barry J. Marshall and John Robin Warren won the 2005 Nobel Prize in Physiology or Medicine for having discovered that a bacterium (H. pylori) is a key culprit in causing ulcers. This finding was contra the accepted wisdom that ulcers were due to, among other things, too much spicy food and excessive stress. The resistance to their idea was so dogged that Marshall resorted to ingesting the bacterium to demonstrate the causal effect. Over the past two centuries, 465 cases of self-experimentation within the medical field have been documented.[15] The orthodoxy is so entrenched that the "I'll show you" adage implies having to conduct the experiment on oneself. In any case, in his Nobel lecture, Marshall wrote: "I realized then that the medical understanding of ulcer disease was akin to a religion. No amount of logical reasoning could budge what people knew in their hearts to be true."[16] Most recently, Victor Ambros, cowinner of the 2024 Nobel Prize in Physiology or Medicine, had been denied tenure in the early nineties at Harvard University.[17]

In 1797, Edward Jenner, a foundational figure in the field of immunology, had his paper rejected by the Royal Society of London wherein he had described the inoculation experiment that led to the eventual eradication of smallpox.[18] Cataract surgery is the most common surgery in the world.[19] Sir Harold Ridley, the pioneering ophthalmologist who developed intraocular lenses to correct cataracts, toiled for decades in a professional ecosystem that had abjectly rejected his work; eventually, though, he was fully vindicated and given his due honors.[20] Bill Hamilton is one of the greatest evolutionary biologists of the twentieth century.[21] He pioneered the theory of kin selection, which explains how kin-based altruism evolves across species. Hamilton's advisers originally thought that his research interests were a waste of time. His visionary insights turned out to be seminal in our understanding of many key evolutionary phenomena. In other words, if one's ideas are feverishly rejected, it could well be because they are of poor quality, or that they are so accurate and pioneering that the orthodoxy is unwilling yet to accept them. But given that science is never settled, there is an autocorrective process that eventually vindicates the pioneering scientists.

Recently, academics invoking the settled science canard have repeatedly utilized an appeal to empathy to justify their positions. Be empathetic, take the vaccine, and accept the draconian COVID policies. Only a heartless and callous person would refrain from doing their part in protecting the community. A similar reality has unfolded regarding climate change. Only dark-hearted science deniers could deny climate change and refuse to accept that trillions of dollars be spent to alleviate the "existential threat." Are you for the raping of Mother Earth? Should the empathy appeal prove ineffective, one could deploy the social proofing appeal via the "97% of scientists agree that man-made climate change is real."[22] Scientific claims are not adjudicated via popularity consensus votes. And of course, the insanity of the transgender craze was largely driven by an appeal to orgiastic empathy. It is incumbent for you to accept that a "woman" with a penis showers with your teenage daughter, as to otherwise refuse this reality would place the transgendered individual at risk of committing suicide. Be empathetic.

COVID-Related Empathy

The COVID pandemic remains fresh in our collective memory. It was extraordinary to watch the COVID policy decisions that were implemented, which resulted in the unnecessary shutdown of the entire world with innumerable negative downstream consequences. Conservatives were apparently less keen on accepting COVID restrictions because they lacked the necessary empathy to care for others.[23] Perhaps no place had a more draconian COVID regime than my home province of Quebec. Late into the pandemic, the Quebec government had instituted a nighttime curfew that forbade people to walk their dogs outside, which they eventually rescinded after a dogged backlash.[24] I hope that Fido does not have diarrhea during the curfew. After all, to walk your dog at 10:00 p.m. in a deserted residential area during a Montreal winter is simply too dangerous. You might pass the COVID virus to the accumulated snow. Much of the snow had yet to be mandatorily vaccinated, so empathetically speaking it was important to be vigilant. Snow Lives Matter. Throughout history, governments have always used exaggerated risk assessments, often couched in a calculus of empathy, as an opportunity to seize greater power, a phenomenon that risk expert Luke Kemp refers to as the "stomp reflex": "Emergency powers tend to only go one way: top-down. During an emergency, the knee-jerk reaction is aways to stomp-down, to reinforce those atop hierarchies in the state and significantly curtail the freedoms, voice and agency of citizens, often in a draconian fashion." Kemp concludes that "[t]his Stomp Reflex is a power-grab: it is built on ideology, not evidence."[25] Political elites are indeed very Machiavellian in their ability to trigger panics,[26] which they subsequently "solve" by assuming greater powers over the Great Unwashed peasants.

Many readers might remember how 1,288 public health officials and activists wrote an open letter explaining that while it was too dangerous for you to visit the funerary home to honor the passing of your grandmother, it was exceedingly important to hold anti-racism protests to support Black Lives Matter. Here are a few snippets from the open letter, which speaks to their immense empathy for Black lives (note that I am capitalizing the word "Black" as a means of being a grammatical ally to all people of color):

> **White supremacy is a lethal public health issue that predates and contributes to COVID-19** [bold in original] . . . COVID-19 among

Black patients is yet another lethal manifestation of white supremacy. In addressing demonstrations against white supremacy, our
first statement must be one of unwavering support for those who
would dismantle, uproot, or reform racist institutions . . . [A]s public
health advocates, we do not condemn these gatherings as risky for
COVID-19 transmission . . . Listen, and prioritize the needs of Black
people as expressed by Black voices.[27]

Hence, while the COVID virus was too dangerous to permit Quebeckers to walk their dogs on a deserted street in the middle of winter, a
gathering of thousands of progressive people did not pose a severe threat
because the risks of new infections were outweighed by the necessary
work of combating white supremacy. I posted a message on X that offered
epidemiological support for this empathetic and progressive understanding of viral transmission: "Noble Protests of Looting though don't spread
the virus because it contains an enzyme (BS-13) that stops the spread
among 'progressive' people."[28] This is indeed settled science.

Speaking of supposed misinformation and disinformation, countless physicians and other health professionals who spoke out against the
COVID restrictions faced severe consequences, including Drs. Jay Bhattacharya, Scott Atlas, Aaron Kheriaty, and Martin Kulldorff, all of whom
have been guests on *The Saad Truth*.[29] Their concerns about the draconian
measures taken have proven to be justified as evidenced by the fact that the
infection fatality rate (pooled across many countries) for the non-elderly
(0 to 59 years old) was estimated to be around 0.034 percent.[30] Much of the
world was shut down for a virus that ultimately had a very low fatality rate
and differentially so across age groups, but we were not allowed to discuss
it. In 2021, I was contacted by one of the representatives of evolutionary
biologist Matt Ridley, who served in the British House of Lords and who
had previously been twice on my show.[31] He wanted to return on the show,
as his latest book coauthored with Alina Chan was about to be released,
wherein they discussed the possible lab leak theory origins of COVID.[32] I
replied that while I was keen on hosting the authors, it was clear to me that
YouTube would likely end up deleting the clip, and possibly canceling my

channel. Two physicians who had questioned the COVID lockdowns in the early part of the pandemic had two of their YouTube videos taken down, so this was justifiable concern on my part.[33] My decision was a very difficult one to take, but I felt that it was perhaps best to modulate my behavior to ensure that I not become a reckless martyr. That decision has never sat well with me. I recently hosted Ridley on my show for the third time, and we ended up discussing that book in some detail.[34] But the mere fact that I had to engage in self-censorship does not bode well for a free society.

I have been a professor for more than thirty-one years. I have sufficient longitudinal data to gauge the number of students who have typically filed requests for accommodations with the university's disability office. The increase of "disabled" students in my classes has been quite remarkable. But the university is so kind and supportive. Instead of inculcating an ethos of resilience in our students, orgiastic empathy requires that we offer an ever-sympathetic ear to students' anxieties. Feeling anxious at the thought of writing an exam or presenting in front of a class is not a "disability." It is called life. Post-COVID, I sat in departmental meetings where faculty were saying that it is now simply too stressful for students to sit and listen to a lecture for a few hours; taking notes was too stressful, let alone taking an exam. We instituted a policy whereby a student could press a "pause" button that allowed them to miss evaluative exercises without having the burden of providing a medical justification for doing so.

Many decisions faced by individuals or organizations are optimization problems, wherein the decision-makers must maximize or minimize some metric subject to one or more constraints. For example, in personal finance, investors seek to maximize their returns on investment subject to risk-taking constraints. The field of operations research is an applied mathematics discipline that operates within this prescriptive realm, namely it offers algorithmic solutions to optimization problems. In single-objective optimization, one is solely trying to optimize one variable, whereas many problems in the real world require multi-objective optimization subject to multiple constraints. In The Parasitic Mind, I used this framework to explain the tension that arises when universities abdicate their key mission statement, namely, to optimize intellectual enrichment and instead use an alternative optimization metric: social justice. When the COVID dictators instituted all their haphazard policies, they were succumbing to the myopia of single-objective optimization (reduce the number of COVID deaths) void of any constraints. But the proper modeling of the COVID crisis would have required multi-objective optimization subject to numerous constraints, an issue that I addressed very early during the pandemic.[35] The great economist Thomas Sowell famously quipped a similar insight: "There are no solutions; there are only trade-offs."[36] Now imagine that for any decision you make, the sole operative optimization metric is to maximize empathy, void of any other optimization metric and subject to no constraints. In other words, the objective function in your worldview is the following: Be maximally empathetic, to the wrong targets, subject to no constraints. Taboo trade-offs are only for mean and callous individuals. Suicidally empathetic people do not worry about such pedestrian concerns.

Climate Activism as Misguided Empathy

If you wish to see how quick my reflexes are, play the SPCA animal cruelty advertisement on television against the backdrop of the haunting sounds of "Angel" as sung by Sarah McLachlan. I will hastily reach for the remote control to change the channel, as I cannot bear to watch these poor souls suffering. I share this story to highlight the fact that I am infinitely empathetic toward the plight of suffering, especially of our animal cousins. It seems that most wildlife documentaries share the same underlying theme, namely that some majestic animal is on the brink of extinction due to various man-made realities (e.g., habitat destruction). My empathy is well in line with Peter Singer's concept of expanding our moral circle to our animal cousins.[37] That said, the reality is that we are less likely to feel empathetic toward animals the further they are from us in the tree of life.[38] In other words, even when it comes to animals, our empathy system does discriminate. Life is about weighing costs and benefits of any action; public policy is about navigating through difficult trade-offs. In a perfect world, it would be wonderful to stop human encroachment in a particular coastline area of Southern California because it might disturb an indigenous frog's mating behavior. But this valid concern must be weighed against all other costs and benefits that are operative in developing a particular stretch of coastline. The eco-activists do not engage in such taboo trade-off calculations. To them, the world is a very simple objective function: maximize empathy toward the environment subject to no constraints. Environmental activism is indeed heavily linked to empathy. Of note, women score higher in their concerns for the environment, and this is driven by their greater emotional empathy.[39]

The Scandinavians are unique in their empathetic climate activism. The same region that delivered us Greta Thunberg, the "How Dare You?" princess of climate-based orgiastic emotional incontinence, is also responsible for having introduced us to the Danish politician Ida Auken. Speaking at the World Economic Forum, Auken explained to the rubes why they should not own personal cars:

> We tend to think of the paradigm of yesterday. So first we would say here's a car, let's put an electric engine into it; let's make this car self-driving. But if it's the same car in a road that is completely congested, it doesn't matter whether this car is autonomous or electric or whatever. You still don't get anywhere; you just get stuck in traffic. So this is why we talk about mobility because actually if you can get people to share a car you can take out a lot of cars in the streets. I think it's Singapore where they looked how they could bring it down to about 40% of the cars. If we would use them smarter, and the interesting thing about technology is that it makes sharing easy and fun and not annoying. It used to be a little bit difficult to share you know; you would have to go in somewhere in the other end of town and get a key and I mean that's not what you want to do if you want to take your car but if you can just use your neighbor's car because you have a smartphone on an app and you don't even need to know the neighbor

to get into his car or if you can find ways of carpooling; this is what technology helps you do it's much easier and much more fun to share and you start then thinking completely different about transport and traffic. I think it's very important that we do not just try to fix yesterday's paradigm but think about how do we want a city to move.[40]

I retorted to Auken as follows on X.

Dear @IdaAuken, I'm trying to create a fun app where people can share sexy time access to their spouses because monogamy removes the ability of undocumented lovemakers from carnal pleasures. Is there someone that I can speak to at the @wef to obtain a Unicornia grant for this app? By sharing one's spouse with the homeless, I can reduce their marginalization, reduce carbon emissions, and create better communities of sharing. Together we can do it!—Prof. Dr. Gad Saad, CEO of Unicornia (he/they)[41]

Auken is so enlightened in her transcendental climate-based empathy that she penned an article titled "Welcome to 2030. I own nothing, have no privacy, and life has never been better." She expands her nonownership vision to include shared homes as follows: "In our city we don't pay any rent, because someone else is using our free space whenever we do not need it. My living room is used for business meetings when I am not there."[42] A truly beautiful setup. When my teenage daughter is coming out of the shower in our communal home, I will need to ensure that a group of men has not booked our shared space for a business meeting, and that none of them are sexual predators. There is a small chance of an increased incidence of sexual assaults, but surely such rapes are negligible compared to the rape of Mother Earth. Together, we can defeat carbon emissions!

In my home city of Montreal, we had our own Greta Thunberg. Valérie Plante, the ecofeminist former mayor of Montreal, spent $800 million creating endless bike lanes in a city that is buried under snow for nearly half the year.[43] She was less concerned with Montreal having become the most

Jew-hating city in North America.[44] Those haughty Jews do not deserve her empathy, which is largely restricted to protecting Mother Earth from the environmental ravages of cars. It is perfectly reasonable that environmental activism is in part shaped by empathy.[45] However, in a world of fixed monetary resources, empathy must be deployed in a strategically discriminating manner.

Zeno of Elea was an ancient Greek philosopher who postulated several paradoxes, one of which is known as the dichotomy paradox. If a runner wishes to travel from point A to point B, he must first travel half that distance, and then half that distance, and so on ad infinitum. The reader who remembers their calculus might recall how the summation of an infinite number of fractions could add up to a finite number. But I digress! I propose that a modern woke instantiation of Zeno's dichotomy paradox is to use an infinite division of evermore granular groups to identify new manifestations of victimhood. Let us apply Zeno's paradox to the "bigotry" of climate change. One could begin by postulating that climate change is racist.[46] This is empathetic, but surely, we can do better. Racism is too broad a term. It is much more empathetic to demonstrate that climate change has a uniquely adverse effect on specific marginalized groups such as the LGBTQ+ communities.[47] I am sure that your empathy juices are now flowing, but surely, using Zeno's infinite divisions, we can come up with an even more empathetic subgroup. I found it! Climate change has uniquely adverse effects on Indonesian trans sex workers.[48] I am certain that some intrepid and infinitely empathetic researcher or journalist is working hard to explore how climate change is uniquely devastating to Indonesian trans sex workers who are obese, deaf, autistic, and in a wheelchair. This could be the empathetic holy grail.

David Suzuki is a prominent Canadian environmental activist with a long and distinguished career in science broadcasting. He founded the David Suzuki Foundation in 1990 to raise people's environmental consciousness, a perfectly laudable objective. You were probably unaware, though, that combating Islamophobia was a central feature of fighting against environmental degradation as explained on their site: "The environmental movement needs to recognize the role it must play to combat

Islamophobia and remain true to its central mission: protecting people and planet."[49] The Stanford University ecologist Paul R. Ehrlich famously warned the world about the existential threat of overpopulation back in 1968.[50] Perhaps the millions of people killed via Islamic conquests over the past fourteen hundred years, or the more recent forty-eight thousand–plus Islamic terror attacks since 9/11 alone in nearly seventy countries could be construed as a pioneering approach to population control? Islam is indeed a religion rooted in environmental consciousness. Incidentally, MIT not long ago held an event to explore how Islamophobia might contribute adversely to climate change. The event was titled "Is Islamophobia Accelerating Global Warming?"[51]

Perhaps US Airways agent Michael Tuohey was fighting against global warming when he chose to ignore his gut instinct when interacting with Mohamed Atta, the mastermind of the 9/11 terrorist attack, on that fateful morning.[52] While it is tragic that nearly three thousand people perished on that day, nothing would have been as catastrophic as Mr. Tuohey being accused of bigotry. It is best to be suicidally empathetic and ensure that Islamic terrorists are not marginalized by the scourge of profiling. In the progressive world of Empathetic Unicornia, two-year-old Japanese girls are just as likely to be terrorists as Mohamed, Muhammad, and Mahmoud, three young Yemini men who spent some time as peaceful camp counselors in Al-Qaeda summer camps. Statistical regularities can be so racist. It is best to ignore reality in the service of community cohesion. I am ashamed to admit that I used to be deeply sexist in that if I was walking down the street and four suspicious-looking young men were following me, it would have triggered a fear response in me. I now know that it is wrong to engage in profiling. Hence, I now abide to *Equitable Fear*, namely, I am just as likely to be afraid of a ninety-year-old elderly woman in a wheelchair waiting at the bus stop. Crime has no sex nor age. It is best to be a non-racist crime victim than to take otherwise bigoted precautions in avoiding becoming a crime statistic. Death before Islamophobia!

In 2016, Europe was shaken by a series of attacks committed by Islamic terrorists. Referring to some of the perpetrators who originated from a neighborhood in Brussels, Councilman Yves Goldstein, a Jewish man, was quick to reassure the world that it had little to do with Islam. Instead, poverty, the inability to integrate within the host society, and lack of art exposure were partly to blame: "These young people will never go to museums until 18 or 20—they never saw Chagall, they never saw Dalí, they never saw Warhol, they don't know what it is to dream."[53] Exactly. Who among us did not worry that failure to attend a museum might radicalize us into joining ISIS to throw the gays off building rooftops? In any case, many ecoterrorists have taken to the destruction of highly valuable art as a means of bringing attention to the "existential crisis" stemming from climate change.[54] If only they knew that to vandalize museums is tantamount to radicalizing otherwise peaceful young Muslim men into becoming terrorists.

Over the past fifty years, experts have made dire, and at times contradictory, predictions about the imminent existential threats posed by climate change and offered specific timelines for the cataclysmic events.[55] Fortunately, the end-of-time dates have come and gone, and you are still here reading this book. It should be possible to point to these failed predictions and accordingly question whether trillions of dollars should be spent on the minimal (if any) reversal of specific climate trends, without being labeled a science denier. But if you are an avowed doomsday climate activist, then the empathy that you have for Mother Earth supersedes all. If the world is about to end, then no policy is too drastic in altering the supposed existential threats. In the words of the political commentator Noah Rothman: "The ban list is forever expanding. And yet the scale of the problem environmentalists claim to want to confront never seems to shrink in scope. It, too, is always growing, which leads skeptical observers to wonder whether restricting consumers' access to life's small pleasures is a remedy to a problem or an end in itself."[56] Another key feature of climate-based empathy is to blame all disasters on climate change. Many experts were quick to posit that the devastating 2025 LA Palisades fires highlighted the deadly consequences of climate change.[57] Reality, though, gets in the way of an empathetic climate narrative, as it was ultimately determined that the fires were allegedly caused by an arsonist.[58] The climate extremists will now undoubtedly pivot to argue that what caused him to commit this grotesque act was his climate-based anxiety, and that the effects of the fires were worsened because of climate change. All roads lead to climate change.

In September 2023, I was invited by the then president of Hungary Katalin Novák to speak at the biannual Budapest Demographic Summit. My talk was titled "The Evolutionary Roots of Family Dynamics and the Parasitic Ideological Detractors of the Family Unit." Some of these parasitic ideas include radical feminism, collectivist ideologies (communism, socialism, Marxism, and BLM), and climate change extremism, all of which are hostile to the nuclear family and/or to the pursuit of our most fundamental drive, to reproduce. Early radical feminists were astoundingly hostile to marriage. Here are two prototypical sentiments: "We can't destroy the inequities between men and women until we destroy marriage."[59] Linda Gordon went much further in her antipathy toward families and, of course, capitalism: "The nuclear family must be destroyed, and people must find better ways of living together. Furthermore, this process must precede as well as follow the overthrow of capitalism, for unless some brave souls develop new living patterns now, the pressures towards retrenchment that seem to follow most revolutions may stifle our advance. Whatever its ultimate meaning, the break-up of families *now* is an objectively revolutionary process."[60] Lest the reader might think that the destruction of the family unit is so passé, Marxist feminist Kathi Weeks has recently reaffirmed the empathetic objective of family abolition.[61] The latest conveyor belt of unhinged hysterics probably believe that the abolition of the family unit will contribute to fight against climate change.

For all sexually reproducing species, including humans, life is a two-step process: survival and reproduction. Or, as I like to say, make sure you get dinner, ensure that you do not become someone's dinner, and have sex. Natural selection selects all the adaptations that yield a survival advantage to an animal (e.g., the evolution of camouflage coloring), whereas sexual selection selects all the adaptations that yield a reproductive advantage (e.g., the evolution of a peacock's majestic tail). An individual animal that is adept at survival but that does not possess the necessary qualities to ever attract a mate faces a Darwinian dead end. The genes of that animal will never be passed on. As such, few things are as natural as the desire to reproduce. I have long argued that our path to immortality is also a two-step process: genetic and memetic immortality.[62] The children whom I sired are my vehicle to the former, whereas my ideas as expressed in my books, scientific papers, articles, lectures, and online content lead to the latter. Not all individuals pursue these two pathways to immortality with equal alacrity. Catholic priests and nuns are expected to be celibate; some people are asexual while others are exclusively interested in same-sex couplings. In other words, notwithstanding the natural variations of life, people typically wish to reproduce. Civilization is built on that premise, literally. If a nation's fertility rate falls below its replacement level, and if this trend were to continue over an extended period, there would be population collapse.

But this is immaterial to suicidally empathetic climate hysterics. According to them, it is perfectly natural to create social movements that are founded on the principle that we must refrain from reproducing to save Mother Earth. One such movement, Birthstrike, explains this quite clearly: "Birthstrike is choosing to forgo having children to protect them from worsening social, economic and environmental conditions . . . You can protect children while fighting climate change and systematic corruption by refusing to procreate!"[63] The anti-natalist movement has spawned a new cottage industry of academic research linking climate anxiety with the decision to forgo having any children.[64] Jade S. Sasser has taken the concept of intersectional victimhood and connected it to the decision to remain childfree as an act of climate empathy.[65] If climate change uniquely affects communities of color and the queer community, it is perhaps "rational" for members of these communities to remain childless. As such, "[i]t's almost shameful to want to have children."[66] If you are truly empathetic toward Mother Earth, not only should you refrain from having children, but perhaps you might consider breathing less, as this, too, apparently has a deleterious effect on the environment.[67] The wasteful act of breathing is destroying our planet. Please suffocate as an act of merciful empathy toward Mother Earth.

Pets are an integral part of our families. Many individuals are more likely to save their dog from being hit by a bus than they would another person.[68] Furthermore, we experience greater empathy when hearing about the suffering of an adult dog or puppy than we do an adult human.[69] Not surprisingly, the climate extremists, who have never been short of creative ways to kill all sources of joy, are now going after our cherished pets.[70] Be empathetic to Mother Earth. Get rid of your pets. At the very least, empathetic governments should decide the reproductive trajectory of your pets. Not long ago, my city's municipal government decreed that all pets must be spayed or neutered as a means of controlling the potential proliferation of unwanted pets.[71] And more recently, in the state of New York, two domesticated animals, P'Nut the Squirrel and Fred the Raccoon, were taken away in a raid and subsequently euthanized due to the possible threat of rabies, for which they eventually tested negative.[72]

The Cult of Climate Alarmism is ultimately nothing more than a redistribution of wealth from "oppressor" first-world nations to their "oppressed" third-world counterparts. The environmental self-flagellation, though, is restricted to your gas-guzzling car, your gas stove, and your pet, whose excessive flatulence is harming the environment. It would be racist to point out that China is the world's largest polluter. This would undoubtedly marginalize the Asian community and lead to an increase of violence targeting them on the streets of San Francisco. It would also be racist to point out that blacks commit the greatest number of hate crimes on Asian Americans. In the empathetic quest to protect Mother Earth from being raped by capitalism, it is vital to protect the Chinese communist regime from climate scrutiny. All attention must be focused on the white Texan cattle farmer who has sired six children. His cattle and his white children are killing Mother Earth.

Trans Activism as Misguided Empathy

On May 10, 2017, I was summoned to the Canadian Senate to offer my expert testimony regarding Bill C-16, which has since passed. The bill sought to incorporate gender identity and gender expression under the rubric of human rights and hate crimes. Here is the transcript of my opening address:[73]

I have spent 20-plus years working at the nexus of evolutionary psychology and the behavioral sciences, a central feature of which is to explore how evolutionary and biological principles shape our human nature. At the root of this grand objective is the profoundly obvious reality that humans are a sexually reproducing, sexually dimorphic species, consisting of reproductively viable males and females. This in no way rejects the equally obvious fact that the rich human tapestry includes other personhoods such as intersexed and transgendered individuals.

Following a 2014 lecture I delivered at Wellesley College on the thought police, I had a conversation with a student who argued passionately that professors should poll their students at the start of class about their gender identities. While most might have construed her position as outlandish back then, some now consider it too tame.

Take the Office of BGLTQ Student Life at Harvard University, which recently distributed a flyer to combat transphobia, where it was stated that one's gender identity and gender expression could change daily and that "fixed binaries and biological essentialism" constitute "transphobic misinformation" and that is tantamount to "systemic violence."

Was the Wellesley student transphobic since she did not potentially consider the daily fluidity of one's gender identity? What about minute-to-minute changes? Should professors poll their students every tenth minute of every lecture to find out if their gender identities have changed since last asked? Should academics no longer design surveys wherein a participant's biological sex is measured as a binary variable? Would this be "transphobic systemic violence" since it perpetuates "fixed binaries and biological essentialism"?

Facebook and NYC allow 50-plus and 31 genders respectively as part of one's profile. Should professors develop surveys that recognize all of these genders? Would it be "systemically violent" to not do so?

Should evolutionists no longer explain how sexual selection works, namely, the fundamental process by which sex differences evolve? This mechanism recognizes two sexes and hence it might "disenfranchise" those who reject "fixed binaries and biological essentialism."

Bottom line: Foundational tenets of evolution might be construed as legal transgressions under Bill C-16, so evolution itself might be a transgression.

Ongoing governmental efforts are pushing for a gender-neutral society to cater to an extraordinarily small number of non-binary or non-gendered people who feel marginalized at having to provide their biological sex as part of their profiles. This is the tyranny of the minority. Ninety-nine percent of the population should acquiesce to having a default feature of their personhood erased because a few individuals might be inconvenienced by it.

The slippery slope of totalitarian lunacy awaits us. Some are now proposing that racial categories constitute "biological essentialism" and instead we should respect racial self-identities. This is known as transracialism, as per Rachel Dolezal who was born white, but who self-identifies as black. How long before the government tables legislation to combat bigotry against the transracial? What about fat phobia? There are many more Canadians who are overweight than transgendered, and the collective abuse that they experience is sizeable. Should the government legislate such hate? The road to hell is indeed paved with good intentions.

As someone who escaped religious persecution in Lebanon and whose parents were kidnapped in Beirut, I fully support the protection of all individuals from institutional discrimination. That said, I am weary of the ethos of victimhood that has parasitized our culture. The operative motto is not "I think therefore I am" but "I am a victim therefore I am." I refer to this condition as *Collective Munchausen*, namely the pathological quest for sympathy and empathy by proclaiming victim status using identity politics and intersection-ality. People have the right to live as equal citizens under the law. They do not have the right to demand that their identities be coddled and celebrated lest they might otherwise get offended. Thank you.

Note that I referenced the gaming of "sympathy and empathy" in the closing paragraph. People should have listened to my warnings in 2017.

Trans activists usually pursue one of two lines to defend their rejection of reality. First, they argue that there are no predictable sex differences and as such biological males who decide to compete in women's competitions as "trans women" hold no distinct advantages. If this argument fails, they then posit that to the extent that there is an advantage, it rarely yields outcomes that are disadvantageous to actual female athletes competing against biological males. A 2024 United Nations report highlighted that in over four hundred athletic competitions spanning twenty-nine sports, more than six hundred actual biological women had lost over 890 medals when competing against biological males.[74] Does the shattering of the dreams of six hundred–plus women serve as a reasonable casualty in the pursuit of suicidal empathy toward trans people? Do the rights of "trans women" supersede those of actual women? Suicidally empathetic individuals do not engage in such taboo trade-offs. Progressive people are very quick to argue that the death penalty is immoral because the dangers of having one innocent person put to death outweighs all other considerations. One innocent life is too great a cost to bear. Apparently, this empathetic calculus does not apply to the innumerable real women who have had their dreams destroyed by "women" with penises.

One of the revealed truths of gender-affirming care, an Orwellian term if I ever saw one, is that to deny such care to young children suffering from gender dysphoria would yield severe consequences to their mental well-being and could potentially lead to suicide. In a perfect manifestation of forbidden knowledge, Johanna Olson-Kennedy, a physician and leading proponent of gender-affirming care, did not release the results of a $10 million study funded by taxpayers because it found that the patients' mental well-being did not improve after receiving such "care."[75]

Hence, in an egregious violation of research ethics, once the "empathetic" hypothesis that puberty blockers improve patients' psychological well-being was refuted, Olson-Kennedy refused to release the results because it would be "empathetic" to do so (as detractors of gender-affirming care might use these findings to their advantage). Both the original hypothesis and the refusal to accept its refutation are rooted in "empathy." All epistemological roads in this case led to a misfiring of the empathy module.

Tremaine Carroll is a recidivist violent criminal who is serving a twenty-five-years-to-life sentence under California's three strikes law (which many progressive Californians reject as too harsh). One of his crimes was for kidnapping and sexual assault. Carroll was known within the penal system to use all possible "empathetic" tools to engage in various scams that garnered him preferential treatments. Undoubtedly, Carroll, who happens to be a six-foot-two-inch man, could not believe it when he learned that he could be transferred to a women's prison if he simply self-identified as a trans woman. He was transferred and ended up raping two female inmates and impregnating another. The female judge presiding over his penal rapes insisted that Carroll be referred to by "her" female pronouns.[76] It is truly difficult to imagine that our society has sunk to such a level of irrational depravity. Incidentally, a Correctional Service of Canada study found that 44 percent of trans women inmates (i.e., men) were incarcerated for sexual crimes.[77] The magical powers of the "trans" prefix are such that it can protect a boy who forcibly sodomized a ninth grader against her will, while wearing a skirt. The boy in question was "trans," so when the father of the victim tried to complain about the rape, he was removed from a meeting of the school board.[78] The bodily integrity of the victim is clearly not as important as the "girl" who sodomized her. The rapist was eventually reassigned to another school, where he apparently committed another sexual attack. Finally, a black nurse who had faced racist abuse from a supposed transgender pedophile was suspended for having misgendered him.[79] She had used "Mr." during a phone conversation, wherein she was discussing his medical case, which dealt with a urinary problem. You truly cannot make this stuff up. The tsunami of empathetic insanity is drowning the West.

The empathetic denial of reality by transgender activists is hardly re-stricted to faculty members in Women's Studies programs. None other than physicists Neil deGrasse Tyson and Sean Carroll have been fully parasitized by their imbecilic misguided empathy. In a tweet from 2022, Carroll shared a figure from *Scientific American* highlighting how various developmental or congenital disorders could result in individuals not fall-ing neatly into the male or female categories. So what? I offered a rebut-tal to his idiocy by pointing to the fact that oligodactyly and polydactyly exist, namely some people are born with fewer or more than five fingers or toes on a hand or foot, respectively.[80] This does not mean that there is finger diversity and finger fluidity.[81] The number of fingers and toes in human beings is a fixed trait, notwithstanding the existence of various disorders that could alter that number. Humans also have two nipples, notwithstanding the fact that polythelia exists. Rather than engaging with me in a discussion, Carroll blocked me on X, I presume because he is unable to rationally defend his suicidal empathy.

Neil deGrasse Tyson's position on the transgender issue is an even greater affront to reality. In his inimitable arrogance and smugness, Ty-son "explained" to all rubes: "The XX, XY chromosomes are insufficient because when we wake up in the morning, we exaggerate whatever fea-ture we want to portray the gender of our choice. Suppose no matter my chromosomes today I feel 80% female, 20% male. Now I'm going to put on makeup. Tomorrow, I might feel 80% male; I'll remove the makeup, and I'll wear a muscle shirt . . . What business is it of yours to require that I fulfill your inability to think of gender on a spectrum?" How empathetic of him! I posted a satirical clip on my show, wherein I demonstrated my transformation from male to female as a function of how much lipstick was on my lips, and which wig I donned.[82] Perhaps Carroll and Tyson could collaborate on a research project to explore the phenomenon of how cosmologists' brains could be sucked into a black hole of imbecilic degeneracy. Until very recently, the 117 billion people to have ever existed on Earth[83] were apparently fully capable of identifying the members of the two sexes. But Tyson and his woke cult have since explained to the simpletons that the determination of one's sex and/or gender is a lot more nuanced. While it is comforting to know that there is a growing push-back against the trans lunacy, as evidenced by the University of Pennsylvania's reversal on the matter in collegiate sports,[84] the trans hysteria is emblematic of what happens to a society when the desire to be suicidally empathetic to a minuscule minority takes precedence over the most fundamental features of biological reality shared by a majority.

The bestselling author Malcom Gladwell recently admitted to the world that he was wrong about the positions that he took regarding transgender "women" (i.e., men) competing in women's sports. He proclaimed that he was cowed into this position by the progressive thought police. Effectively, he was a walking manifestation of the Asch conformity experiment, wherein people were pressured to go against their lying eyes. In his tardy mea culpa, he stated, "I was objective in a dishonest way."[85] Hence, even when supposedly backtracking, he is incapable of being honest. Gladwell saw that the winds were changing regarding the trans issue, and as such he had the edifying epiphany that biological sex matters. He did not have any empathy toward all the people who were victimized by this gargantuan delusion. He had a progressive image to uphold, and cool liberal parties to attend.

This chapter has highlighted what happens when suicidal empathy destroys reason, reality, and common sense in the pursuit of a more "noble" goal. In the next chapter, the ravaging tentacles of this weaponized virtue seek to destroy the ethos of excellence: meritocracy.

6

Selling Indulgences

Nothing is more unequal than the equal treatment of unequals.[1]

Evidently the poor souls believe that when they have bought indulgence letters they are then assured of their salvation. They are likewise convinced that souls escape from purgatory as soon as they have placed a contribution into the chest. [footnotes omitted][2]

There are many pathways for seeking divine forgiveness for one's sins. The rite of confession in Catholicism is one such practice. More controversially is the selling of indulgences by the Catholic Church as a means of erasing an individual's earthly sins, a practice challenged by Martin Luther, the founder of Lutheranism in the sixteenth century. Now imagine that you are a "greedy capitalist pig" transgressing by virtue of your profit-seeking objectives. One means by which you can seek penance is by engaging in woke capitalism. The currency of woke capitalism is orgiastic empathy, even if it comes in lieu of profit maximization. Hiring the best employees is less empathetic than recruiting nonbinary and two-spirit people. Drilling for natural gas is less empathetic than protecting Mother Earth from being "raped" by energy companies. Creating ads that celebrate transgender women of color is more empathetic than creating ads that increase sales. Building a hedge fund that maximizes sustainability markers and minimizes the carbon footprint is more empathetic than maximizing investment returns via "greedy" dollars. Do you feel guilty about standing on stolen land? Indigenize and decolonize the university curriculum. Do you wish to be an ally to trans people? Hire professors who specialize in queer computing. Does your white skin disgust you, considering the American history of slavery? Set up preferential college admissions for people of color and institute equitable grading. The suicidally empathetic destroy meritocracy as a form of selling indulgences. I empathize, therefore I am.

According to the *Oxford English Dictionary*, the "American dream" is defined as follows: "the ideal that every citizen of the United States should have an equal opportunity to achieve success and prosperity through hard work."[3] I was born in Lebanon to a Jewish family. Suppose that we had not been forced to flee Lebanon at the start of the Lebanese civil war in 1975, and let us presume that I held aspirations of running for the highest political offices of my homeland. I would be out of luck, as Lebanon has long had a confessional system wherein specific political positions can be held only by an individual of a given faith. Specifically, the president must be a Christian Maronite, the prime minister is set aside for a Sunni Muslim, whereas the speaker of the house is reserved for a Shiite Muslim.[4] In the context of the Middle East, this has historically been viewed as a laudable political model of pluralistic coexistence. From the perspective of the American dream, though, it seems unthinkable that one's religion could disqualify you from ascending to a specific political office. Hence, the "equal opportunity" component to the American dream refers to the absence of institutional (or other) barriers that would cause specific individuals from having an equal chance at competing for any goal or aspiration. Now let us contrast this concept of "equality of opportunities" with the "equality of outcomes" that progressives, in general, and Kamala Harris, in particular, repeatedly espouse. In a 2021 speech, Harris stated the following: "We have always fought for equality. But now we are also talking much more, rightly, about equity. Understanding that we must be clear-eyed about the fact that yes, we want everyone to get an equal amount, that sounds right. But not everyone starts out from the same place. Some people start out on first base. Some people start out on third base. And if the goal is truly about equality, it has to be about a goal of saying everybody should end up in the same place. And since we didn't start in the same place, some folks might need more."[5]

The "we did not start at the same place" canard can be falsely applied to all innate or environmentally induced differences, even those that are otherwise not rooted in anything nefarious. I have been told that innate differences in intelligence are inherently unfair because dim-witted individuals did not choose to be so. Imagine how sinister this worldview is. Genetic differences become an instantiation of cosmetic injustice to be remedied via institutional interventions. Suppose that you are a parent who reads to your children as part of their bedtime ritual. It turns out that you are a grotesque human being because you are placing children who are not read to by their parents at an unfair disadvantage.[6] Shame on you. Please starve your children, beat them, and ensure that they are illiterate. Do it out of empathy for the children who might tragically be facing such hardships.

Harris's position, which she has repeated in countless speeches, is perfectly antithetical to the American dream. It stems from a cancerous belief that all individual differences or group differences in outcomes arise because of some nefarious factor typically associated with unfair bigotry. As such, it becomes incumbent on the empathetic and benevolent central government to intervene to ensure, in Harris's words, that we end up at the same final place. People are equal under the law. They are not equal in their innate talents, ambitions, proclivities, or preferences. It is impossible for me to overstate the extent to which this misguided form of equity is antithetical to the American dream. The Biden administration was fully committed in its adherence to the equity ethos.[7] Pete Buttigieg did not have any relevant qualifications to be secretary of transportation, but he made up for it by being gay. Under his leadership, he fought for racial equity across American roads, and gender equity via crash test dummies.[8] Rachel Leland Levine, the US assistant secretary of health, was hailed for being the first woman to hold this prestigious position. This was particularly laudable because she happened to be a biological man who sired two children. But as a progressive physician, she knew that one's genitalia do not define one's sex. You go, girl! The White House press secretary Karine Jean-Pierre had the eloquence of sand, but she made up for it by being gay and black. Finally, Sam Brinton was appointed deputy assistant secretary of Spent Fuel and Waste Disposition (Office of Nuclear Energy). Brinton dresses in women's clothes, is nonbinary, and uses the "they" pronoun. They also have the predilection of stealing luggage at airports.[9] A truly explosive combination for a nuclear energy expert.

That the persistent attack on meritocracy stems largely from the Democrats is expected since they have long fashioned themselves as the Party of Empathy. Bill Clinton was reputed to make anyone interacting with him feel as though they were the only person in the room. His famous "I feel your pain" became a staple of his persona. Clinton's supposed empathy paled in comparison to his Democratic successor, the Empathizer in Chief Barack Obama, who could not complete a sentence without appealing to the empathy deficit that was supposedly plaguing our societies.[10] Incidentally, longitudinal studies of empathy in the United States from 1979 to 2018 do not fully support Obama's contention regarding an endemic empathy deficit.[11] As the 2008 US presidential elections were unfolding, an intrepid political scientist saw the growing focus on the vacuous calls to empathy that politicians were making: "The politics of hope? The politics of change? How about the politics of empathy? To judge from the 2008 campaign so far, a candidate could do worse than to promote herself, above all, as a person of feeling. Solicitude is—or is on the verge of becoming—the preeminent qualification for our nation's highest office. . . . The politics of empathy is a new and invidious corrosive of our political life. Obviously, appeals to emotion, questions of motivation and sincerity, and the like always have been and always will be part of the political life of a liberal democracy. What distinguishes today's politics of empathy is its lack of political content, the way in which it utterly divorces questions of feeling from the important problems of the day. Good intentions can replace good ideas as a qualification only if politics are no longer serious."[12]

Democrats, though, are much less empathetic than Republicans toward fellow Americans, friends, family members, and romantic partners who might hold differing political opinions.[13] I recently experienced liberals' "empathy" in my personal life. Having been invited to speak at a Republican club event in Savannah, Georgia, I reached out to an old friend whom I had not seen in years. I consider him to be a gentle and sensitive person, albeit I found out that his empathetic disposition does not extend to those who might be favorably disposed to Donald Trump. He sent me a note advising me that considering my apparent support of Trump (I am Canadian), it was infeasible for us to maintain our friendship. He alluded to the fact that Trump was apparently harming his community (perhaps he was referring to the fact that he is black or maybe some other affiliation group). While there is some evidence that liberals are more likely to be empathetic than conservatives, individuals from both sides of the political aisle are predisposed to exhibit greater empathy to in-group members.[14] That I disagree with the premise that transgender "women" of color should receive preferential treatment on job applications makes me unworthy of this individual's friendship. Perhaps in the eyes of my former friend, my muscular defense of meritocracy makes me a mean person lacking in the requisite amount of empathy.

Empathetic Mandatory Training

Universities are no longer exclusively committed to intellectual pursuits. They also serve as empathetic molders of your personhood. Over the past few years, I have had to take several mandatory trainings at Concordia University. These were under the empathetic rubric of the "It Takes All of Us" training program. I have had to follow a training titled "Recognizing Attitudes, Changing Behaviour [annual training for 'sexual violence awareness and prevention']" and a second one "Systems of Oppression and Intersectionality." I feel fortunate to have a benevolent employer that patiently teaches me the proper ways to interact with women (including women with penises). I had apparently spent my entire life, well into my fifties, floundering in utter darkness when it came to knowing how to act as a civilized human being. But through my employer's empathetic mandatory seminars, I was guided, mentored, and channeled into becoming a good person.

I also learned about the hierarchy of oppression and victimhood that shapes our bigoted privileges. Let me remind the reader about my family's history. As Lebanese Jews, we faced endemic Jew-hatred in Lebanon, culminating in our having to leave Lebanon at the start of the civil war to avoid being executed. My parents were kidnapped by Fatah, and they faced some terrible realities during their captivity. Some of my grandparents had long ago escaped Syria to settle in Lebanon because of the Jew-hatred that they faced in Syria. My brother-in-law's family are Egyptian Jews who escaped from Alexandria due to the endemic Jew-hatred in Egypt. My wife's family are Lebanese Armenians who also had to leave Lebanon to escape the civil war. Their ancestors came to Lebanon to escape the Armenian genocide at the hands of the Turks. Hence, within the past one hundred years, my own family's reality and that of my wife are defined by an endless escape from literal executions and genocides. But apparently, I knew nothing about oppression until I was again taught about my privilege via the empathetic employer training seminar.

The Orwellian chutzpah is simply astounding, if not deeply offensive and insulting. It is a means of signaling to the world that "we are empathetic. We care. We want to create a safe space." But of course, the safe space does not apply to mouthy and pesky Jewish students and Jewish professors, and especially not to me. As I explained in a *National Post* article after the October 7, 2023, Hamas massacre, it is dangerous to be Jewish at my university, but the administration has largely ignored the problem.[15] All lives are important but some a lot more so than others. As a matter of fact, I was told by a senior administrator that there was no Jew-hatred at my university, notwithstanding the fact that the university's president testified on Parliament Hill (the Canadian government) that Concordia University did indeed have a problem with Jew-hatred.[16] Sorry, no empathy for Jews.

The Empathy of the Diversity, Inclusion, and Equity (DIE) Cult

The DIE cult has taken over academia along with countless other industries, all of which should be strictly guided by meritocracy (e.g., surgeons or airplane pilots). Using a sample of 999 academic job postings in the United States, close to 20 percent required an explicit commitment to DIE principles as part of a candidate's application dossier.[17] At Canadian universities, the situation is much worse. Of 489 job postings, 477 referenced DIE requirements.[18] The University of Michigan, where I faced one of the most hostile academic audiences back in 2008, has over 500 DIE positions costing $30 million in payroll.[19] Imagine the number of leading professors who could have been hired with that wasted money. This is what happens when the implementation of parasitic ideologies such as DIE supersedes the pursuit of scientific truths and academic excellence.[20] If there is an "inequitable" distribution of employees on some irrelevant DIE markers, it must be due to structural inequities that must be redressed through corrective actions. If there aren't enough full professors of mathematics at Princeton University who are black trans women, it must be that the mathematics department is racist and transphobic. If there aren't enough female Nobel Prize winners in physics, it can only be because of the deep patriarchal misogyny of the Nobel committees that adjudicate this award.

While there has been some recent pushback against this cancerous ideology, it remains a well-entrenched reality at many universities.[21] Let me begin with Concordia University, which I joined in 1994. A few years ago, researchers at my university were awarded a substantial research grant from the government (New Frontiers in Research Fund) to decolonize light. Dear Sir Isaac Newton, Christiaan Huygens, Thomas Young, James Maxwell, Albert Einstein, and other white physicists. We appreciate your contributions, but they are tainted by your whiteness. Apparently, a full explanation of light cannot be achieved void of Indigenous knowledge. On the Decolonizing Light website, the grand goal of the project is clearly stated: "Tracing and countering colonialism in contemporary physics." More specifically, though, "[t]he Decolonizing Light project explores ways and approaches to decolonize science, such as revitalizing and restoring Indigenous knowledges, and capacity building. The project aims to developing a culture of critical reflection and investigation of the relation of science and colonialism."[22] This project is well in line with the effort to decolonize the entire field of physics, one of the strongest proponents of which is Chanda Prescod-Weinstein, an associate professor of physics at the University of New Hampshire and a core faculty member in Women's and Gender Studies. On her personal page, she reminds people that she is both a theoretical physicist and a black feminist,[23] and in a separate article she offers readers a "decolonize science" reading list, wherein she begins by highlighting how empathetic and compassionate she is: "Thank me for my free labor maintaining this list by making a donation to funds [hyperlink removed] for the Kānaka Maoli Protectors of Mauna a Wākea, and if you are using it for academic work cite and/or acknowledge it. Citation is care."[24] I should add that she is also queer and agender,[25] so this places her in a unique position to access both black and queer epistemologies in understanding the cosmos, unlike the heterosexual white physicists blinded by their whiteness and heteronormative orientation. Incidentally, given that she is half Jewish (of Ukrainian and Russian descent) and half Barbadian, she seems to focus a lot more on the black half in presenting herself to the world. Given that Jews have won an extraordinary number of Nobel Prizes, does she rejoice at that fact, or does she lament that Jews are "stealing" Nobel Prizes from black scientists? It can be so difficult to navigate the empathy minefield of identity politics.

Dr. Michael Hart, vice provost of Indigenous engagement at the University of Calgary, explained the importance of moving beyond the scientific method as the epistemology of choice. He states, "We are embracing new ways of knowing, ways of doing, ways of connecting and ways of being. We are exploring our past, incorporating Indigenous knowledge into our research and practices, breaking down barriers to access education and seeking guidance from our Elders to teach us ancient wisdom that was once silenced."[26] This is fully congruent with my own university, which recently released its five-year strategic plan, central to which is the stated grand objective of decolonizing and indigenizing all curricula and associated pedagogy.[27]

For my undergraduate degree, I majored in mathematics and computer science. I greatly enjoyed studying these fields because they catered to my sense of epistemological purity. A mathematical proof is either correct, or it is not. A computer program either has a bug in it, or it does not.

I remember learning to code in several computer languages (e.g., Pascal, C, Lisp), one of which, assembly, consisted of instructions expressed in the binary language of 0s and 1s. Of course, Boolean algebra (a form of mathematical logic) yields truth values that are either true or false (i.e., 0 or 1). Hence, binary processing is the most elemental and granular unit of analysis in computer science. Yet as we now know from Queer Biology, we must reject antiquated binary labels such as male and female. The empathy wand allows us to have a multiplicity of sexes and an even much larger number of genders. You might ask, how might one engage in the queering of computer science? Rest assured, Queer Theorist Dylan Paré (they/them), who is the founder of Queer Code,[28] has solved this challenge. Here is the opening paragraph of their article on queer computing:

> Centering queer and trans perspectives through a critical phenomenological framing are an essential reorientation away from the largely cisheteronormative body of technoscientific scholarship that predominantly defines computing and computing education. I examine historical and ongoing relationships between computing education and queering, an act of reorientation of computing objects, practices, and disciplinarity away from cisheteropartriarchal [sic] hegemonies, particularly in the context of computing education. I argue that a critical, intersectional queer and trans phenomenological analysis of computing and computing education, can offer an essential epistemological and axiological challenge to cisheteropatriarchal, militaristic, and intersectionally oppressive, carceral technologies.[29]

It is regrettable and deeply shameful that when I studied computer science, we focused on topics such as Turing machines, NP-complete problems, alpha-beta searches in artificial intelligence, the computational complexity of algorithms, and Gödel's incompleteness theorem. In retrospect, we should have spent more time focusing on how to queer prime numbers and indigenize differential equations. Luckily for me though, my favorite course was Formal Languages, wherein Alan Turing's work was a central feature. As some of the readers know, Turing was gay (and

in all seriousness he was severely persecuted, resulting in his tragic suicide), so perhaps I can count myself as part of the original acolytes of
Queer Computing.

The University of Waterloo has historically been a leading Canadian institution in engineering and computer science. WATFOR, a compiler for
the early computer coding language FORTRAN, was developed at the university, which is often referred to as the Massachusetts Institute of Technology of Canada. It continues to rank very highly nationally and globally in
these fields, as evidenced by several recent rankings.[30] Its Cheriton School
of Computer Science not long ago advertised for two open and highly prestigious Natural Sciences and Engineering Research Council Tier 1 Canada
Research Chairs. The precise call was as follows (bold in the original).[31]

Position 1, all areas of artificial intelligence. The call is **open only
to qualified individuals who self-identify as women, transgender,
gender-fluid, non-binary, or Two-spirit.**

Position 2, all areas of computer science. The call is **open only to
qualified individuals who self-identify as a member of a racialized
minority.**

It is comforting to see that Canada's leading experts in artificial intelligence will be steeped in queerness.

Not wishing to be "outwoked," the University of British Columbia, another prestigious Canadian university, recently advertised an open position for a Tier 1 Canada Research Chair in Oral Cancer Research. The call
sets out the types of dossiers that they are looking for: "The selection will
be restricted to members of the following federally designated groups:
people with disabilities, Indigenous people, racialized people, women,
and people from minoritized gender identity groups. Currently, UBC has
a gap in representation for people with disabilities. Until such time as this
is remedied, the names of those self-identifying as having a disability will
be provided separately to the search committee in order for them to follow preferential hiring strategies."[32] In order to truly innovate in the field

of oral cancer, the research community needs to hire a blind Indigenous nonbinary and obese individual. Speaking of oncology, it is difficult to overestimate the extent to which the Canadian government and its funding agencies have promulgated cancerous social justice nonsense, a topic that I addressed in my recent testimony in front of the Canadian House of Commons.[33]

The attacks on meritocracy take many forms, one of which is to remove standardized testing as part of a student's application dossier. A growing number of business schools have decided to drop the GMAT from their application requirements because it serves to attract more students. This movement of getting rid of standardized testing has taken place for the SAT (undergraduate admission), GRE (graduate admission), MCAT (medical school), and LSAT (law school). In *The Parasitic Mind*, I discussed how the number of credits that were required when I obtained my MBA was astoundingly greater than many MBA programs today. Many medical schools are now reducing the standard four-year curriculum to three years. Universities need to be "empathetic" to the new generation of students. It is simply too onerous to expect them to adhere to the same requirements that were expected of past generations of students. In any case, to promote a meritocratic ethos is apparently tantamount to supporting white supremacy.[34] American meritocracy is apparently a myth that serves to justify race-based economic inequalities.[35] Merit is inherently tyrannical, and it breeds resentment and divisiveness.[36] Finally, to promulgate meritocracy is akin to unleashing a pathogen on African Americans because "[m]eritocratic ideology may be a source of stress. If social status tends to be attributed to individual responsibility, meritocratic ideology may be associated with adverse health outcomes among African Americans by increasing the risk of internalizing negative self-attributions for failure to obtain the American Dream."[37] Incidentally, meritocracy is hardly the only instantiation of "racism." Luckily for us, *The College Fix* has generated a handy list of items that are racist in 2024, including romance.[38] In my quest to combat white supremacy and serve as an anti-racism ally, I have informed my wife that I shall be removing romance from our marriage. My desire to be empathetic to communities of color has forced me to forgo foreplay and flowers; my wife is simply going to have to accept this new reality.

In *The Parasitic Mind*, I explained how my mother was horrified when she wrongly thought that after having just obtained my MBA, I might take a break prior to pursuing my PhD. She felt that people might view me as someone who "dropped out of school" and as such this would be shameful. I recount that story to highlight the level of academic excellence that is typically expected in a Jewish home. Now contrast this to the regrettable accusation of "acting white" that has been levied by some black students toward their race cohorts who excel academically.[39] Doing well in school becomes a performative form of "whiteness." This is hardly a recipe for success. Now imagine that the data show that black students do not perform as well on standardized tests, on their grades, and in their likelihood of taking advanced placement classes in high school. One possibility might be to look inward to explore ways by which they might be responsible for these failures. But this would not be "empathetic," as it might marginalize these communities of color. Hence, a "better" solution is to get rid of standardized tests, eliminate advanced placement classes, and of course get rid of grading (or perhaps create "equitable grading").[40] Then, when Amy Wax, a University of Pennsylvania law professor (and former neurologist) remarked that black students did not typically perform well in her classes, she was eventually punished for sharing this "forbidden knowledge."[41] If facts are non-empathetic, it is best to never utter them as a means of promoting social cohesion. On the other hand, when Russell Rickford, a history professor at my alma mater Cornell University, stated that the October 7, 2023, massacre of Jews by Hamas was "exhilarating," he was quietly reinstituted after a brief leave.[42] #BlackGradesMatter and #JewishLivesDoNotMatter seem to be the operative hashtags in academia. Not all victims are created equal.

Ian Roberts was celebrated for being the first black individual to serve as the superintendent of the Des Moines Public Schools, a clear remedy to Iowa's whiteness problem. Another glorious victory for the DIE cult. It turns out, though, that he was an illegal alien who had lied about his academic credentials.[43] When US Immigration and Customs Enforcement agents arrested the illegal alien with a loaded gun and a hunting knife,[44] the first reflex of Jackie Norris, the white woman and chair of the school board, was to quickly invoke empathy toward Roberts: "[I]t seems fitting to take a page out of Dr. Roberts' book [he had proclaimed that his leadership approach would be 'anchored in empathy'] and ask the community to engage in radical empathy as we work through this situation together. Radical empathy is the recognition that we can disagree and still empathize with each other, the respect of others' humanity. This concept will be essential as we wait to learn more."[45] Sure, he might have lied about his credentials, stayed in the country illegally, had prior weapons charges, evaded the ICE agents, and had a loaded gun and hunting knife when arrested, but for goodness' sake, he is black. Jackie Norris was radically empathetic, ergo suicidally empathetic. The illegal alien Ian Roberts was "anchored in empathy" but the law is not deserving of any empathy.

When Argentina and Lionel Messi won the 2022 World Cup, I was ecstatic because the greatest soccer player of all time had finally obtained the ultimate trophy. To my chagrin, I later discovered that the Argentinian national team was nothing more than a vehicle for white supremacy, as some parasitized degenerates lamented the fact that no black players were on the national team.[46] I trust that those individuals levying this complaint will be equally angered that the Angolan national soccer team does not have any white players. The DIE cult destroys everything that is beautiful in life in the pursuit of misguided empathy. Imagine if an NBA team were to suddenly decide that, more important than fielding the most competitive team possible, it is crucial to create a maximally diverse team rooted in the principles of DIE. Mark Cuban, the former owner of the Dallas Mavericks, and a vocal supporter of the cancerous principles of DIE, was unhappy with me when I posted the following: "Dear @mcuban, I noticed recently that you've come out in favor of the DIE principles. Fair enough. That said, I've noticed that the @dallasmavs have never had a Lebanese-Jew as their starting point guard. I hope that you'll consider making me an offer to redress the systemic inequities baked into your organization. I'm happy to share some of my basketball clips. Let's stop anti-Mizrahi Jew discrimination."[47] Cuban has since unfollowed me on X, and he has feverishly deleted most if not all of his pro–Kamala Harris posts. He also refused to accept my repeat invitation to chat on my show because apparently folks like me and Elon Musk exist in an echo chamber, and Cuban can never learn anything in interacting with us. People who firmly believe in their positions never have to delete anything (unless they have genuinely revised their opinion about an issue). Cuban's e-shredding of his imbecilic posts, as well as Occasional Cortex's (AOC) removal of her pronouns from her bio on X (shortly after Trump's 2024 victory) unequivocally highlight that these parasitized ideologues are merely engaging in performative progressive purity tests.

Empathetic Research Ethics

I often lecture about some of the most famous psychology experiments ever conducted. These include Solomon Asch's group conformity studies, Stanley Milgram's obedience to authority work, and Philip Zimbardo's Stanford prison experiment.[48] They are all uniquely powerful in that they demonstrate difficult truths about human nature. If you were a participant in any of these three experiments, you might not want to know that you are a weak-minded conformist to group pressure (Asch), a person capable of administering an electric shock that might severely harm another (Milgram), or that you can assume the role of a sadistic corrections officer (Zimbardo). Hence, even if the researchers end up debriefing you about the deception used in the studies in question, the cat is out of the bag. It is a common ploy in the behavioral sciences to use deception as an integral element of the experimental design.[49] In many instances, this is necessary because you do not wish to provide participants with the real purpose of the study, as this might alter their natural behaviors. Accordingly, you provide a false cover story to get them off the scent of the real purpose of the study, and at the end of the experiment you debrief them accordingly. In some instances, the deception can result in an enduring harmful effect on the participants. Take, for example, false feedback studies, wherein experimenters wish to explore how the reception of ego-reducing feedback might affect a person's ability to perform on a subsequent task. Let us suppose that the experimenter administers an IQ test to participants and subsequently offers them the following false negative feedback. "Mr. Jones, have you ever taken an IQ test before? No? Well, according to the results of the IQ test that you just took, you have the intelligence of a gerbil. OK, let's move on to the second part of the experiment." Even though at the end of the experiment, the researcher debriefs Mr. Jones about the fact that the feedback was bogus, the doubt has been introduced. Mr. Jones is likely to wonder whether the debriefing is false, meant to simply assuage his hurt feelings. "Am I truly as dumb as a gerbil?" Mr. Jones might forevermore wonder. Hence, there are clear and legitimate reasons to have ethical research guidelines prior to conducting a study. Regrettably, though, the current university institutional review boards that provide ethical clearance for research have been fully parasitized by an ethos of misguided empathy and care. The pathological need to cause no harm has reached new heights of bureaucratic lunacy.

In all of my courses, be it at the undergraduate, MSc, MBA, or PhD level, I have always assigned a semester-long project where students have to identify a research question, posit hypotheses, conduct the relevant literature review, develop the data collection procedure (e.g., survey, lab experiment, field experiment, or observation), conduct the appropriate inferential statistics on the data, and arrive to the correct conclusions. The project requires a tremendous amount of supervision on my part, but I find it an indispensable pedagogic tool in highlighting the importance of the scientific method to my students. I always make sure to explain to the students the proper research ethics that must be adhered to when conducting primary research (e.g., how to design a consent form). For the first two decades or so of my career, I was the one who would provide the students with the ethical clearance to collect their data. Over the past decade or so, the Office of Research decided that even for class projects, the ethical clearance had to go through a third party. This places an astounding administrative and bureaucratic burden, especially when trying to conduct such a laborious project within the timeline of any given semester. This breathtakingly silly process stems from the overregulation of all aspects of a university. What if a student were to ask a survey question that offends someone? Make sure to ask about the 873 possible genders. Refrain from asking any income questions because it might make someone feel bad that they are not wealthy. Refrain from asking anything that might be culturally insensitive to the different cultures represented on campus. What if a participant is deeply puritanical and they are exposed to a print ad with sexy models as part of an advertising experiment? Heaven forbids that anyone might be offended in any one of a trillion trivial ways. In *The Parasitic Mind*, I explained how victimology is akin to a homeostatic system, namely, keep diluting the definition of victimhood until one attains the desired societal threshold of victimology. Suicidal empathy is a homeostatic system as well. Set the bar of what is considered potentially harmful, insulting, or sensitive to such an absurd level that it necessitates new monitoring systems within the confines of a class assignment. This has caused me to question whether I should remove this project from my courses. If I were to do so, the students would bear a huge pedagogic cost, but at least we are being maximally empathetic.

Reject the Hippocratic Oath, Choose the Woke Oath—Be Empathetic

It is one thing to ensure that the Intersectional Lesbian Dance Therapy major at Oberlin College adheres to the DIE cult. It goes without saying that no Queer Dance choreography should ever start without the appropriate land acknowledgment ("we are dancing on the stolen land of the Ojibwe") and without the recognition that we must eradicate white supremacy from all forms of dance, and as such elevate the indigeneity of choreographies of color. Sure, this is all great, as no one wants to see queer choreographies laced with white supremacy. But in the real world, where actual decisions matter, it is perhaps not a good idea to focus on DIE principles. Take, for example, medicine. Historically, we used to aspire to put physicians and surgeons through a rigorous objective training, given that they hold our lives in their hands. But as we all now know, meritocracy and scientific knowledge are tantamount to white supremacy. Hence, the suicidally empathetic members of the Anti-Racism Expert Working Group of CanMEDS (an organization that develops evolving training codes for physicians and surgeons in Canada) came up with the following conclusion: "A new model of CanMEDS would seek to centre values such as anti-oppression, anti-racism, and social justice, rather than medical expertise."[50] You read that correctly. Medical expertise should take a back seat to the real global disease, white supremacy. Here is their full statement on the matter (for the CanMEDS renewal 2025 guidelines):

Anti-racism is an explicit stance, a process and a systematic method of analysis requiring a proactive course of action for individuals, institutions, and societies to undertake. Anti-racism sheds light on the structures of racism rooted in the justification of colonization, slavery, and white supremacy, with manifestations at the individual, interpersonal and systemic levels. Anti-racism actively seeks to identify, remove, prevent, and mitigate racially inequitable outcomes and power imbalances and change the structures that sustain inequities. Anti-racism is deeply rooted in anti-oppression, which analyzes the world through the lens of power, including the historical and ongoing structures of racism, white supremacy, settler colonialism, heteropatriarchy, capitalism, ableism, classism, sexism, homophobia, transphobia and more. Anti-racism and anti-oppression call for action on the manifestations of oppression based on race, ethnicity, religion, sex, gender identity, sexual orientation, socioeconomic status, immigration status and more. Anti-racism in medicine and healthcare requires us to examine, acknowledge and work to mitigate and dismantle the deep roots and manifestations of racism and other intersecting oppressive structures in our day-to-day work.[51]

The report makes it clear that this new outlook in the training of healthcare providers is done in the name of "inclusive compassion." This "empathetic" insanity engendered much backlash and concern.[52]

American medical schools are also parasitized by suicidal empathy.

Here is the exact oath taken at the White Coat ceremony at the University of Minnesota Twin Cities Medical School:

> With gratitude, we the students of the University of Minnesota Twin Cities Medical School class of 2026 stand here today among our friends, families, peers, mentors, and communities who have supported us in reaching this milestone. Our institution is located on Dakota land. Today, many indigenous people throughout the state including Dakota and Ojibwe called the Twin Cities home. We also recognize this acknowledgment is not enough. We commit to uprooting the legacy and perpetuation of structural violence, deeply embedded within the health care system. We recognize inequities built by past and present traumas rooted in white supremacy, colonialism, the gender binary, ableism, and all forms of oppression. As we enter this profession with opportunity for growth, we commit to promoting a culture of anti-racism, listening, and amplifying voices for positive change. We pledge to honor all indigenous ways of healing that have been historically marginalized by Western medicine. Knowing that health is intimately connected to our environment, we commit to healing our planet and communities. We vow to embrace our role as community members and strive to embody cultural humility. We promise to continue restoring trust in the medical system and fulfilling our responsibilities as educators and advocates. We commit to collaborating with social, political, and additional systems to advance health equity. We will learn from the scientific innovations made before us and pledge to advance and share this knowledge with peers and neighbors. We recognize the importance of being in community with and advocating for those we serve.[53]

Imagine the solace that Americans must feel knowing that their future physicians will no longer abide to the antiquated Hippocratic oath but will instead root out white supremacy as a public health measure.

Aviation is another industry that one would hope is strictly rooted in an ethos of meritocracy. But this is precisely what an ableist bigot would say. On its website, the Federal Aviation Administration (FAA) recognizes that "[i]ndividuals with targeted or 'severe' disabilities are the most under-represented segment of the Federal workforce."[54] Accordingly, they have implemented a targeted recruitment and hiring program that includes "hearing, vision, missing extremities, partial paralysis, complete paralysis, epilepsy, severe intellectual disability, psychiatric disability and dwarfism."[55] Imagine how much safer passengers on a plane would feel if the captain were a blind, paranoid schizophrenic queer transwoman elevated by dwarfism. That all industries have been so utterly parasitized by this orgiastic quest to appear evermore suicidally empathetic in their inclusive hiring speaks to a deep-seated problem. Meritocracy is the only game in town in any free society that is rooted in individual dignity.

The 2025 Los Angeles fires caused unimaginable damage resulting in the death of twenty-nine people and the destruction of more than sixteen thousand properties.[56] Fortunately, though, the Los Angeles Fire Department was fully committed to DIE principles. LA Deputy Fire Chief Kristine Larson, who obtained a DIE certification at Cornell University (my alma mater), explained the importance of DIE as follows: "You want to see somebody that responds to your house, your emergency, whether it's a medical call or a fire call, that looks like you. It gives that person a little bit more ease, knowing that somebody might understand their situation better."[57] Exactly. Let us suppose that you are a queer woman who weighs as much as a California seal, and you are trapped in a burning house; the last thing you want to see is a tall and muscular heterosexual male firefighter trying to rescue you. He probably does not understand your plight. Now imagine if a supersized big-boned fellow queer woman were to break down that door; you would immediately feel safe knowing that she looks like you. When questioned about a female firefighter's ability to carry a man out of a dangerous situation, Larson replied: "He got himself in the wrong place if I have to carry him out of a fire." Precisely! The male victim should have known that the firefighter might be an obese queer woman and hence should have explained this to the fire. DIE burns everything in its wake, including human decency. The empathy owed to obese queer transgender women to feel seen is certainly greater than that owed a white heterosexual man about to succumb to a fire in his apartment. Incidentally, Larson's insanity about achieving a match on irrelevant markers between the firefighter and the person being saved is a concept that has been covered in the academic literature in other helping domains. For example, it has been explored within the mental health profession and in medicine.[58] Imagine how insulting it is to posit that a therapist's skin color or a physician's race should be matched to that of their patients. And yet, here we are.

Woke Capitalism—Maximize Corporate Empathy

When profit-seeking corporations compete in the free market, they are implicitly abiding to a form of meritocracy. It is a central feature of the capitalist ethos, wherein the ultimate objective is to maximize shareholder profits. Woke capitalism, though, rejects this premise; maximizing profits takes a back seat to being an empathetic organization rooted in the pursuit of social justice. Let me backtrack and provide a brief historical timeline of how we got here. The social contract to which for-profit corporations must abide has gone through four stages over the past century or so.[59] The first stage coming out of the Industrial Revolution was driven by the desire to create manufacturing systems that met consumer demand. This is best captured by Henry Ford's somewhat flippant remark that "[a]ny customer can have a car painted any colour that he wants so long as it is black." This is now referred to as Fordism's mass production approach, wherein the manufacturing process was inflexible to the heterogeneity of consumer preferences. The second stage precisely addressed this lacuna by recognizing that consumer demand must be met while catering to various market segments. This led to the rise of the marketing-centric organization. During my MBA (1988–1990), I was first exposed to the concept of mass customization, which incorporates elements of stages 1 and 2.[60] The goal is to create flexible manufacturing systems that cater to consumer heterogeneity using economies of scale. The third stage expands the delineation of corporate responsibility by requiring that no third party or entity is harmed in the pursuit of meeting consumer demand and consumer heterogeneity. Green companies are an instantiation of this third stage in that they recognize that corporate social responsibility must incorporate the non-harming of the environment, within their sphere of influence. And this leads us to the current fourth stage, namely, woke capitalism, which posits that in addition to the requirements implicit to stages 1, 2, and 3, companies must actively affect societal changes beyond their fiduciary responsibility of maximizing their shareholders' short-term profit stakes. Companies must fight against the glass ceiling that has kept women away from the boardrooms; they must explicitly support #BlackLivesMatter; they have to implement the woke ethos of ESG (environmental, social, and governance) as part of their central mission statement; they must hire a woman with a penis as their beer spokesperson (as per Dylan Mulvaney and the Bud Light fiasco); they must fight toxic masculinity (as per the Gillette ad of 2019); they must explicitly combat the patriarchy and white supremacy by repeatedly creating ad copy where the white husband is depicted as a babbling buffoon; all couples depicted in ads should be interracial; they must hire transgender women of color, for it is only through queer wisdom of color that we can truly understand business dynamics; and for God's sake, do not succumb to your eugenicist impulse by using the ravishing white woman Sydney Sweeney to sell jeans (American Eagle).[61]

The entire currency of woke capitalism is rooted in hyperactive empathy. It is perfectly reasonable for a business to adhere to an ethos of empathy if this does not grossly conflict with its fiduciary responsibility of maximizing short-term profits for its shareholders. Some have argued that greater empathy in business yields superior commercial success.[62] Tell that to Jaguar when they unleashed in late 2023 an astoundingly woke advertisement consisting of a bunch of weirdly dressed people of color (including some apparent nonbinary and transgender folks) sashaying around.[63] Not a single car was shown in the ad to which Elon Musk sarcastically posted on X: "Do you sell cars?"[64] To destroy the massive intergenerational brand equity that Jaguar has accrued via a suicidally empathetic advertising campaign is apparently well worth it if the objective is to elevate the visibility of transpeople of color.

Whether in academia, medicine, business, aviation, firefighting, or any other worthy endeavor, meritocracy must always serve as the defining ethos. Competition is a central feature of the human spirit. No one is existentially owed anything because of some misguided victimology narrative. Suicidal empathy, when used to attack merit-based pursuits, is a cancer that ravages human innovation and individual dignity.

7

Govern Me Harder, Daddy!

Of all tyrannies a tyranny sincerely exercised for the good of its victims may be the most oppressive. It may be better to live under robber barons than under omnipotent moral busybodies. The robber baron's cruelty may sometimes sleep, his cupidity may at some point be satiated; but those who torment us for our own good will torment us without end for they do so with the approval of their own conscience.[1]

Empathy forms the foundation for welfare state and its liberal social welfare programmes.[2]

A foundational tenet of the US Constitution is the principle of limited government. This is in sharp contrast with overreaching centralized governments, which are always justified via an appeal to empathy. Franklin D. Roosevelt's New Deal, which laid the groundwork for the American welfare state, as well as Joseph Stalin's Soviet propaganda both relied heavily on mass empathy appeals.[3] How ironic that the two great adversaries of the eventual Cold War each recognized the effectiveness of empathy-based appeals to justify their respective societal visions. People's levels of empathy and their beliefs in communism are positively correlated.[4] To the extent that communism purports to create utopian equality for all, it makes sense that the more empathetic you are, the more you are likely to support this failed ideology. Interpersonal empathy is positively correlated with one's score on a governmental intervention scale, an item of which is "I think that the government needs to be a part of leveling the playing field for people from different racial groups."[5] In other words, woke social justice, as instituted by the benevolent welfare state, runs through the empathy module. If you score high on empathetic ability and you do not believe that you possess personal agency over your successes or failures in life, you are more likely to support social welfare programs.[6]

If children go through a predictable set of cognitive and moral developmental stages (see the works of Jean Piaget and Lawrence Kohlberg), could the same apply for one's political orientation throughout the human lifespan?[7] In other words, because of the sampling from life's experiences, is one more likely to start off as a liberal and become more conservative, or vice versa? The maxim "If you are not a liberal when you are young, you have no heart, and if you are not a conservative when old, you have no brain" implies a recurring pattern, which has been empirically validated across several cultures.[8] People tend to become more conservative as they get older because many of the progressive tenets are rooted in an infantile ethos of empathy. What sounds nice to a young and naive mind is autocorrected by life's experiences. "Sharing is caring" is a very nice motto when you are in grade one, but it is less so when more than 50 percent of your earnings are taxed by the socialist welfare state. It is not surprising that as people get older, their views of socialism worsen, whereas their views toward capitalism become more favorable.[9] Longitudinal data across the lifespan show no empathy effect,[10] suggesting that people's greater conservatism as they age is shaped by life experiences and not by changes in their empathy scores. Reality has a way of slapping the misguided empathy and utopian imbecility out of you. Interestingly, given that women score higher on empathy than men, they are more likely to prefer socialism over capitalism, whereas men prefer capitalism.[11] In other words, even within the United States, American women who benefit directly from the liberating force of capitalism succumb to the empathy-based appeal of socialism. For those dissatisfied both with socialism and capitalism, the empathetic people at the World Economic Forum have found the optimal economic system: "Finding a midway point between traditional capitalism and socialism, empathicalism would be about bridging concepts, regions and people. It would be about ending divisions and promoting collaboration, driving individuals towards a real sense of community. Empathic societies remind us that we are just a part of the whole, and that without the whole we are nothing. If we want to promote change in the world, there is no other way than to be empathetic with one other—as well as with our planet."[12] How kind!

Communism and socialism are roughly the same system, albeit they vary in how Unicornia, the land of mythical egalitarianism, is implemented. Marxism is the philosophy that guides the implementation of socialism and communism. Socialists are somewhat "nicer" in the ways by which they seek to create the socialist dream (e.g., via the ballot box), whereas communists are less concerned with such niceties and prefer a swift implementation of their goals (be it by killing their detractors or sending them off to gulags and other "rehabilitation" centers). Notwithstanding these small differences in how Unicornia is to be implemented, these ideologies are all rooted in misguided empathy. Several evolutionary-based scholars have argued that since the human mind evolved within an ecosystem consisting of small groups, the economic intuitions that people hold apply to small-scale economic systems (e.g., zero-sum thinking and the supposed unfairness of economic inequality).[13] Hence, the persistent appeal of socialism and communism, despite their abject failure everywhere that they have been implemented, rests in a naive understanding of economic systems known as folk economics.[14] It seems inherently unfair that some people make $50 million per year whereas others have to get by on $50,000. This might perhaps explain why people living in capitalist societies continue to be enticed by the promise of the supposed fairness of communism, notwithstanding the fact that "[c]ommunism's redistribution of wealth, abolition of private property, and economic control are quite an alluring vision to the general populous because of the equality and stability it promises. Although communism masquerades as justice, it is the worst kind of inverted egalitarianism."[15]

Of note, well before Karl Marx espoused his failed vision of how societies should be organized, the Utopian Socialist Robert Owen had founded New Harmony (Indiana) in 1824.[16] Owen thought that a structured society might eliminate some of our "dark" instincts such as the desire to own private property. He would create a well-designed society where everyone lived happily ever after. How empathetic! New Harmony failed miserably. Robert Dale Owen, Robert Owen's son, arrived at the following conclusion regarding his dad's efforts to implement Utopian Socialism via the New Harmony community: "All cooperative schemes which provide equal remuneration to the skilled and industrious and the ignorant and idle, must work their own downfall, for by this unjust plan of remuneration they must of necessity eliminate the valuable members—who find their services reaped by the indigent—and retain only the improvident, unskilled, and vicious members."[17] The quest for radical equality as envisioned by the Utopians, socialists, and communists will always fail because it is contrary to human nature. The establishment of hierarchies within human societies is a universal reality, albeit there are ecological conditions wherein it would have been adaptive to promote a form of egalitarianism to maintain cohesion among a group.[18] Socialism relies on a misguided application of the egalitarian ethos, dooming it to always fail: "The advocates of socialism generally condemn selfishness and advocate altruism. They want to make a better world, improve human relationships, establish fairness and equality. These are, indeed, noble goals, but they ignore the emotions that guaranteed equality in our evolutionary past. And they ignore the inescapable fact that the conditions that produced equality in ancestral human bands no longer exist."[19] Perhaps no Western leader was more adept at explaining the falsity of radical socialist egalitarianism as the former British prime minister Margaret Thatcher.[20] The Iron Lady fully recognized that socialism was a gigantic Ponzi scheme, as evidenced by her now famous quote: "Socialist governments traditionally do make a financial mess. They always run out of other people's money."[21] While it is often argued that the welfare state is a generous entity, there is nothing generous about exhibiting largesse with other people's hard-earned money: "The concept of generosity is not operative, one way or the other, in any of the roles that are essential or distinctive to the welfare state."[22] Despite its failure in every society in which it has been tried, the socialism phoenix rises from the ashes of devastation fueled by the allure of empathetic fairness.

Political systems and associated policies that are incongruent and antithetical to key features of our evolved human nature will always fail, of which socialism/communism is a telling example. It has been repeatedly tried in countless countries with the same outcome: abject failure. Of course, the refrain is always the same. If only True Socialism were implemented, we would achieve Unicornia, a mythical utopia that solely exists in the deep recesses of the minds of leftist utopians. Perhaps no animal has more often been used to extol the virtues of communism than insects in general, and ants in particular. Trophallaxis, or the mutual regurgitation of nutrients between insects, was extended as a metaphor to be applied to human societies. Most notably, the avowed socialist Auguste-Henri Forel, who was a psychiatrist by training, argued that this "social stomach" highlighted the virtues of cooperative socialism within the human context.[23] Countless other entomologists and other scholars have warned against this ant-human comparison.

> Innumerable comparisons have been made between human society and the social organization of ant, bee, or termite; theories have been advanced and morals pointed, Utopian schemes encouraged and whole theories of the State built up for man on the basis of analogy with these little insects. Almost without exception the moral has been false, the analogy used misleadingly.[24]

> I'm not saying that everyone should be paid the same. People have tried and it was a dismal failure. Karl Marx was right, but he picked the wrong species. With the ants, he was right. In their world, the individual is nothing, the society is everything.[25]

> [W]hile ants naturally embody a form of communism where the society is everything, this model does not translate well to human beings, whose evolutionary history and social dynamics are fundamentally different. The altruistic, collective behavior of ants is driven by genetic imperatives that are absent in humans, making the seamless operation of a communist society feasible for ants but

untenable for people. This highlights a key insight from sociobiology: that the social structures and behaviors of different species are deeply rooted in their evolutionary biology, and what works for one species does not necessarily apply to another.[26]

All the misguided empathy inherent to the supposed "fairness" of communism/socialism cannot eradicate the fact that humans are not social ants, and as such to impose a system that is against our nature is the epitome of lacking empathy in recognizing our phylogenetic history.[27]

To delusional empaths, income inequality is so unfair and mean. Taxing people to death can be so kind and liberating. An effective way of creating a utopian ant-like society of imposed equality within capitalist nations is via parasitic taxation, to which I turn next.

Parasitic Taxation

Taxation is theft, purely and simply, even though it is theft on a grand and colossal scale which no acknowledged criminals could hope to match. It is a compulsory seizure of the property of the State's inhabitants, or subjects.[28]

May 2, 2022, was a marking day for me, as it irrevocably altered my sense of individual dignity and personal freedom. It was the deadline for me to settle any "owed" taxes with the Quebec and Canadian governments. My wife called me and calmly asked for my bank account's password, which I entered compliantly. Right there, on the home page of my bank statement, were two boxes, each corresponding to the Quebec and Canadian governments, respectively. I clicked both boxes, entered two very large numbers (corresponding to well over 50 percent of all my earned money), pressed the send button, and the money disappeared. I went from having succeeded financially (e.g., having saved some money for retirement) to having next to nothing left. I have two broad sources of income: my salary as a professor and all other revenues earned from my other professional activities, including book royalties, online revenue (e.g., YouTube ad revenue stemming from my show), and speaking engagements. Whereas my professor's salary is taxed at the source, the other revenue streams are not, so the total sum of money that I had to transfer to the two governments on that fateful day were truly life-altering, if not existentially shattering.

Let me backtrack. That year was a successful one for me, a culmination of an entire career of hard work. My book *The Parasitic Mind* was a certified international bestseller, with more than twenty translation rights already signed. The book features key elements of my personal and professional life. It captures my neuronal firings, my thoughts, my words, my ideas, my expertise, my humor, and my lived experiences. When writing this book, I was laying it all on the line. I was presenting myself to the world in the most intimate of ways, knowing that I was taking great personal and professional risks. And yet, when it comes to the financial proceeds of my life's work, the Quebec and Canadian governments have decided that they own most of the royalties, even though nearly all the royalties were generated outside of Canada.

To state that I felt as though I had been robbed blind is a grotesque understatement. I walked around for nearly one month thereafter consumed by anger, resentment, and a deep sense of having been violated in the most depraved of ways. Let me explain: No one likes to pay taxes. Millions of people work very hard for their money, and as such none feels particularly happy about being fleeced for the "greater good." That said, all sources of income are not created equal. The richness of a society is in part determined by its cultural and intellectual heritage. Surely, the hedge fund manager who is taxed on his yearly bonus is not experiencing the same intrusion to his sense of personhood as the author who is being taxed on his life's story. In the same way that the tax code recognizes that different sources of revenue are taxed at varied rates (e.g., business income versus dividends), there is no moral, philosophical, or ethical reason to suggest that all sources of personal income should be treated as though they constitute one indistinguishable lump. This is precisely why Ireland has a tax dispensation for artistic creations and book royalties. The Irish recognize that such creations constitute fundamental contributions to the richness of a society. The proceeds of my life's work should not be stolen from me at a rate greater than 50 percent of my book's royalties.

Let us look at the concept of intellectual property. As an author, if you wish to quote a passage that is longer than five hundred words, you may need to obtain permission from the copyright holder of the passage. In other words, it takes very little to trigger the due copyright protection that is afforded to authors and/or publishers. And yet, while we protect authors from having more than say five hundred words of their work quoted properly, it is perfectly "acceptable" for the Quebec and Canadian governments to levy more than 50 percent of my book's royalties. You cannot quote more than five hundred words without obtaining permission, but you can steal more than 50 percent of my book's earnings.

The amount of taxes that I pay on my professor's salary is already exorbitantly high. In other words, the amount that is levied from my regular salary already places me in the bracket of citizens who pay the most taxes in Quebec and Canada. At this point, the two governments could say: Okay, we have already fleeced you more than the great majority of Canadians. Any extra money that you make from your additional creative initiatives is yours to keep. Ultimately, a moral and just society would place a ceiling on the amount of taxes that you could levy from any individual in any given year. But the opposite occurs under our so-called progressive taxation system. The more money that I make, the more entrepreneurial I am, the more risks that I take, the harder that I work, the more intellectual content that I create, the more punitive and confiscatory the tax rate becomes. So much so that I am left with well under 50 percent of my earnings.

I should add that the great majority of additional revenue that I make beyond my professor's salary does not originate from Quebec or Canada. But the confiscatory taxation system is such that the two governments do not care about such geographic matters. If my book sells in China, Croatia, or Brazil, the two governments want their majority cut. If I were to sell my book on other planets or galaxies, my book royalties could not achieve the escape velocity of the gravitational pull of the Quebec and Canadian governments. The tentacles are infinitely reaching in their omnipresence. There is no mechanism by which a supposedly free individual can ever escape from the financial grip of the two governments. And of course, this is all done in the name of collective and empathetic "fairness," albeit it is certainly not fair to the person who created the intellectual output and associated financial remuneration. Incidentally, not even death frees you from the tentacles of parasitic taxation. Here is what one British author wrote regarding a 100 percent inheritance tax: "The idea that we should be able to pass on our life's accumulated wealth to descendants is deeply embedded. It appeals to the fundamental biological urge to protect your offspring and propagate your genes. . . . Instinct seems to override common sense. . . . Yes, the desire to pass on property to your descendants may be natural—but why should we be slaves to our biology? Social progress has frequently depended on our ability to transcend individualistic urges and work together for the common good."[29] Suicidal empathy, couched in the ethos of collective "fairness," erases biological imperatives.

Our current tax system is as far removed as possible from any calculus of moral, ethical, or fair considerations. It posits that your tax rate increases the more income that you make, all the way to a maximum of around a 53 percent progressive tax rate. Note that in 2022, the highest tax bracket for the federal government was set at 33 percent and that of the Quebec government at 25.75 percent. Once you add the two sales taxes (provincial and federal), which are levied on your spending, school tax, property tax, gas tax, etc., I am left with roughly one-third of my earned revenue. If I make $100, I take home around $30 to $35. In other words, from January 1 to August 31, I work for free for the government. Starting in September, the Quebec and Canadian governments allow me to keep my hard-earned money, much of which stems from my creative initiatives (e.g., book royalties). How can you get people to willingly give up much of their earnings? Cue their empathy. When people's empathy is primed in a laboratory setting, they end up engaging in greater tax compliance.[30] This is precisely how Canada went from first levying income tax in 1917 as a temporary measure to more than a century later stealing more than 50 percent of your income (once all taxes are combined).[31] It is all justified under the banner of being an empathetic citizen. When parasitic socialists such as Bernie Sanders scream that the wealthy should pay their fair share of taxes, one wonders what that might be. The Tax Foundation states, "In 2016, the top 1 percent of taxpayers accounted for more income taxes paid than the bottom 90 percent combined."[32] This seems more than fair using any reasonable calculus, but parasitic taxation can never be satiated. If the mafia extorts 3 percent of your revenue to provide you with some much-needed neighborhood protection, this is illegal. If your government empathetically takes more than 60 percent of your income, this is legal. Once the insatiable taxation apparatus is unleashed, the parasitic gluttony only worsens. The United States income tax code grew from 27 pages when it was first enacted in 1913 to 17,427 pages as of April 2024; furthermore, the opportunity and out-of-pocket costs to comply with the tax system in 2024 in the United States was estimated at $414 billion.[33] How do we go from an income tax of 0 percent to one greater than 50 percent and from a tax code that expands from 27 to 17,427 pages? The following two quotes explain it perfectly, as does the parable of the boiling frog:

> Power concedes nothing without a demand. It never did and it never will. Find out just what any people will quietly submit to and you have found out the exact measure of injustice and wrong which will be imposed upon them, and these will continue till they are resisted with either words or blows, or with both. The limits of tyrants are prescribed by the endurance of those whom they oppress.[34]

––––

> [A]ccordingly all experience hath shewn, that mankind are more disposed to suffer, while evils are sufferable, than to right themselves by abolishing the forms to which they are accustomed.[35]

The newly formed Department of Government Efficiency headed by Elon Musk has publicized and subsequently eliminated a breathtaking amount of corruption, waste, and fraud. When governments have the legal authority to forcefully take your hard-earned money from you via parasitic taxation, and if there are no consequences to how they spend the money, it is nearly impossible to expect that the money will be spent properly. Politicians view your money as rightfully belonging to them, and as such, if the money is improperly spent, this is perfectly fine. Raise taxes, spend carelessly, rinse and repeat. While a significant percentage of misspending stems from governmental ineptitude, third-party fraud, or political corruption, much governmental waste is rooted in the reflex of misguided empathy. Both Canada and the United States view the entire world as within their empathetic circle. In other words, the globalist ethos does not delineate its reach to national borders. Hence, the suicidally progressive politicians think that it is perfectly fine that your hard-earned money is spent as follows, as reported by Rep. Brian Mast, the chairman of the Foreign Affairs Committee: "half-a-million dollars to expand atheism in Nepal, $50,000 to do, let's see, a transgender opera in Colombia, $47,000 to do an LGBTQ trans comic book in Peru, $20,000 a pop to do drag shows in Ecuador."[36] DOGE released a list of vanity global projects, funded by American taxpayers, in Cambodia, Czech Republic, Serbia, Moldova, India, Bangladesh, Nepal, Liberia, Mali, and South Africa, among other countries that serve zero national interests, other than of course the $10 million allocated for "Mozambique voluntary medical male circumcision."[37] Uncircumcised men in Mozambique pose a national security threat to the United States, not to mention the devastation that this would reap on American farmers. Senator Rand Paul released his 2024 Festivus Report, wherein he highlighted more than $1 trillion of wasted taxpayer funds, including "to advance fertilizer use in Pakistan, Vietnam, Colombia, and Brazil," "to teach Kyrgyzstan youth to go viral," and on a "new Sesame Street show in Iraq," among countless other outlandish displays of orgiastic excess.[38] Citizens Against Government Waste produce a yearly report that documents the astounding governmental waste that is inherent to pork barrel spending.[39] Parasitic taxation does not have to worry about how wisely your hard-earned money is spent. Your money is to be distributed to politicians in a way that advances their career. Shut up and be empathetic.

Speaking of Musk, suicidally empathetic socialists would love to see him taxed at a nearly 100 percent rate as he is apparently "unfairly" wealthy when other Americans must rely on food stamps to survive. These same folks fail to realize that Musk's companies have injected $338+ billion into the US economy over the past five years alone, stemming from $110.7 billion in salaries, $46 billion in levied taxes, and $182.2 billion in procurements.[40] Musk's ability to generate and allocate capital is astoundingly greater than would be the case of a "caring and empathetic" centralized government agency. The parasitic reflex to punish successful capitalists who otherwise inject extraordinary economic activity is a manifestation of the tall poppy syndrome and is also captured by a cross-cultural insight stemming from Bono (the lead singer of U2) who said: "In the United States, you look at the guy that lives in the mansion on the hill, and you think, you know, one day, if I work really hard, I could live in that mansion. In Ireland, people look up at the guy in the mansion on the hill and go, one day, I'm going to get that bastard."[41] Pathological envy bathing in suicidal empathy fuels socialism.

The empathetic equalization of income is not solely within the purview of the parasitic welfare state. Many years ago, the ice cream manufacturer Ben & Jerry's had created the 5 to 1 ratio as relating to the company's compensation structure, meaning that the chief executive officer (CEO) could not make more than five times the lowest-paid employee. The logic was that in the spirit of fairness, the ratio had to be reasonable. This ratio was then increased to 7 to 1, then 17 to 1, and ultimately the policy was shed when the ice cream manufacturer was bought out by Unilever.[42] A 2021 study found that the ratio of CEO pay to that of the typical worker was 399 to 1.[43] Hence, socialists use a multipronged approach in achieving empathic income equality, be it by flattening the variance between the highest- and lowest-paid individuals in an organization, and by requiring that the wealthiest members of society pay astronomically more taxes than others. Whenever I air my frustration on social media at the amount of taxes that I pay, many people are not in the least bit sympathetic. Rather, driven by a deep sense of parasitic entitlement and fueled by pathological envy, they are aghast that I would "whine" at having to pay such hefty taxes. After all, according to them, if I am paying a huge tax bill, it must be because I made a lot of money, so "quit your whining and perhaps help others in need." In their view, there is something existentially unfair about having winners and losers in the competitive game of life. If person A makes more money than person B in a socialist utopia, it can only stem from the dynamics between the oppressors (those who succeed) and the oppressed (those who failed). In other words, that one person is greatly more successful than another must be inherently and existentially unfair. Hence, true to the Marxist ideal of "we should all be equally miserable under the sun," the successful ones must have their money confiscated to be distributed to those whom we fetishize as being romantically oppressed. Hence, when people react with the "stop whining and pay your fair share of taxes," they are expressing this criminally parasitic mindset. But there is no moral, ethical, or rational reason that people should arrive to equal outcomes. From a fairness perspective, there is no conceivable reason that countless Canadians do not pay any taxes while others pay hundreds of thousands of dollars in taxes. Some people are more talented, hardworking, driven, smarter, and innovative. In a free society, there is nothing unfair about the fact that distinct individuals end up with different outcomes. The system cannot change because the great majority of the population benefits from the parasitic socialist Ponzi scheme. You need to destroy my financial viability to maintain the illusion of the utopian greater good.

Some beneficiaries of the taxation Ponzi scheme will angrily tell me that since Quebec and Canada had accepted us as war refugees in 1975, I was perpetually in their debt. Yet others believe that I was able to make my money because I benefited from being a Canadian citizen (e.g., safe and peaceful country) and hence it was only natural that I would pay the society that provided me with the daily conditions to flourish. Those arguments are deeply flawed as well as morally bankrupt. All immigrants who benefit in equal measure from being members of Canadian society do not end up paying the same amount of taxes. As such, some immigrants are apparently more equal than others. Furthermore, the amount of taxes that I have paid in my lifetime suggests that I have settled my "debt" long ago. Finally, a few posit that since Canadian universities are public institutions, professors are paid by the public coffers, and hence I am "benefiting" from taxation. This is perhaps the most imbecilic of all justifications for parasitic taxation. I am providing a highly desired service for the salary that I am drawing, and I should add that I am being grossly underpaid compared to my market value. Hence, the governments are using my talent and expertise while paying much less for my professorial services. If anything, they owe me a lot more than I owe them.

It is often a natural progression for the welfare state to become a nanny state. This almost always happens via the use of an empathy appeal. All the governmental intrusions into the minutia of your daily lives exist to protect you from yourself. I may have survived the brutality of the Lebanese civil war as a child, but I am certainly not capable of determining when I can cross a one-way street in a quiet residential area. My eyes are insufficiently honed to understand that the absence of any cars barreling toward me suggests that I can cross the street. This is why the loving paternalistic government places a cop in hiding, who is younger and less experienced than some of my socks, to intercept jay walkers who do not abide by the nurturing guidance of the crossing signs. The government is effectively telling me: "We cannot trust you to make such an important decision. It is best that we manage the crossing of the street for you, rube. Failure to accept our nurturance will result in a hefty fine precisely because we love you." This is why the Quebec government tells us when we must switch to winter tires. It also stipulates when restaurants are allowed to open their outdoor terraces in spring. All these intrusions have led me to appreciatively scream: "Govern me harder, Daddy!" Ronald Reagan was indeed prescient when he famously quipped: "I think you all know that I've always felt the nine most terrifying words in the English language are: I'm from the Government, and I'm here to help."[44] As the French philosopher Albert Camus proclaimed "The welfare of the people in particular has always been the alibi of tyrants, and it provides the further advantage of giving the servants of tyranny a good conscience."[45] If the government is intruding into the minutia of your lives, it is because they are overflowing with empathy toward you.

"Free" Canadian Healthcare

In 2012 I authored a *Psychology Today* article titled "Don't Romanticize the Canadian Healthcare System."[46] It is remarkable to witness the utopian fantasy prism through which many Americans view our crumbling healthcare system. It is indeed "true" that the Canadian healthcare system is "free," only if you ignore the pesky fact that I pay hundreds of thousands of dollars in taxes. Over the entirety of my professional career, I have paid astronomically more taxes than any governmental services that I might have gotten in return. Hence, it is certainly not free for me, or more generally to the main victims of the so-called socialist utopia, namely the few suckers who sustain the gigantic and immoral socialist Ponzi scheme by paying an astronomical share of all levied taxes. Now it is true that healthcare is free to the 40 percent of Canadians who do not pay a cent of income tax, as our former dear leader Justin Trudeau correctly stated.[47] Hence, the Canadian healthcare system is free in a similar manner to how my meal at a steakhouse is free if you exclude the $150 bill that I paid.

As mentioned earlier, another feature of a social welfare society is that it engenders criminal waste because our parasitic overlords are not held accountable for their governmental largesse. It is always easy to be generous and noble with other people's money. Case in point, the medical insurance cards that Canadians present when receiving "free" healthcare used to be bereft of a photo ID. A running joke in Montreal was that the entire country of Lebanon received free healthcare from Canada. When a man from Beirut, who had never set foot in Canada, had to have heart surgery, it was easy to fly to Montreal and use his nephew's health insurance card. Empathetic socialism breeds contempt for other people's money. Of note, the Democrats exhibit even greater global healthcare empathetic largesse than does Canada. In the 2019 primary debate for the 2020 presidential election, all ten Democrats raised their hands when asked if they would support free healthcare for illegal migrants.[48]

The Quebec healthcare system is so overburdened that many people are placed on waiting lists for years to be matched up to a personal physician. If you do not like your matched physician, too bad, rube. The government will tell you who your physician will be, and you will obey, smile, and nod in subservient gratitude. Good luck trying to find a medical specialist within a reasonable time frame. If you require a visit to the emergency room, prepare to wait for interminable hours. Whenever my wife visits her gynecologist for her yearly checkup, we usually prepare her a six-week survivalist backpack, since it is unclear how long it will take her to be seen, notwithstanding that she has an appointment. I should mention that the waiting times for various screening tests and important surgeries are breathtakingly long, but at least the Canadian healthcare system is "free." "Dear Mr. Joliette, the scheduled date for the lifesaving surgery that you require will take place in nine months. We realize that this might be too late to save you, but at least you can rejoice knowing that your death would not have cost you a penny. Your death was free of charge." Tragically, a young thirty-nine-year-old man from Montreal recently died of an aneurysm after deciding to leave the emergency room after having waited in vain for six hours.[49]

The healthcare system is so overburdened that many Quebec residents (me included) must pay for private medical insurance. But wait, I thought that healthcare was a free universal right. To conclude, yes, Canada has free universal healthcare with the following small caveats: I pay for everyone else's healthcare; I receive substandard healthcare; and I must take out private medical insurance to obtain proper timely care. This all sounds like a gigantic fraudulent racket, but as my American friends remind me, we are uniquely privileged in Canada for having "free" and empathetic healthcare unlike the "inhumane" dog-eat-dog American healthcare system.

Quebec's Empathetic Language Police

In bilingual Canada, all immigrants who move to Quebec must send their children to French school. The only exemption is for those who had a parent who had received English instruction as part of their education. Apparently, personal freedoms do not apply when one is trying to save the French language from the sea of English hostility. The Quebec government has resorted to breathtakingly silly if not draconian laws to protect the French language from apparent annihilation. Quebec's language police, the Office Québécois de la Langue Française, will harass storeowners if their bilingual signs do not adhere to the rule that the French sign must be clearly more prominent than its second-language counterpart.[50] And of course, it is taxpayers who fund the defense against such linguistic crimes. Even trademarks and brand names that, by definition, might not be in French, have come under legal scrutiny.[51]

The Quebec government is so desperate to ensure that the evil English language does not take over, they supported a lax immigration policy that threatens the very cultural fabric of Quebec. For many years, the Quebec government allowed entry of a bewildering number of immigrants from Islamic countries, many of whom were very hostile to central features of Quebec society (e.g., secularism). The Quebec government, though, had a strong logic on their side: Sure, Islamic extremists in Quebec might eventually behead the kuffar (the non-Muslims), but at least they will say "bonjour" first before the beheadings. The beheadings will be carried out in French, so rest assured, folks: *Ici on parle Français. Tout est bien qui finit bien.* (Here we speak French. All's well that ends well.)

On my eleven appearances on Joe Rogan's podcast, we have tackled innumerable thorny issues, be it in science, politics, or culture, none of which generated as much ire as a joke that I made on his show in July 2023. While discussing various accents, I committed the ultimate linguistic genocide: I stated that the French Canadian accent was "an affront to human dignity." This is part of an ongoing signature gag that I have been using for years. The Beatles, U2, and musicals are an affront to human dignity. In other words, the use of an exaggerated hyperbolic term to communicate one's aesthetic preference is the central feature of this form of humor. Well, Quebec society was not very understanding, forgiving, or empathetic. I received an email from a Quebec journalist, Marc Cassivi, asking me to explain my comments. I replied that there was nothing to add, namely, people have auditory preferences (e.g., Italian is more beautiful than Dutch). He proceeded to write an Orwellian article about my unforgivable "crime" in *La Presse*, a leading Quebec newspaper,[52] which set off an avalanche of breathtaking hate, threats, and calls to have me fired from Concordia University. For the next few weeks, I was public enemy number one of Quebec. Even leading Quebec ministers weighed in on my linguistic genocide, and my university disavowed my comment. Hence, rather than rallying around me, they threw me under the bus. Here was part of my reply in an article that I wrote in the *National Post*: "Such is the death trap of the humourless. To lead a good life, one must be anti-fragile to innumerable stressors including jokes at one's expense. A hallmark of a confident person is the ability to engage in self-deprecating humour. Similarly, a secure and proud society does not lose its head because someone joked about the local accent whilst having fun with Joe Rogan in Austin, Texas."[53] Be empathetic, say no to humor!

Woke Empathy in the Military

Si vis pacem, para bellum. (He who desires
peace, let him prepare for war.)[54]

Speak softly and carry a big stick.[55]

The antithesis of the welfare and nanny states is a government that stays out of your way other than providing key domestic services (e.g., snow removal, police force) and protecting the populace from foreign enemies. Military readiness is a fundamental responsibility of any government. However, suicidal empathy destroys this social contract. The military becomes a venue from which to elevate the self-esteem of marginalized people. We might be conquered by people who hate us, but at least our transgender soldiers will be able to surrender on the battlefield in their preferred gender identity. Perhaps the most operative dynamic throughout history is the following: There are two tribes, one on either side of a river. The men of both tribes look across the river at the resources of the other tribe with eyes of covetousness (hence its prohibition in the Ten Commandments). The only mechanism stopping either tribe from forcefully taking that which does not belong to them from the other tribe is the reality that it would be costly and bloody to do so. The recognition that individuals will violently protect what is theirs is a fundamental law of nature. Now imagine if a society were to be parasitized by a worldview that removes that threat. Enlightened progressive men show compassion to their enemies. They extend a welcoming hand to refugees hell-bent on destroying their societies. In Progressive Unicornia, only barbarians would ever respond violently; only Neanderthals would seek to protect their civilizations, heritage, religion, women, children, and resources. The invertebrate castrati can commit Civilizational Seppuku emboldened by their misguided suicidal moral vanity. To defend one's possessions and territory is an indelible feature of our human nature, a reality of which the 1973 Nobel laureate and ethologist Konrad Lorenz and the screenwriter Robert Ardrey were only too aware. In the 1960s, they each wrote highly successful books explaining the innate penchant for territoriality.[56] Many anthropologists at the time were promulgating the idea that humans, in their natural state, are all about peace and love. As such, they were highly critical of the position that humans are inherently territorial. Notwithstanding the illusory kumbaya of these social scientists, the long path of history is paved with rivers of blood. This is why nations need a strong military.

The enlistment oath in the United States armed forces is as follows: "I, [fill-in the name], do solemnly swear (or affirm) that I will support and defend the Constitution of the United States against all enemies, foreign and domestic; that I will bear true faith and allegiance to the same; and that I will obey the orders of the President of the United States and the orders of the officers appointed over me, according to regulations and the Uniform Code of Military Justice. So help me God."[57] Now imagine that when it comes to domestic threats, the former chairman of the Joint Chiefs of Staff, General Mark Milley, reaffirmed in 2021 what his boss, President Joe Biden, had intimated on numerous occasions: the greatest threat faced by the United States stems from "white rage" and white supremacy.[58] This is why, according to Milley, it was important for the US military to immerse itself in critical race theory. Critical race theory is astoundingly more dangerous and corrosive than the nonexistent "white" threats that they are so keen on eradicating. This reflex to create a unicorn threat from those suffering from Dermatological Original Sin (being white) is an "empathetic" correction for historical wrongs of the past. By repeatedly throwing white Americans, especially those who are male, under the bus, this will demonstrate that "hate has no place here." Intergenerational guilt must be dealt with. Not only are there no statutes of limitations when it comes to past historical grievances, but those who share the dermatological hue of the past culprits are guilty today. For the sake of empathetic reparative justice, we must eradicate the nonexistent "white rage," which was insufficiently enraged when it elected Barack Hussein Obama in 2008 and 2012.

What about foreign enemies? Do not worry, the US military under Joe Biden had fully internalized Justin Trudeau's "Diversity Is Our Strength" motto by seeking to cater to the LGBTQIA2+ community with a series of truly unbelievable recruitment ads. Ancient Roman armies, the Nazis, Genghis Khan, Attila the Hun, and Islamic military conquerors would have been easily defeated had they faced battalions of gender-fluid slobs with "Ask Me About My Pronouns" etched on their military uniforms. That is simply settled science. A military that seeks to maximize its commitment to empathetic celebration of marginalized groups rather than maximizing military readiness is optimizing the wrong metric. Pete Hegseth, the current US secretary of defense (since renamed secretary of war), explained how parasitic ideological capture in the form of wokeism has deeply degraded the military, as has Lieutenant-General (ret.) Michel Maisonneuve, who is arguably the top-ranking anti-woke military man stemming from the Canadian Forces.[59]

The British army put together a plan to phase out its "Be the Best" motto, which it had used since 1993.[60] This was construed as too ableist and elitist, and as such was non-inclusive of losers. It is more important to be empathetically mindful of the feelings of unemployed couch potatoes than to develop an elite military fully ready to defeat its avowed foreign enemies. Nothing is more important than military empathy. True to form, Scandinavian anthropologists have found a way to link military anthropology to empathy: "Through the term *ethnography of things military*, we propose to reposition military anthropology as intense engagements with militarisation through empathic immersion in things military. We develop this term through feminist critiques of militarisation and compassion . . ."[61] Feminism is never too far away from suicidal empathy.

The Tunnel to Towers Foundation, of which actor Mark Wahlberg is a staunch endorser, provides a wide range of support to the families of fallen or severely injured first responders and soldiers.[62] The foundation often airs a plea for donations on Fox News, and each time that I view the commercial I am left with the gnawing thought: Imagine if the taxes levied from Americans were properly used, there would be no need for this foundation. How is it that a country as great as the United States cannot take care of its heroes? Well, if you are spending the money on the housing and medical care of illegal aliens, this might explain the lack of funds.

The parasitically gluttonous welfare state rooted in the spirit of utopian socialism destroys the spirit of freedom and liberty. It imposes a punishing system of taxation meant to create empathetic equality across people. The compassionate nanny state is unconcerned with the bloating of governmental programs and the asphyxiating intrusion into our daily lives. Remember, they enslave the most productive members of society for a greater collective good. Once the suicidal empathy of socialism is coupled with the degeneracy of woke ideology, you are no longer a free and dignified human being but an empathetic worker ant slaving for a greater common goal.

Inoculation Against Suicidal Empathy

Ideas, not armies, rule the world. We believed too easily that tanks, barbed wire, secret police and instruments of thought control and to-talitarian power were decisive and that slaves could never be free. The events of the last several years have proved us wrong. It was false belief, not barbed wire, that enslaved. In the end, the wire was cut and the Iron Curtain broken by simple human choice, not arms. Those who had been trapped behind the barricades said, "Enough!" and were freed.[1]

Since Donald Trump's victory in the 2024 presidential election, I have often been asked whether this spells the end of the lunacy that has gripped the West. My answer is an emphatic no! The parasitic ideas and suicidal empathy that have obliterated our edifices of reason have taken many decades to fester first within the university ecosystem and then within the greater society at large. While Trump's victory has helped to quickly reverse some of the insanity, the battle is far from over. The shingles virus can remain dormant for decades until it painfully flares up in your fifties or sixties. The same applies to these idea pathogens and associated mis-guided empathy. They must be completely eradicated in a manner akin to how smallpox was extinguished. This can only take place when people's cognitive and emotional systems are free of the dreadful ideological parasites that have hijacked their capacity to reason. The Spanish painter Francisco Goya famously produced an aquatint titled *The Sleep of Reason Produces Monsters*.[2] The West's capacity to reason has indeed taken a long-unwelcomed nap, but I hope that this book, along with *The Parasitic Mind*, will awaken people from their stupor. Below, I offer a set of actionable prescriptions that provide protection against the pull of suicidal empathy, and in doing so will liberate us from the ghastly ideas that have enslaved us, as per the epigraph above.

Resist the Immediate Gratification of the Empathy-Based Dopamine Hit

The ability to optimally navigate between immediate and delayed rewards has countless downstream effects in one's life. Should you have that dessert now (immediate reward) or forgo it to remain thin? Should you buy that expensive car now, or perhaps save the money for a rainy day? These decisions and countless others amount to a temporal trade-off. Life is one long series of temptations, and how you navigate through these will have a profound impact on your success, health, and happiness. Some of the early work on self-control and delayed gratification was conducted by psychologist Walter Mischel on children in the 1960s, but a burgeoning literature has since explored this profoundly important issue.[3] I posit that suicidal empathy is the dysregulation of such intertemporal choices, namely, notwithstanding that a decision might have disastrous long-term consequences, these are ignored in the pursuit of an immediate dopamine hit fueled by one's empathetic largesse. It is perhaps not surprising then that women are more likely to suffer from suicidal empathy. While across decisional domains, women are better able than men to delay gratification, this general sex effect varies as a function of the task.[4] When it comes to signaling to the world that one is infinitely empathetic, women are more likely to seek the immediate rewards of the empathy-laced dopamine hit. This is why women are much more likely than men to be seen with the #RefugeesWelcome signs across many ports of entry in the West. Sure, some of these noble refugees might end up raping the empathetic women, but the immediate empathy hit is too alluring to worry about the downstream negative consequences. Similarly, by exhibiting infinite financial largesse to illegal migrants, you are increasing the financial burden that future generations will bear (in terms of the ballooning national debt). But if you see the world only through the prism of maximizing empathy now, then such intertemporal calculations are no longer an issue. The world is solely made of an empathy landscape, of which your job is to always find its most immediate and optimal manifestation. That this might lead to the destruction of your society downstream is immaterial because the much-desired empathy dopamine hit happens now.

Avoid the Empathetic Myopia of First-Order Effects

The classic domino effect occurs by tilting a single domino, resulting in a long series of linked dominoes to falter. People understand that there is a first cause that sets off the chain reaction, which then propagates across the chain, network, or system. The butterfly effect, as originally postulated by meteorologist Edward Lorenz, recognizes that a minuscule perturbation in a complex system can yield sizable downstream effects precisely because of webs of causal interconnections.[5] To fully understand the world around us requires that we build causal explanations for a given phenomenon. A central feature of such causal reasoning necessitates an understanding of the downstream effects of a given first cause. By virtue of their cognitive immaturity, children are in many instances unable to engage in complex causal reasoning, but this cognitive ability develops as an individual matures in ways that are driven by evolutionary forces.[6]

Suicidal empathy is inherently blind to causal thinking. It wallows in the world of first-order effects. If millions of refugees wish to come into your country illegally, please be empathetic and let them stay. Problem solved. Future consequences be damned. If millions of people enter your country legally, albeit they stem from societies that are perfectly antithetical to your values, do not worry about it. It will all work out. They will assimilate. The death of George Floyd at the hands of cops necessitates that you exhibit empathy with communities of color. Thus, if you support with great alacrity the need to defund the police, it is all fine. That fewer cops will yield an increase of crime rates in the communities in question is something in a far-distant future. Be empathetic now. The future will sort itself. Empathy now, for tomorrow we might be dead. Rational people who are not suicidally empathetic can see beyond the prism of first-order effects.

Do Not Succumb to the Singular Exemplar Bias—Statistical Regularities Matter

When I explain biological truths that are operative at the population level, I will often hear from a detractor about an exemplar that supposedly "falsified" said truths. Men are taller and heavier than women, notwithstanding the reality that your aunt Martha is heavier and taller than your uncle Jethroe. Statistical distributions overlap such that not every man is taller and heavier than every woman. Suicidally empathetic people, though, willfully succumb to this singular exemplar bias. The United States is currently attempting to deport millions of illegal aliens, some of whom are violent criminals. If there are 20 million illegals currently living in the United States, it is statistically expected that such a massive deportation program might yield singular exemplars of incorrect deportations. "Look, Alejandro Rodriguez is a sweet and caring father who was unfairly deported. This proves that the deportation of illegal migrants is cruel." No! Surgeries save lives, notwithstanding that surgical mishaps do occur. Lifesaving drugs work, notwithstanding that at times there are severe side effects. We cannot be rendered impotent in defending our societies by imposing a zero-error expectation. But to the suicidally empathetic, the rights of a wrongly deported individual supersede the rights of hundreds of millions of Americans to live in a nation with secure borders. Hence, let us abandon all deportations to ensure that no errors occur. Incidentally, many of the "wrongly deported" people end up being violent criminals who should have not been privy to anyone's empathy. But such is the trap of the infinitely kind. MS-13 gang members magically become fathers of the year. It is precisely how the suicidally empathetic refuse to criticize Islam: "My friend Mahmoud is married to a Jewish man, he eats prosciutto, drinks whiskey, and owns two black dogs. This proves that Islam loves the Jews, respects homosexuality, permits the eating of pork and the drinking of alcohol, and adores black dogs." The orgiastic industrial-scale rape of white British girls by Muslim Pakistani men is erased once you repeat the words "Jeffrey Epstein was Jewish" three times. Suicidal empathy can flourish only when overwhelming statistical realities are "falsified" by a singular exemplar that is contrary to the general pattern.

Do Not Succumb to the False Equality Bias

Individuals are equal under the law, but they are not equal in their talents or potentials. Individuals stemming from different cultures are equal under the law, but not all cultures are equally likely to assimilate within the foundational values of a host society. Men and women are equal under the law, but they are not indistinguishable in their abilities, preferences, or interests. Religions might be equally protected (and foolishly so) under the law, but they are not equally likely to assimilate within a Western system of personal freedoms and liberties. Suicidal empathy requires that we shed these important distinctions. By preaching a message of faux and imposed equality, this is construed as tolerant and empathetic. But it is a full departure from reality. Individual differences do exist. Men and women are different. Cultures are distinct. Religions preach radically diverse messages. To waive the magic wand of indistinguishable and indiscriminate equality as a means of creating sameness is an attack on the fabric of reality. Bowling is a sport, as is boxing. They are both sports that start with the letter "b" but they are not equally likely to yield brain injuries. Sane people recognize these obvious realities. The suicidally empathetic reject these distinctions. Suicidal empathy lobotomizes you.

Another feature of the false equality bias is to shut off people's natural and adaptive capacity to discriminate. All children might be equal in the eyes of God, but this does not mean that parents are equally likely to sacrifice their lives for their biological children versus random children. All women might be equal under the law; this does not imply that I love all women equally (at least not if I wish to remain happily married). As mentioned earlier, I was recently invited to speak in Iceland, a very small nation of nearly four hundred thousand people. Many Icelandic people suffer from stage 4 suicidal empathy. In one of my interactions, I asked whether given the small population of Iceland, would two hundred thousand people from Waziristan be equally likely to assimilate in Iceland as, say, two hundred thousand from Denmark?[7] You should have seen the uncomfortable squirming. Everyone knew the correct answer, but it was so difficult for many to admit that cultures are not equally homophilic.

Reject the Urge to Be an Empathetic Fence-Sitter

Lex Fridman is a podcaster who has amassed a very large audience stemming from his long-form conversations with many high-profile guests. Not long ago, I critiqued his unabated positivity, laced with endless empathetic pleas for spreading love, as a means of solving all social ills.[8] It is not laudable to be a fence-sitter who seldom takes a hard-line position to appear open-minded and impartial. The dogged defense of Truth is the highest form of empathy, namely epistemological empathy. I love Truth more than I love the desire to appear kind. Fridman's misplaced empathy is, in the best case, profoundly naive; in the worst case, it is a carefully curated act meant to strategically alienate no one: "Look, I am so accepting of everyone's point of view that I welcome everyone into my tent of empathy and love." No! Women do not have penises. It is empathetic to reject this delusion. Islam is not a religion of peace. More than thirty years ago, the political scientist Samuel P. Huntington explained that Islam is always in conflict with its neighbors,[9] and this continues to be true today based on an analysis of the world's war zones. It is empathetic to reject this falsehood. Moral people take positions on consequential matters. They do not equivocate endlessly to appear tolerant of all viewpoints. Effectively speaking, Fridman is the ultimate postmodernist (there are no objective truths), albeit he cloaks it in the sartorial robe of empathetic love. Be kind as a default value but a ferocious honey badger in the defense of the deontological principles that permit truth and freedom to flourish. Life is replete with unequivocal rights and wrongs; the moral and empathetic person recognizes this. Judge those who are unwilling to make this distinction under the faux guise of empathetic understanding. There is nothing more existentially empathetic than the dogged defense of the truth. To reiterate a point that I made in *The Parasitic Mind*, activate your inner honey badger in defending truth.

Expect and Demand Reciprocity—Otherwise, You Are in a Parasitic Relationship

Game theory is an applied mathematics field that models optimal behavior when multiple parties are interacting with one another. Perhaps the most famous game theoretic example is the Prisoner's Dilemma.[10] Two co-criminals are caught by the police and are interrogated separately. Each of the two criminals can either testify or not, yielding four possible outcomes. If both stay silent, they will each serve one year in prison. If one testifies while the other remains silent, the one who testified is set free, whereas the other receives a sentence of three years. If they both testify, they each receive two years. The optimal strategy is to testify irrespective of what the other criminal does, but of course if they both pursue this strategy, it leads to an outcome that is worse than had they both stayed silent. This is known as a One-Shot Prisoner's Dilemma, whereas the more general form is to play an Iterated Prisoner's Dilemma game, where the two parties will engage in multiple rounds of iterations. The question then becomes: Which of all possible strategies will yield the optimal outcome? The political scientist Robert Axelrod conducted a tournament pitting many submitted strategies against one another, and the one that came out victorious was the Tit-for-Tat strategy.[11] Start off by staying silent in the first round and subsequently mimic the behavior of your opponent. In other words, reciprocate in kind. It makes perfect evolutionary sense for rational choice actors to pursue their self-interests, an element of which is to offer and expect reciprocity. It is perfectly reasonable to be empathetic toward others, as this helps promote prosocial behavior, altruism, and cooperation.[12] But our empathy must be tethered to rational boundaries rooted in reciprocity. Otherwise, it leads to the gaming of our emotional system.

There are conditions under which reciprocity is not sought (i.e., non-reciprocal altruism). Under such circumstances, though, the altruist stands to benefit from the reputational signal of this unidirectional largesse. This can yield a form of competitive altruism wherein multiple parties engage in a bout to signal their generosity and beneficence. As a matter of fact, extreme forms of altruism could be a manifestation of Amotz Zahavi's handicap principle, namely for the signal to be an honest one, it must constitute a costly signal (i.e., one that handicaps the altruist).[13] That said, there is an upper limit to one's penchant for non-reciprocal altruism, and it falls far short of the suicidally empathetic altruism that the West engages in vis-à-vis countless parties.

If a dyadic relationship is not based on reciprocity, wherein both parties reap equal benefits and incur equal costs, it will ultimately be an unstable one. Many interactions work well because the parties involved all have a shared sense of the expectations, norms, and rituals implied to that context. Once this no longer holds true, you have created a scenario for free riding, or parasitic behavior. Now let us apply this principle to foreign aid between nations. For a relationship to be symbiotic, there needs to be a clear calculus of reciprocity between two nations. However, because of the suicidally empathetic largesse of the West in general, and the United States in particular, foreign aid does not impose any reciprocal accountability on the recipients of the foreign aid. According to the Council on Foreign Relations, from 1946 to 2021, the United States defrayed $3.71 trillion in foreign aid (or $49.5 billion per year) while readily admitting that it is unclear whether this staggering sum of money was well spent.[14] No worries. Simply increase the tax burden on your citizens, and the problem is solved. As a politician, it is always easy to be suicidally empathetic with other people's hard-earned money. Canada is such an empathetic country that it concerns itself with sanitary issues in Ghana to the tune of nearly $20 million in Canadian taxpayer funds.[15] Part of being sanitary is to teach Ghanaians that they should not use beaches as open toilets, and as such

$850,000 was spent by Canadian taxpayers on a campaign, including the use of billboards, in Ghana.[16] Will Ghanaians ever reciprocate Canadians' empathy? They will not have to because to expect reciprocity would be too mean.

Choose the Targets of Your Empathy Wisely

A fundamental feature of human sociality is altruism, which can be directed toward family members or toward nonkin (friends or strangers). These two Darwinian mechanisms are known as kin selection and reciprocal altruism.[17] Kin selection explains the evolutionary roots of kin-based altruism (e.g., why a parent jumps in front of a bus to save three of their children) whereas reciprocal altruism explains nonkin-based altruism (e.g., why a person jumps into a burning building to save a friend or even a stranger). These two forms of altruism need not solely occur in the context of lifesaving scenarios; rather, humans have evolved the strategic capacity to modulate their investments in others, as a function of their closeness to the beneficiary of the altruistic act. In my own work, I have shown how gifts are allocated to various recipients as a function of the evolutionary importance of the relationship in question. With one of my former doctoral students, I explored how people allocate their gift budgets across various possible recipients.[18] The largest gift is reserved for one's romantic partner, followed by close kin, then closest friends, and then further kin. In other words, people's gift-giving budget allocations map closely to the Darwinian importance that specific recipients hold in the eyes of their gift givers. The same holds true when people are choosing whom to save in the classic trolley problem.[19] Few people offer gifts to random strangers because our cognitive and emotional systems did not evolve to be nondiscriminating. We also found a positive correlation between the amount spent on a gift and the genetic relatedness between giver and recipient. It is perhaps not surprising that one might spend more on a sibling than a second cousin. In a subsequent paper with three Israeli coauthors, I found again that the size of monetary gifts at Israeli weddings is positively correlated to the genetic relatedness between wedding guests and the brides and grooms.[20] The animal kingdom is replete with countless such manifestations of kin-based discrimination. It makes perfect evolutionary sense to discriminate across targets for your affection, investment, and empathy. People experience on average nine daily opportunities to empathize with others, and the likelihood to empathize is correlated with the closeness of the relationship.[21] In other words, our empathy system has evolved to be preferentially focused on evolutionarily important relationships. Suicidal empathy shatters this reality by altering the order of importance to whom one should most care for.

Visual agnosia is a neurological disorder wherein people lose the ability to recognize faces (e.g., due to a stroke). I posit that suicidal empathy is a form of agnosia, namely an inability to identify the appropriate targets of one's empathy. I refer to this as "empathy agnosia," wherein people become blind to the evolutionary mechanisms that would have shaped how our empathy is dispensed. Do not succumb to this empathy disorder. Choose the recipients of your empathy carefully and wisely.

Adaptive Empathy Is Noble—Suicidal Empathy Is Fatal

Empathy is an evolutionarily selected virtue, which, when properly deployed, serves as a reminder that human beings are a social species capable of immeasurable good. But never forget that it must be invoked at the right time, in the right amount, and to the right targets. Otherwise, it becomes a liability that is gamed by those who wish to destroy us.

Nobody is against empathy. Nonetheless, it's insufficient. These days empathy has become a shortcut. It has become a way to experience delicious moral emotions without confronting the weaknesses in our nature that prevent us from actually acting upon them. It has become a way to experience the illusion of moral progress without having to do the nasty work of making moral judgments. In a culture that is inarticulate about moral categories and touchy about giving offense, teaching empathy is a safe way for schools and other institutions to seem virtuous without risking controversy or hurting anybody's feelings.[22]

I end with the following reminder, which I first posted on my social media: "A society dies when it cares more about exhibiting infinite tolerance and empathy than invoking its survival instinct. It truly is that simple."[23]

ACKNOWLEDGMENTS

On March 19, 2024, I posted some thoughts on my X feed regarding the suicidal empathy that I theorized was sending the West into a death spiral.[1] Shortly thereafter, I received an email from Eric Nelson, executive editor at HarperCollins and publisher of Broadside Books, containing the link to my post, and with the following subject heading: "Here's your book idea." From the onset, he has been incredibly supportive of the theme of my book and even intimated that he was a champion of anything that I wanted to write. It is difficult to hope for greater encouragement from one's editor and publisher. Thank you, Eric, for your unwavering support of this book.

I would like to thank Concordia University for having granted me a leave of absence that allowed me the necessary freedom to write this book. I spent 2024–2025 as a visiting professor and global ambassador at Northwood University, and 2025–2026 as a scholar at the University of Mississippi's Declaration of Independence Center for the Study of American Freedom. Both institutions have been highly supportive of my work.

Finally, I am thankful to the innumerable people who, upon first hearing of my suicidal empathy concept, made sure to spread it globally. I have been very pleased by the viral speed with which the term has proliferated around the world. The avalanche of reason is upon us. May we restore sanity to our once glorious societies by ensuring that the noble virtue of empathy is properly deployed.

NOTES

Preface

1. Irene Blanken, Niels Van De Ven, and Marcel Zeelenberg (2015). A meta-analytic review of moral licensing. *Personality and Social Psychology Bulletin*, 41(4), 540–558; Rob Henderson (2024). *Troubled: A Memoir of Foster Care, Family, and Social Class*. New York: Gallery Books; Maja Kutlaca and Helena R. M. Radke (2023). Towards an understanding of performative allyship: Definition, antecedents and consequences. *Social and Personality Psychology Compass*, 17(2), e12724.

2. Carolyn Pedwell (2012). Economies of empathy: Obama, neoliberalism, and social justice. *Environment and Planning D: Society and Space*, 30(2), 280–297.

3. Alan Levinovitz and Awais Aftab (2025). The Rumpelstiltskin effect: Therapeutic repercussions of clinical diagnosis. *BJPsych Bulletin*, doi: 10.1192/bjb.2025.10137.

4. Nicholas A. Christakis and James H. Fowler (2013). Social contagion theory: Examining dynamic social networks and human behavior. *Statistics in Medicine*, 32(4), 556–577.

5. Nicholas A. Christakis and James H. Fowler (2007). The spread of obesity in a large social network over 32 years. *New England Journal of Medicine*, 357(4), 370–379; James H. Fowler and Nicholas A. Christakis (2008). Dynamic spread of happiness in a large social network: Longitudinal analysis over 20 years in the Framingham Heart Study. *British Medical Journal*, 337, doi: https://doi.org/10.1136/bmj.a2338.

6. Leslie P. Boss (1997). Epidemic hysteria: A review of the published literature. *Epidemiologic Reviews*, 19(2), 233–243; Robert E. Bartholomew and Simon Wessely (2002). Protean nature of mass sociogenic illness: From possessed nuns to

chemical and biological terrorism fears. *The British Journal of Psychiatry*, 180(4), 300–306; Robert E. Bartholomew and Erich Goode (2000). Mass delusions and hysterias. *Skeptical Inquirer*, 24(3), 20–28; Robert E. Bartholomew and Bob Rickard (2014). *Mass Hysteria in Schools: A Worldwide History Since 1566.* Jefferson, NC: McFarland; Robert E. Bartholomew (2001). *Little Green Men, Meowing Nuns and Head-Hunting Panics: A Study of Mass Psychogenic Illness and Social Delusion.* Jefferson, NC: McFarland.

Chapter 1: A Good Virtue Gone Bad

1. Jeremy Rifkin (2009). *The Empathic Civilization: The Race to Global Consciousness in a World in Crisis* (2–3). New York: Penguin Books.

2. Stephanie D. Preston and Frans B. M. de Waal (2002). Empathy: Its ultimate and proximate bases. *Behavioral and Brain Sciences*, 25(1), 1–20; Frans B. M. de Waal (2009). *The Age of Empathy: Nature's Lessons for a Kinder Society.* New York: Crown; Jean Decety (2011). The neuroevolution of empathy. *Annals of the New York Academy of Sciences*, 1231(1), 35–45.

3. Normal P. Li, J. Michael Bailey, Douglas T. Kenrick, and Joan A. W. Linsenmeier (2002). The necessities and luxuries of mate preferences: Testing the tradeoffs. *Journal of Personality and Social Psychology*, 82(6), 947–955.

4. Donna E. Youngs, Miroslava A. Yaneva, and David V. Canter (2023). Development of a measure of kindness. *Current Psychology*, 42(7), 5428–5440.

5. Jonathan G. Kimmes, Anne B. Edwards, Joseph L. Wetchler, and Jerome Bercik (2014). Self and other ratings of dyadic empathy as predictors of relationship satisfaction. *The American Journal of Family Therapy*, 42(5), 426–437.

6. Joseph Ciarrochi, Philip D. Parker, Baljinder K. Sahdra, Todd B. Kashdan, Noona Kiuru, and James Conigrave (2017). When empathy matters: The role of sex and empathy in close friendships. *Journal of Personality*, 85(4), 494–504.

7. Peter Kardos, Bernhard Leidner, Csaba Pléh, Péter Soltész, and Zsolt Unoka (2017). Empathic people have more friends: Empathic abilities predict social network size and position in social network predicts empathic efforts. *Social Networks*, 50, 1–5.

8. Robert Elliott, Arthur C. Bohart, Jeanne C. Watson, and David Murphy (2018). Therapist empathy and client outcome: An updated meta-analysis. *Psychotherapy*, 55(4), 399–410.

9. Jean Decety and Aikaterini Fotopoulou (2015). Why empathy has a beneficial impact on others in medicine: Unifying theories. *Frontiers in Behavioral Neuroscience*, 8, 457. doi:10.3389/fnbeh.2014.00457; Ingrid M. Nembhard, Guy David,

Iman Ezzeddine, David Betts, and Jennifer Radin (2023). A systematic review of research on empathy in health care. *Health Services Research*, *58*(2), 250–263.

10. Elisa Silvia Colombo, Franca Crippa, Tessa Calderari, and Emanuela Prato-Previde (2017). Empathy toward animals and people: The role of gender and length of service in a sample of Italian veterinarians. *Journal of Veterinary Behavior*, *17*, 32–37; Nancy Stackhouse, Jared Chamberlain, Annette Bouwer, and Angela M. Mexas (2020). Development and validation of a novel measure for the direct assessment of empathy in veterinary students. *Journal of Veterinary Medical Education*, *47*(4), 452–464.

11. David Jeffrey (2016). Empathy, sympathy and compassion in healthcare: Is there a problem? Is there a difference? Does it matter? *Journal of the Royal Society of Medicine*, *109*(12) 446–452; Aaron Simmons (2014). In defense of the moral significance of empathy. *Ethical Theory and Moral Practice*, *17*, 97–111.

12. Benjamin M. P. Cuff, Sarah J. Brown, Laura Taylor, and Douglas J. Howat (2016). Empathy: A review of the concept. *Emotion Review*, *8*(2), 144–153.

13. Emma J. Lawrence, Philip Shaw, Dawn Baker, Simon Baron-Cohen, and Anthony S. David (2004). Measuring empathy: Reliability and validity of the Empathy Quotient. *Psychological Medicine*, *34*(5), 911–920; Martin C. Melchers, Mei Li, Brian W. Haas, Martin Reuter, Lena Bischoff, and Christian Montag (2016). Similar personality patterns are associated with empathy in four different countries. *Frontiers in Psychology*, *7*, 290, doi:10.3389/fpsyg.2016.00290.

14. Lior Abramson, Florina Uzefovsky, Virgilia Toccaceli, and Ariel Knafo-Noam (2020). The genetic and environmental origins of emotional and cognitive empathy: Review and meta-analyses of twin studies. *Neuroscience & Biobehavioral Reviews*, *114*, 113–133.

15. Ashley Abramson (2021). Cultivating empathy: Psychologists' research offers insight into why it's so important to practice the "right" kind of empathy, and how to grow these skills. *Monitor on Psychology*, *52*(8), https://www.apa.org/monitor/2021/11/feature-cultivating-empathy; Dominique Harz, Arabella Simpkin Begin, Reem Alansari, Ramiro Esparza, Corinne Zimmermann, Brooke DiGiovanni Evans, Staci Eisenberg, and Joel T. Katz (2023). The art of empathy: Teaching empathy through art. *The Clinical Teacher*, *20*(5), e13643; Pablo González Blasco and Graziela Moreto (2012). Teaching empathy through movies: Reaching learners' affective domain in medical education. *Journal of Education and Learning*, *1*(1), 22–34; P. Matthijs Bal and Martijn Veltkamp (2013). How does fiction reading influence empathy? An experimental investigation on the role of emotional transportation. *PloS One 8*(1), e55341.

16. Kathy A. Stepien and Amy Baernstein (2006). Educating for empathy: A review. *Journal of General Internal Medicine*, *21*, 524–530; Joshua D. Rosenberg

(2001). Teaching empathy in law school. *University of San Francisco Law Review*, 36, 621–658; Bridget Cooper (2011). *Empathy in Education: Engagement, Values and Achievement*. New York: Bloomsbury Publishing; Diane F. Baker (2017). Teaching empathy and ethical decision making in business schools. *Journal of Management Education*, 41(4), 575–598.

17. Douglas Hollan (2012). Emerging issues in the cross-cultural study of empathy. *Emotion Review*, 4(1), 70–78; Parvaneh Yaghoubi Jami, David Ian Walker, and Behzad Mansouri (2024). Interaction of empathy and culture: A review. *Current Psychology*, 43(4), 2965–2980; William J. Chopik, Ed O'Brien, and Sara H. Konrath (2017). Differences in empathic concern and perspective taking across 63 countries. *Journal of Cross-Cultural Psychology*, 48(1), 23–38.

18. Axel Franzen, Sebastian Mader, and Fabian Winter (2018). Contagious yawning, empathy, and their relation to prosocial behavior. *Journal of Experimental Psychology: General*, 147(12), 1950–1958.

19. Ivan Norscia and Elisabetta Palagi (2011). Yawn contagion and empathy in Homo sapiens. *PloS One*, 6(12), e28472; Ramiro M. Joly-Mascheroni, Atsushi Senju, and Alex J. Shepherd (2008). Dogs catch human yawns. *Biology Letters*, 4(5), 446–448.

20. Linda Kamas and Anne Preston (2020). Does empathy pay? Evidence on empathy and salaries of recent college graduates. *Journal of Labor Research*, 41, 169–188.

21. Svetlana Holt and Joan Marques (2012). Empathy in leadership: Appropriate or misplaced? An empirical study on a topic that is asking for attention. *Journal of Business Ethics*, 105, 95–105.

22. Adam Waytz (2016). The limits of empathy. *Harvard Business Review*, 94(1), 68–73.

23. Sven Form and Christian Kaernbach (2018). More is not always better: The differentiated influence of empathy on different magnitudes of creativity. *Europe's Journal of Psychology*, 14(1), 54–65; Andreas König, Lorenz Graf-Vlachy, Jonathan Bundy, and Laura M. Little (2020). A blessing and a curse: How CEOs' trait empathy affects their management of organizational crises. *Academy of Management Review*, 45(1), 130–153; See also p. 65, in Adam M. Grant and Barry Schwartz (2011). Too much of a good thing: The challenge and opportunity of the inverted U. *Perspectives on Psychological Science*, 6(1), 61–76, for a brief discussion of the inverted-U as relating to empathy.

24. Nancy Eisenberg, Natalie D. Eggum, and Laura Di Giunta (2010). Empathy-related responding: Associations with prosocial behavior, aggression, and intergroup relations. *Social Issues and Policy Review*, 4(1), 143–180.

25. Marita A. M. Van Langen, Inge B. Wissink, Eveline S. van Vugt, Trudy Van der Stouwe, and Geert Jan J. M. Stams (2014). The relation between empathy and offending: A meta-analysis. *Aggression and Violent Behavior, 19*(2), 179–189.

26. Emily V. Robinson and Richard Rogers (2015). Empathy faking in psychopathic offenders: The vulnerability of empathy measures. *Journal of Psychopathology and Behavioral Assessment, 37,* 545–552.

27. Nils Bubandt and Rane Willerslev (2015). The dark side of empathy: Mimesis, deception, and the magic of alterity. *Comparative Studies in Society and History, 57*(1), 5–34.

28. Frans B. M. de Waal (2009). *The Age of Empathy: Nature's Lessons for a Kinder Society* (p. 128). New York: Crown.

29. Chaoli Huang, Zifeng Wu, Sha Sha, Cunming Liu, Ling Yang, Peng Jiang, Hongxing Zhang, and Chun Yang (2025). The dark side of empathy: The role of excessive affective empathy on mental health disorders. *Biological Psychiatry,* https://doi.org/10.1016/j.biopsych.2024.12.020; Erin B. Tone and Erin C. Tully (2014). Empathy as a "risky strength": A multilevel examination of empathy and risk for internalizing disorders. *Development and Psychopathology, 26*(4 part 2), 1547–1565.

30. Adam Smith (2006). Cognitive empathy and emotional empathy in human behavior and evolution. *The Psychological Record, 56*(1), 3–21.

31. Nicola Cavanagh, Grayson Cockett, Christina Heinrich, Lauren Doig, Kirsten Fiest, Juliet R. Guichon, Stacey Page, Ian Mitchell, and Christopher James Doig (2020). Compassion fatigue in healthcare providers: A systematic review and meta-analysis. *Nursing Ethics, 27*(3), 639–665; Natália Ondrejková and Júlia Halamová (2022). Prevalence of compassion fatigue among helping professions and relationship to compassion for others, self-compassion and self-criticism. *Health & Social Care in the Community, 30*(5), 1680–1694.

32. Victoria E. Maringgele, Martin Scherr, Wolfgang Aichhorn, and Andreas K. Kaiser (2023). Helper Syndrome and Pathological Altruism in nurses—a study in times of the COVID-19 pandemic. *Frontiers in Psychology, 14,* 1150150.

33. Jess Baker and Rod Vincent (2023). *The Super-Helper Syndrome: A Survival Guide for Compassionate People.* Cheltenham, UK: Flint.

34. Paul Bloom (2016). *Against Empathy: The Case for Rational Compassion.* New York: HarperCollins; Paul Bloom (2017). Empathy and its discontents. *Trends in Cognitive Sciences, 21*(1), 24–31.

35. Barbara Oakley, Ariel Knafo, Guruprasad Madhavan, and David Sloan Wilson (Eds.). (2012). *Pathological Altruism.* New York: Oxford University Press.

36. Fritz Breithaupt (2019). *The Dark Sides of Empathy*. Ithaca, New York: Cornell University Press.

37. Allie Beth Stuckey (2024). *Toxic Empathy: How Progressives Exploit Christian Compassion*. New York: Penguin.

38. Derek Beres (2013). Idiot compassion and mindfulness. *Big Think*, https://bigthink.com/articles/idiot-compassion-and-mindfulness/. Many thanks to Jacek Blaszczynski, who alerted me to this Buddhist example.

39. C. A. Soper (2018). *The Evolution of Suicide*. Cham, Switzerland: Springer International Publishing; Diya Chatterjee and Rishabh Rai (2021). Choosing death over survival: A need to identify evolutionary mechanisms underlying human suicide. *Frontiers in Psychology*, 12, 689022, https://doi.org/10.3389/fpsyg.2021.689022; Gad Saad (2007). Suicide triggers as sex-specific threats in domains of evolutionary import: Negative correlation between global male-to-female suicide ratios and average per capita gross national income. *Medical Hypotheses*, 68(3), 692–696; Craig R. Kirkpatrick (2000). The evolution of human homosexual behavior. *Current Anthropology*, 41(3), 385–413; Andrew B. Barron and Brian Hare (2020). Prosociality and a sociosexual hypothesis for the evolution of same-sex attraction in humans. *Frontiers in Psychology*, 10, 2955, https://doi.org/10.3389/fpsyg.2019.02955.

40. Jodi Magness (2019). *Masada: From Jewish Revolt to Modern Myth*. Princeton, NJ: Princeton University Press.

41. Margaret Pabst Battin (Ed.). (2015). *The Ethics of Suicide: Historical Sources* (p. 285). New York: Oxford University Press.

42. Hawre Ahmed Mohammed (2023). The last genocide against the Yazidi People. *Review of Middle East Studies*, 56, 108–122.

43. Kathy Cordes (1988). The ritual of the Mesoamerican Ballgame. *Journal of Physical Education, Recreation & Dance*, 59(9), 44–47; Mary Ellen Miller (1989). The ballgame. *Record of the Art Museum, Princeton University*, 48(2), 22–31.

44. Vincent D. Riordan (2019). Suicide and human sacrifice; sacrificial victim hypothesis on the evolutionary origins of suicide. *Suicidology Online*, 10(2), 1–10.

45. Accessed via Project Gutenberg: https://www.gutenberg.org/ebooks/12096.

46. Bradley A. Thayer and Valerie M. Hudson (2010). Sex and the shaheed: Insights from the life sciences on Islamic suicide terrorism. *International Security*, 34(4), 37–62; John Orbell and Tomonori Morikawa (2011). An evolutionary account of suicide attacks: The kamikaze case. *Political Psychology*, 32(2), 297–322.

47. Kawon Victoria Kim, Cayley Russell, Mark S. Kaplan, Jürgen Rehm, and

Shannon Lange (2023). Types of suicide pacts: A comparative analysis using the National Violent Death Reporting System. *Frontiers in Psychiatry, 14*, 1139305, https://doi.org/10.3389/fpsyt.2023.1139305.

48. Yoshitomo Takahashi and Douglas Berger (1996). Cultural dynamics and suicide in Japan. In Antoon A. Leenaars and David Lester (Eds.). *Suicide and the Unconscious* (pp. 248–258). Northvale, NJ: Jason Aronson; See also K. Ohara and David Reynolds (1970). Love-pact suicide. *OMEGA-Journal of Death and Dying, 1*(3), 159–166; Fumiko Satoh, Junpei Nagato, Wataru Irie, Chizuko Sasaki, Eriko Ochiai, Maho Kondo, and Kino Hayashi (2023). Double suicide in Japan in the post-war reconstruction period, with reference to contemporary Japan. *Medicine, Science and the Law, 63*(3), 222–226.

49. Dennis R. Cooley (2020). Was Jesus an assisted suicide? *Ethics, Medicine and Public Health, 14*, 100514.

50. Abba Eban and Natan Aridan (2006). The Toynbee Heresy. *Israel Studies, 11*(1), 91–107.

51. Seth D. Kaplan (2019). How do America's elites stack up? *The American Interest, 15*(4), https://www.the-american-interest.com/2019/10/30/how-do-americas-elites-stack-up/.

52. James Burnham (1964). *Suicide of the West: An Essay on the Meaning and Destiny of Liberalism* (p. 25 and p. 35, respectively). New York: The John Day Company. Accessed at: https://archive.org/details/suicideofwestess00burn/page/24/mode/2up?q=suicide.

53. Donald J. Robertson (October 17, 2024). The Saad Truth about Happiness, *Substack*, https://donaldrobertson.substack.com/p/the-saad-truth-about-happiness.

54. Jack G. Rayner, Samantha L. Sturiale, and Nathan W. Bailey (2022). The persistence and evolutionary consequences of vestigial behaviours. *Biological Reviews, 97*(4), 1389–1407.

55. John Archer (2006). Testosterone and human aggression: An evaluation of the challenge hypothesis. *Neuroscience & Biobehavioral Reviews, 30*(3), 319–345; Aaron Sell, John Tooby, and Leda Cosmides (2009). Formidability and the logic of human anger. *Proceedings of the National Academy of Sciences, 106*(35), 15073–15078; Michael E. McCullough, Robert Kurzban, and Benjamin A. Tabak (2013). Cognitive systems for revenge and forgiveness. *Behavioral and Brain Sciences, 36*(1), 1–15.

56. Laith Al-Shawaf, Daniel Conroy-Beam, Kelly Asao, and David M. Buss (2016). Human emotions: An evolutionary psychological perspective. *Emotion Review, 8*(2), 173–186.

57. See Gad Saad (2006). Sex differences in OCD symptomatology: An evolutionary perspective. *Medical Hypotheses 67*(6), 1455–1459, and references therein.

58. Asmir Gračanin, Lauren M. Bylsma, and Ad J. J. M. Vingerhoets (2018). Why
only humans shed emotional tears: Evolutionary and cultural perspectives.
Human Nature, 29(2), 104–133.

59. The ethical precept originates from a poem by Bessie Anderson Stanley titled
Success, albeit it has been misattributed to various other authors.

60. Gad Saad (August 4, 2016). Confronting a Human Pig on a Pristine SoCal
Beach (*The Saad Truth*, 233), https://youtu.be/QHzSLAop4DM.

61. Will Worley (April 8, 2016). Norwegian rape survivor "feels guilty" the man
who assaulted him was deported. *Independent*, https://www.independent.co
.uk/news/world/europe/norwegian-rape-victim-feels-guilty-the-man-who
-raped-him-was-deported-a6975041.html.

62. David Livingstone Smith (2020). *On Inhumanity: Dehumanization and How to
Resist It*. New York: Oxford University Press; David Moshman (2007). Us and
them: Identity and genocide. *Identity: An International Journal of Theory and
Research, 7*(2), 115–135.

63. Eric J. Vanman (2016). The role of empathy in intergroup relations. *Current
Opinion in Psychology, 11*, 59–63.

64. Daniel Balliet, Junhui Wu, and Carsten K. W. De Dreu (2014). Ingroup favoritism
in cooperation: A meta-analysis. *Psychological Bulletin, 140*(6), 1556–1581; Jim A.
C. Everett, Nadira S. Faber, and Molly Crockett (2015). Preferences and beliefs
in ingroup favoritism. *Frontiers in Behavioral Neuroscience, 9*, 126656; Mina Cikara,
Emile Bruneau, Jay J. Van Bavel, and Rebecca Saxe (2014). Their pain gives
us pleasure: How intergroup dynamics shape empathic failures and counter-
empathic responses. *Journal of Experimental Social Psychology, 55*, 110–125.

65. Gad Saad (December 2, 2015). My Chat with Evolutionary Medicine Pioneer
Randy Nesse (*The Saad Truth*, 101), https://youtu.be/VokpuzXtqXs; Gad Saad
(June 12, 2023). My Chat with Psychiatrist Dr. Randy Nesse, Pioneer of Evo-
lutionary Medicine (*The Saad Truth*, 1581), https://youtu.be/1mhuspKoRtg;
Randolph M. Nesse and George C. Williams (1996). *Why We Get Sick: The New
Science of Darwinian Medicine*. New York: Vintage Books; Martin Brüne and
Wulf Schiefenhövel (Eds.). (2019). *The Oxford Handbook of Evolutionary Medi-
cine*. Oxford, UK: Oxford University Press.

66. Margie Profet (1988). The evolution of pregnancy sickness as protection to
the embryo against Pleistocene teratogens. *Evolutionary Theory, 8*(3),
177–190; Samuel M. Flaxman and Paul W. Sherman (2000). Morning sickness:

A mechanism for protecting mother and embryo. *Quarterly Review of Biology*, *75*(2), 113–148.

67. Michael McGuire and Alfonso Troisi (1998). *Darwinian Psychiatry*. New York: Oxford University Press; Marco Del Giudice (2018). *Evolutionary Psychopathology: A Unified Approach*. New York: Oxford University Press.

68. The two Nesse quotes stem from Randolph M. Nesse (2019). *Good Reasons for Bad Feelings: Insights from the Frontier of Evolutionary Psychiatry* (p. 65 and p. 122). New York: Dutton.

69. Leonardo Christov-Moore, Elizabeth A. Simpson, Gino Coudé, Kristina Grigaityte, Marco Iacoboni, and Pier Francesco Ferrari (2014). Empathy: Gender effects in brain and behavior. *Neuroscience & Biobehavioral Reviews*, *46*, 604–627; David M. Greenberg, Varun Warrier, Ahmad Abu-Akel, Carrie Allison, Krzysztof Z. Gajos, Katharina Reinecke, P. Jason Rentfrow, Marcin A. Radecki, and Simon Baron-Cohen (2023). Sex and age differences in "theory of mind" across 57 countries using the English version of the "Reading the Mind in the Eyes" Test. *Proceedings of the National Academy of Sciences*, *120*(1), e2022385119; Magali Jane Rochat (2023). Sex and gender differences in the development of empathy. *Journal of Neuroscience Research*, *101*(5), 718–729.

70. Oskari Lahtinen (2024). Construction and validation of a scale for assessing critical social justice attitudes. *Scandinavian Journal of Psychology*, *65*(4), 693–705; Noah Carl (December 2, 2021). Did women in academia cause wokeness? More women means more censorship, more discrimination, more advocacy—and less debate. *The Critic*, https://thecritic.co.uk/did-women-in -academia-cause-wokeness/; Melinda R. Roberts, Wendy Turner, Leigh Anne Howard, Erin E. Gilles, and Anne Statham (2019). Gender and social justice: An examination of attitudes and behaviors among undergraduate liberal arts students. *Affilia*, *34*(4), 552–567; Cory Clark (April 28, 2021). The gender gap in censorship support: Research suggests women favor inclusivity over academic freedom. *Psychology Today*, https://www.psychologytoday.com /ca/blog/the-antisocial-psychologist/202104/the-gender-gap-in-censorship -support; Leigh Revers (October 14, 2024). The dark side of the feminization of higher education: Universities are matriarchal enterprises run by women for women, in pursuit of retribution for the patriarchy of the past. *National Post*, https://nationalpost.com/opinion/the-dark-side-of-the-feminization-of -higher-education; Barbara Kay (April 2, 2023). Women are fuelling the crisis of wokeism on campus, and in society. *National Post*, https://nationalpost .com/opinion/women-are-fuelling-the-crisis-of-wokeism-on-campus-and -in-society; Glenn Geher, Olivia Jewell, Richard Holler, Julie Planke, Kian Betancourt, Amanda Baroni, Jacqueline Di Santo, Morgan Gleason, and Jacqueline Eisenberg (2020). Politics and academic values in higher education:

Just how much does political orientation drive the values of the Ivory Tower? unpublished manuscript, https://osf.io/495nc; Glenn Geher (November 26, 2020). Politics in academia: A case study. *Psychology Today*, https://www.psychologytoday.com/ca/blog/darwins-subterranean-world/202011/politics-in-academia-case-study.

71. Heather Mac Donald (March 5, 2023). In Loco Masculi: The feminization of the American university is all but complete. *City Journal*, https://www.city-journal.org/article/in-loco-masculi.

72. Elizabeth A. Segal, M. Alex Wagaman, and Karen E. Gerdes (2012). Developing the social empathy index: An exploratory factor analysis. *Advances in Social Work*, *13*(3), 541–560.

73. Gad Saad (2007). *The Evolutionary Bases of Consumption* (chapter 5). Mahwah, NJ: Lawrence Erlbaum; Gad Saad (2011). *The Consuming Instinct: What Juicy Burgers, Ferraris, Pornography, and Gift Giving Reveal About Human Nature* (chapter 6). Amherst, NY: Prometheus Books; Gad Saad (2012). Nothing in popular culture makes sense except in the light of evolution. *Review of General Psychology*, *16*(2), 109–120.

74. Julian B. Rotter (1966). Generalized expectancies for internal versus external control of reinforcement. *Psychological Monographs: General and Applied*, *80*(1), 1–28.

75. Emily Ekins (2019). What Americans think about poverty, wealth, and work (p. 25). The Cato Institute, https://www.cato.org/publications/survey-reports/what-americans-think-about-poverty-wealth-work.

76. Amy H. Mezulis, Lyn Y. Abramson, Janet S. Hyde, and Benjamin L. Hankin (2004). Is there a universal positivity bias in attributions? A meta-analytic review of individual, developmental, and cultural differences in the self-serving attributional bias. *Psychological Bulletin*, *130*(5), 711–747.

77. Otto Kernberg (2009). The concept of the death drive: A clinical perspective. *International Journal of Psychoanalysis*, *90*(5), 1009–1023.

78. William Voegeli (2014). The case against liberal compassion. *Imprimis*, *43*(10), https://imprimis.hillsdale.edu/the-case-against-liberal-compassion/.

79. Diane N. Solomon (May 1, 2024). Why do I still feel guilty for my privilege? *Psychology Today*, https://www.psychologytoday.com/us/blog/the-narrative-nurse-practitioner/202404/why-do-i-still-feel-guilty-for-my-privilege.

80. Dena M. Bravata, Sharon A. Watts, Autumn L. Keefer, Divya K. Madhusudhan, Katie T. Taylor, Dani M. Clark, Ross S. Nelson, Kevin O. Cokley, and Heather K. Hagg (2020). Prevalence, predictors, and treatment of impostor syndrome: A systematic review. *Journal of General Internal Medicine*, *35*, 1252–1275.

81. Mary Namnyak, Nicola Tufton, R. Szekely, M. Toal, S. Worboys, and Elizabeth L. Sampson (2008). "Stockholm syndrome": Psychiatric diagnosis or urban myth? *Acta Psychiatrica Scandinavica*, 117(1), 4–11.

82. Rebecca Bailey, Jaycee Dugard, Stefanie F. Smith, and Stephen W. Porges (2023). Appeasement: replacing Stockholm syndrome as a definition of a survival strategy. *European Journal of Psychotraumatology*, 14(1), 2161038.

83. Kenneth Levin (2005). *The Oslo Syndrome: Delusions of a People Under Siege*. Hanover, NH: Smith & Kraus.

84. David Suissa (October 19, 2024). Yahya Sinwar's Brain. *Jewish Journal*, https://jewishjournal.com/commentary/columnist/editors-note/375955/yahya-sinwars-brain/; Judith Miller (March 18, 2024). Saving Sinwar. *Tablet*, https://www.tabletmag.com/sections/israel-middle-east/articles/saving-sinwar-hamas-gaza.

85. EBSCO Knowledge Advantage™. The Firebugs by Max Frisch, https://www.ebsco.com/research-starters/literature-and-writing/firebugs-max-frisch.

Chapter 2: Forbidden Knowledge

1. John Milton (1674; 2005). In David Scott Kastan (Ed.), *Paradise Lost* (p. 127). Indianapolis, IN: Hackett Publishing Company.

2. Ayn Rand (1964). *The Virtue of Selfishness: A New Concept of Egoism* (p. 19). New York: Signet.

3. Roger Shattuck (1996). *Forbidden Knowledge: From Prometheus to Pornography* (p. 327). New York: St. Martin's Press.

4. Rob Montz (April 15, 2022). Why did Harvard University go after one of its best black professors? *Quillette*, https://quillette.com/2022/04/15/why-did-harvard-university-go-after-one-of-its-best-black-professors/.

5. Ben Clerkin (January 2, 2024). Harvard president resigns but will stay on as lecturer making nearly $1m a year. *The Jewish Chronicle*, https://www.thejc.com/news/usa/harvard-president-resigns-over-plagiarism-weeks-after-infamous-congressional-hearing-ljwdy5fc.

6. Isabel Vincent (January 9, 2024). Harvard board facing probe over Claudine Gay cover-up and censorship demands. *New York Post*, https://nypost.com/2024/01/09/news/harvard-facing-probe-over-claudine-gay-cover-up-censorship/.

7. Philippe J. Rushton (1996). *Race, Evolution, and Behavior: A Life History Perspective*. New Brunswick, NJ: Transaction Publishers.

8. Joanna Kempner, Jon F. Merz, and Charles L. Bosk (2011). Forbidden knowledge: Public controversy and the production of nonknowledge. *Sociological Forum, 26*(3), 475–500.

9. Gad Saad (April 30, 2023). The Deontological Pursuit of Truth—The Slippery Slope of Forbidden Knowledge (*The Saad Truth*, 1550), https://youtu.be/AMCtTLQtgro.

10. Bari Weiss, Isaac Grafstein, Suzy Weiss, et al. (December 15, 2022). Why Twitter really banned Trump. *The Free Press*, https://www.thefp.com/p/why-twitter-really-banned-trump.

11. Kenneth Pennington (2003). Innocent until proven guilty: The origins of a legal maxim. *The Jurist, 63*, 106–124.

12. Lee Brown (August 19, 2022). Sam Harris: Censoring The Post's Hunter Biden exposés "warranted" to beat Trump. *New York Post*, https://nypost.com/2022/08/19/sam-harris-defends-silencing-the-post-on-hunter-biden/.

13. Post Editorial Board (March 18, 2022). Spies who lie: 51 "intelligence" experts refuse to apologize for discrediting true Hunter Biden story. *New York Post*, https://nypost.com/2022/03/18/intelligence-experts-refuse-to-apologize-for-smearing-hunter-biden-story/.

14. Robert R. Reilly (2010). *The Closing of the Muslim Mind: How Intellectual Suicide Created the Modern Islamist*. Wilmington, DE: ISI Books.

15. Francisco Bethencourt (2009). *The Inquisition. A Global History, 1478–1834*. Cambridge, UK: Cambridge University Press.

16. Alberto A. Martinez (2018). *Burned Alive: Giordano Bruno, Galileo, and the Inquisition*. Chicago: University of Chicago Press.

17. Steven Nadler (2013). Why Spinoza was excommunicated. *Humanities, 34*(5), https://www.neh.gov/article/why-spinoza-was-excommunicated; see also Steven Nadler (1999). *Spinoza: A life*. Cambridge, UK: Cambridge University Press.

18. James Lynch (September 29, 2024). John Kerry says the First Amendment is getting in the way of online censorship. *National Review*, https://www.nationalreview.com/news/john-kerry-says-the-first-amendment-is-getting-in-the-way-of-online-censorship/.

19. Nikki Schwab (February 3, 2021). New climate czar John Kerry said taking his family's private jet to a climate change conference in Iceland in 2019 was "the only choice for somebody like me." *Daily Mail*, https://www.dailymail.co.uk/news/article-9220535/Kerry-said-taking-private-jet-climate-conference-choice-somebody-like-me.html.

20. Tufayel Ahmed (September 30, 2019). Leonardo DiCaprio criticized for private jet use after calling out climate change deniers at Global Citizen Festival, *Newsweek*, https://www.newsweek.com/leonardo-dicaprio-climate-change-private-jet-yacht-global-citizen-1461990; Associated Press (February 2, 2024). Why Taylor Swift's globe-trotting in private jets is getting scrutinized, *U. S. News & World Report*, https://www.usnews.com/news/entertainment/articles/2024-02-02/why-taylor-swifts-globe-trotting-in-private-jets-is-getting-scrutinized.

21. Fox News (October 6, 2024). Hillary Clinton warns that allowing free speech on social media means "we lose control," *New York Post*, https://nypost.com/2024/10/06/us-news/hillary-clinton-warns-that-allowing-free-speech-on-social-media-means-we-lose-control/.

22. Sean Burch (September 17, 2024). Hillary Clinton says some Americans who share political misinformation should be criminally charged, Yahoo! News, https://www.yahoo.com/news/hillary-clinton-says-americans-share-150735862.html.

23. Gad Saad (February 5, 2019). My Chat with Twitter Co-Founder Jack Dorsey (*The Saad Truth*, 843), https://www.youtube.com/watch?v=U7u2oJ_HX3U.

24. https://x.com/ThierryBreton/status/1823033048109367549.

25. AtlanticCouncil (June 22, 2021). A conversation with former Wikimedia CEO, Katherine Maher, https://www.youtube.com/watch?v=y-JRPJnVvOU&t=3s [36:39–37:06].

26. David Inserra and Jennifer Huddleston (August 11, 2024). Actually, Tim Walz, the First Amendment does protect misinformation and "hate speech." *Cato Institute*, https://www.cato.org/commentary/actually-tim-walz-first-amendment-does-protect-misinformation-hate-speech; Alexandria Ocasio-Cortez (January 13, 2021). What happens after the Capitol attacks? | Alexandria Ocasio-Cortez, https://www.youtube.com/watch?v=PBC8LeXb_6s.

27. Sabrina Strings (2023). How the use of BMI fetishizes white embodiment and racializes fat phobia. *AMA Journal of Ethics*, *25*(7), 535–539.

28. Marisa Crane (April 27, 2023). Diet culture is rooted in racism, white supremacy, and colonialism. *Within*, https://withinhealth.com/learn/articles/diet-culture-rooted-in-racism-white-supremacy-and-colonialism.

29. Olivia B. Waxman (December 28, 2022). The white supremacist origins of exercise, and 6 other surprising facts about the history of U.S. physical fitness. *Time*, https://time.com/6242949/exercise-industry-white-supremacy/.

30. https://think.taylorandfrancis.com/special_issues/indigenously-fat-fatly-indigenous/.

31. Angela Last (2018). In Gurminder K. Bhambra, Dalia Gebrial, and Kerem Nişan-cıoğlu (Eds.), *Decolonizing the University* (pp. 208–230). London: Pluto Press.

32. James Gordon (December 17, 2024). San Francisco hires taxpayer funded "weight stigma" czar Virgie Tovar, *Daily Mail*, https://www.dailymail.co.uk/news/article-14203981/san-francisco-hires-weight-czar-virgie-tovar-taxpayer-funded.html.

33. https://www.spj.org/spj-code-of-ethics/.

34. Charles Fain Lehman (April 14, 2022). Yes, the media bury the race of murderers—if they're not white. *Washington Free Beacon*, https://freebeacon.com/media/yes-the-media-bury-the-race-of-murderers-if-theyre-not-white/.

35. David Bauder (July 20, 2020). AP says it will capitalize Black but not white. Associated Press, https://www.ap.org/media-center/ap-in-the-news/2020/ap-says-it-will-capitalize-black-but-not-white/.

36. Catherine Savini (January 26, 2021). 10 ways to tackle linguistic bias in our classroom. *Inside Higher Ed*, https://www.insidehighered.com/advice/2021/01/27/how-professors-can-and-should-combat-linguistic-prejudice-their-classes-opinion.

37. Dan Lerman (August 31, 2025). The war on knowledge. *The Free Press*, https://www.thefp.com/p/the-war-on-knowledge-education-schools-teachers.

38. Sonya Gugliara (July 16, 2025). Straight white author's career finally takes off after he tells woke publishers he's gender queer Nigerian. *Daily Mail*, https://www.dailymail.co.uk/news/article-14912627/Poet-Aaron-Barry-Vancouver-faked-woke.html.

39. Khaleda Rahman (November 21, 2024). Why Laken Riley's killer isn't facing death penalty in Georgia, *Newsweek*, https://www.newsweek.com/why-laken-riley-killer-not-facing-death-penalty-georgia-1989397.

40. Josh Boak, Michelle Price, and Jill Colvin (March 10, 2024). Trump blasts Biden over Laken Riley's death after Biden says he regrets using term "illegal." Associated Press, https://apnews.com/article/biden-illegal-riley-marjorie-taylor-greene-trump-04924ffb3be76d60e1b6e8796a968051.

41. Charlie Spiering (September 13, 2024). Kamala Harris moved to probe "gender-bias" language in top secret reports. *Daily Mail*, https://www.dailymail.co.uk/news/article-13848007/kamala-harris-gender-bias-vice-president-intelligence.html.

42. Jennifer Thomson (2020). What's feminist about feminist foreign policy? Swe-

den's and Canada's foreign policy agendas. *International Studies Perspectives*, *21*(4), 424–437.

43. Paul Bois (December 19, 2024). Spending bill includes woke language: Criminal offender becomes "justice-involved individual." *Breitbart*, https://www .breitbart.com/politics/2024/12/19/spending-bill-includes-woke-language -justice-involved-individual/.

44. Sara Jahnke, Nicholas Blagden, and Laura Hill (2022). Pedophile, child lover, or minor-attracted person? Attitudes toward labels among people who are sexually attracted to children. *Archives of Sexual Behavior*, *51*(8), 4125–4139. See also https://nypost.com/2021/11/25/prof-who-referred-to-pedophiles-as -minor-attracted-persons-to-resign/.

45. Craig A. Harper, Rebecca Lievesley, Nicholas J. Blagden, and Kerensa Hocken (2022). Humanizing pedophilia as stigma reduction: A large-scale intervention study. *Archives of Sexual Behavior*, *51*(2), 945–960.

46. New Scientist (February 14, 2024). Is it time for a more subtle view on the ultimate taboo: Cannibalism? https://www.newscientist.com/article /mg26134783-600-is-it-time-for-a-more-subtle-view-on-the-ultimate-taboo -cannibalism/.

47. Leo Strauss (1953). *Natural Right and History* (p. 3). Chicago: University of Chicago Press. Accessed at: https://archive.org/details/naturalrighthist00stra /page/2/mode/2up?q=%22the+principles+of+cannibalism+are+as%22.

48. https://www.nextbigfuture.com/2023/11/have-the-top-us-cities-in-homelessness -had-democrat-mayors.html; https://www.usnews.com/news/best-states/slide shows/cities-with-the-largest-homeless-populations-in-the-u-s?slide=28. For a detailed report of homelessness in the United States, see https://www.huduser .gov/portal/sites/default/files/pdf/2022-AHAR-Part-1.pdf.

49. Barrett A. Lee, David W. Lewis, and Susan Hinze Jones (1992). Are the homeless to blame? A test of two theories. *Sociological Quarterly*, *33*(4), 535–552; Robert J. Pellegrini, Sergio S. Queirolo, Victor E. Monarrez, and Dona M. Valenzuela (1997). Political identification and perceptions of homelessness: Attributed causality and attitudes on public policy. *Psychological Reports*, *80*(3_suppl), 1139–1148; Jack Tsai, Crystal YS Lee, Jianxun Shen, Steven M. Southwick, and Robert H. Pietrzak (2019). Public exposure and attitudes about homelessness. *Journal of Community Psychology*, *47*(1), 76–92.

50. Jack Tsai, Crystal Yun See Lee, Thomas Byrne, Robert H. Pietrzak, and Steven M. Southwick (2017). Changes in public attitudes and perceptions about homelessness between 1990 and 2016. *American Journal of Community Psychology*, *60*(3–4), 599–606.

51. Christopher F. Rufo (March 10, 2020). Plot twist: The progressive narrative on homelessness has always been wrong—and new data undermine it further. *City Journal,* https://www.city-journal.org/article/plot-twist; Howard Husock (October 13, 2023). Liberals reap consequences of their homeless policies. *American Enterprise Institute,* https://www.aei.org/op-eds/liberals-reap-consequences-of-their-homeless-policies/.

52. Marc Cota-Robles (June 20, 2024). New high-rise building to house homeless in $600K units in downtown Los Angeles, ABC7 News, https://abc7news.com/post/new-high-rise-building-house-skid-row-homeless/14976180/.

53. Michael Shellenberger (April 25, 2024). The dirty little secret about homelessness is the key to ending it, https://fixhomelessness.org/2024/the-dirty-little-secret-about-homelessness-is-the-key-to-ending-it/.

54. Amy Swearer (June 20, 2019). This New York man got arrested after defending his own home. *Heritage Foundation,* https://www.heritage.org/gun-rights/commentary/new-york-man-got-arrested-after-defending-his-own-home; Associated Press (February 18, 2019). Court overturns conviction in killing of home intruder, https://www.wric.com/news/local-news/court-overturns-conviction-in-killing-of-home-intruder/1791365891/.

55. Mark Daniell (September 8, 2025). Hollywood stars mock York Regional Police chief advice on how to deal with home intruders. *Toronto Sun,* https://torontosun.com/entertainment/celebrity/hollywood-stars-mock-york-regional-police-chief-advice-on-how-to-deal-with-home-intruders.

56. Jonathan Turley (July 3, 2023). "Fairly big problem": Squatters invade homes and refuse to leave. How is this legal? *USA Today,* https://www.usatoday.com/story/opinion/2023/07/03/squatters-rights-leave-homeowners-forgotten/70364321007/.

57. Elena Salvoni (January 14, 2025). French leftist theatre faces bankruptcy after opening its doors to 250 African migrants for a free show . . . and they refused to leave and remain in the building five weeks later. *Daily Mail,* https://www.dailymail.co.uk/news/article-14282399/French-theatre-bankruptcy-250-African-migrants-refused-leave-remain-building.html.

58. Shane Galvin (August 26, 2025). Homeless man kills mom of 3 with mallet after she invites him to say in her London apartment. *New York Post,* https://nypost.com/2025/08/26/world-news/uk-woman-killed-by-homeless-man-she-invited-to-stay-in-her-apartment/.

59. David Smith (November 14, 2011). Humphrey the pet hippo kills owner in South Africa, *The Guardian,* https://www.theguardian.com/world/2011/nov/14/pet-hippo-humphrey-kills-owner.

60. http://www.simplycycling.org/blog/2018/3/25/22.

61. CBS News (August 1, 2018). D.C. couple killed in ISIS-claimed attack were cycling around world, https://www.cbsnews.com/news/washington-dc -couple-american-cyclists-tajikistan-isis-lauren-geoghegan-jay-austin/.

62. Colum Lynch (September 13, 2017). U.N. to join Congolese authorities in hunt for killers of U.N. experts. *Foreign Policy*, https://foreignpolicy .com/2017/09/13/u-n-to-join-congolese-authorities-in-hunt-for-killers-of-u-n -experts/.

63. Peter Allen (August 27, 2008). British journalism student gang-raped in Calais, *The Telegraph*, https://www.telegraph.co.uk/news/worldnews/europe /france/2637452/British-journalism-student-gang-raped-in-Calais.html.

64. Gad Saad (August 22, 2025). Spreading reason & common sense in Iceland (*The Saad Truth*, 1879), https://www.youtube.com/watch?v=aAVflncjwKY [1:55:11–2:01:24].

65. Jennie Taer (November 21, 2024). Venezuelan migrant charged with raping his boss' 14-year-old daughter while living in their Colorado home. *New York Post*, https://nypost.com/2024/11/21/us-news/venezuelan-migrant-charged -with-raping-bosss-teen-daughter/.

Chapter 3: Cultural Theory of Mind

1. Niccolò Machiavelli (as translated by Luigi Ricci, 1921). *The Prince* (p. 9). London: Oxford University Press, https://archive.org/details/princemac00ma chuoft/princemac00machuoft/page/n7/mode/2up.

2. As quoted by Bimal H. Ashar (2017). An ounce of prevention? *Medical Clinics*, *101*(4), xv–xvi.

3. Frederick S. Perls (1969; 1972). *In and Out the Garbage Pail* (p. 52). New York: Bantam Books.

4. Associated Press (April 14, 2019). Cassowary attack: Giant bird kills owner in Florida after he fell. *The Guardian*, https://www.theguardian.com/us -news/2019/apr/14/cassowary-attack-giant-bird-kills-owner-in-florida-after -he-fell.

5. J. David Smith, Alexandria C. Zakrzewski, Jennifer M. Johnson, and Jeanette C. Valleau (2016). Ecology, fitness, evolution: New perspectives on categorization. *Current Directions in Psychological Science*, *25*(4), 266–274; J. David Smith (2014). Prototypes, exemplars, and the natural history of categorization. *Psychonomic Bulletin & Review*, *21*, 312–331; Jeremy N. Bailenson,

Michael S. Shum, Scott Atran, Douglas L. Medin, and John D. Coley (2002). A bird's eye view: Biological categorization and reasoning within and across cultures. *Cognition*, 84(1), 1–53.

6. Lawrence W. Barsalou (1991). Deriving categories to achieve goals. In Gordon H. Bower (Ed.), *The Psychology of Learning and Motivation: Advances in Research and Theory, vol. 27* (pp. 1–64), San Diego, CA: Academic Press; Tobia Brosch, Gilles Pourtois, and David Sander (2010). The perception and categorisation of emotional stimuli: A review. *Cognition and Emotion*, 24(3), 377–400; Tonghe Zhuang and Angelika Lingnau (2022). The characterization of actions at the superordinate, basic and subordinate level. *Psychological Research*, 86(6), 1871–1891.

7. David Premack and Guy Woodruff (1978). Does the chimpanzee have a theory of mind? *Behavioral and Brain Sciences*, 1(4), 515–526; Martin Brüne and Ute Brüne-Cohrs (2006). Theory of mind—evolution, ontogeny, brain mechanisms and psychopathology. *Neuroscience & Biobehavioral Reviews*, 30(4), 437–455; Simon Baron-Cohen, Alan M. Leslie, and Uta Frith (1985). Does the autistic child have a "theory of mind"? *Cognition*, 21(1), 37–46.

8. Jonathan Dvash and Simone G. Shamay-Tsoory (2014). Theory of mind and empathy as multidimensional constructs: Neurological foundations. *Topics in Language Disorders*, 34(4), 282–295.

9. Gad Saad (December 5, 2023). The West suffers from cultural self-delusion. *National Post*, https://nationalpost.com/opinion/gad-saad-the-west-suffers-from-cultural-self-delusion.

10. For a list of human universals, see Donald E. Brown (1991). *Human Universals*. Boston, MA: McGraw-Hill. The work of Geert Hofstede is arguably the best-known effort to catalogue cross-cultural differences in values. See Geert Hofstede (1980). *Culture's Consequences: International Differences in Work Related Values*. Beverly Hills, CA: Sage.

11. Claire Yorke (2023). Is empathy a strategic imperative? A review essay. *Journal of Strategic Studies*, 46(5), 1082–1102.

12. https://docs.house.gov/meetings/FA/FA16/20171206/106698/HHRG-115-FA16-Wstate-LenczowskiJ-20171206.pdf.

13. GBD 2021 Fertility and Forecasting Collaborators (2024). Global fertility in 204 countries and territories, 1950–2021, with forecasts to 2100: A comprehensive demographic analysis for the Global Burden of Disease Study 2021. *The Lancet*, 403(10440), 2057–2099; Pew Research Center (April 2, 2015). The future of world religions: Population growth projections, 2010–2050, https://www.pewresearch.org/religion/2015/04/02/religious-projections-2010-2050/.

14. Raymond Ibrahim (October 1, 2008). Islam's doctrines of deception. *Middle East Forum*, https://www.meforum.org/islams-doctrines-of-deception.

15. Andrew C. McCarthy (2010). *The Grand Jihad: How Islam and the Left Sabotage America*. New York: Encounter Books.

16. Emma Diggins, Hein Heuvelman, Mar Pujades-Rodriguez, Allan House, David Cottrell, and Cathy Brennan (2024). Exploring gender differences in risk factors for self-harm in adolescents using data from the Millennium Cohort Study. *Journal of Affective Disorders*, *345*, 131–140.

17. https://rotary7910.org/stories/tolerance-is-one-of-the-most-important -virtues-in-the-rotary-spirit/.

18. Charles Foran (January 4, 2017). The Canada experiment: Is this the world's first "postnational" country? *The Guardian*, https://www.theguardian .com/world/2017/jan/04/the-canada-experiment-is-this-the-worlds-first -postnational-country.

19. Douglas Todd (March 13, 2016). The dangers of Trudeau's "postnational" Canada. *Vancouver Sun*, https://vancouversun.com/news/staff-blogs/the-dang ers-of-trudeaus-postnational-canada.

20. Jarryd Jäger (June 9, 2025). WATCH: Carney says Muslim values are Canadian values. *Western Standard*, https://www.westernstandard.news/news /watch-carney-says-muslim-values-are-canadian-values/65290.

21. https://x.com/MayorOliviaChow/status/1842293389024477457.

22. https://www.parliament.scot/chamber-and-committees/official-report /search-what-was-said-in-parliament/meeting-of-parliament-10-06-2020?meet ing=12685&iob=114774.

23. Julia Bryson (August 26, 2024). Rotherham child abuse: what was the Jay Report. BBC News, https://www.bbc.com/news/articles/cy4ynzppk80o; Martin Hanson (September 2017). Muslim grooming gangs. *New English Review*, https://www.newenglishreview.org/articles/muslim-grooming-gangs/; Kish Bhatti-Sinclair and Charles Sutcliffe (2020). Group localised child sexual exploitation offenders: Who and why? *SSRN 3248665*, https://papers.ssrn.com /sol3/papers.cfm?abstract_id=3248665; Soeren Kern (July 11, 2013). Britain: "Rape jihad" against children. *Gatestone Institute*, https://www.gatestonein stitute.org/3846/britain-child-grooming.

24. Mark Easton (October 19, 2018). Huddersfield grooming: Twenty guilty of campaign of rape and abuse, BBC, https://www.bbc.com/news/uk -england-45918845.

25. Dominic Green (January 5, 2025). The biggest peacetime crime—and

cover-up—in British history. *The Free Press*, https://www.thefp.com/p /muslim-grooming-gangs-cover-up-keir-starmer-elon-musk.

26. Lizzie Dearden (August 11, 2017). Muslim community "absolutely disgusted" by Newcastle grooming gang: Communities fear backlash as far-right seeks to "exploit exploitation." *Independent*, https://www.independent.co.uk/news /uk/home-news/grooming-gang-newcastle-asian-pakistani-bangladeshi-musl im-response-faith-leaders-operation-shelter-police-convictions-a7888946.html.

27. Steve Bird (December 9, 2017). Grooming gangs of Muslim men failed to integrate into British society, *The Telegraph*, https://www.telegraph.co.uk /news/2017/12/09/grooming-gangs-muslim-men-failed-integrate-british -society/.

28. Bythomas Brooke (October 14, 2024). Italy: 10-year-old child undergoes abortion after rape by Bangladeshi migrant in asylum center. *Remix News*, https:// rmx.news/article/italy-10-year-old-child-undergoes-abortion-after-rape-by -bangladeshi-migrant-in-asylum-center/.

29. Justin Trudeau (April 17, 2013). CBC News: *The National*, https://www.you tube.com/watch?v=BlYBVpa49gk&t=440s [14:08-15:16]. I edited the transcript to remove extra utterances of "and" and "or"; Mitch Wolfe (April 18, 2013). Trudeau's Boston bombing comment should cost him, *HuffPost*, https:// www.huffpost.com/archive/ca/entry/trudeaus-boston-bombing-comment -should-cost-him_b_3106351https://www.youtube.com/watch?v=BlYB Vpa49gk&t=440s.

30. Aaron Kliegman (December 22, 2017). Trudeau: ISIS fighters returning home to Canada "can be an extraordinarily powerful voice for preventing radicalization." *Washington Free Beacon*, https://freebeacon.com/national -security/trudeau-isis-fighters-returning-canada-can-powerful-voice -preventing-radicalization/.

31. BBC (July 13, 2017). Trudeau feels blowback from $8m Khadr settlement, https://www.bbc.com/news/world-us-canada-40598484.

32. Eric Blum (January 2, 2025). Sugar Bowl sponsor sparks outrage with "shameful" comments following New Orleans terror attack, *Daily Mail*, https:// www.dailymail.co.uk/sport/college-football/article-14245881/Sugar-Bowl-co mments-New-Orleans-terror-attack-Tom-Wilson.html.

33. For a list of 24 such lies, refer to my X post from March 30, 2024, https://x .com/GadSaad/status/1774166352191737962.

34. Deirdre Bardolf (December 14, 2024). Gaza death toll inflated to promote anti-Israel narrative, study finds. *New York Post*, https://nypost

.com/2024/12/14/world-news/gaza-death-toll-inflated-to-promote-anti-israel
-narrative-study/.

35. Louisa Loveluck (July 12, 2015). Isil releases new video of 2014 Speicher
     massacre of Shia army recruits. *The Telegraph*, https://www.telegraph.co.uk
     /news/worldnews/islamic-state/11734606/Isil-releases-new-video-of-2014
     -Speicher-massacre-of-Shia-army-recruits.html.

36. Matthew Lapierre (August 28, 2025). Quebec plans to table bill banning
     prayer in public. CBC News, https://www.cbc.ca/news/canada/montreal
     /public-prayer-ban-quebec-1.7619985.

37. Peter Hammond (2013). *Slavery, Terrorism, and Islam: The Historical Roots and
     Contemporary Threat*. Cape Town, South Africa: Frontline Fellowship. See
     Appendix III for the relevant breakdown.

38. Daily Mail Reporter (October 29, 2011). "Our human rights have been vio-
     lated": Muslim students accuse Catholic University in 60-page dossier. *Daily
     Mail*, https://www.dailymail.co.uk/news/article-2055047/Muslim-students-ac
     cuse-Catholic-University-violating-human-rights-Washington-DC.html.

39. Joe Rogan Experience #2148 (May 9, 2024)—Gad Saad, https://www.youtube
     .com/watch?v=zzU_UrhmCEs.

40. There are several variants of this proverb including "After Saturday Comes
     Sunday": Bernard Lewis (January 1976). The return of Islam. *Commentary*,
     https://www.commentary.org/articles/bernard-lewis/the-return-of-islam/;
     Susan Adelman (June 27, 2019). After Saturday Comes Sunday. *De Gruyter
     Conversations*, https://blog.degruyter.com/after-saturday-comes-sunday/;
     Lela Gilbert (November 30, 2023). Saturday people, Sunday people, and
     Americans at risk. *Hudson Institute*, https://www.hudson.org/religious
     -freedom/saturday-people-sunday-people-americans-risk-lela-gilbert.

41. See my review of the film here: Gad Saad (November 3, 2024). My Review
     of Conclave (Film)—Wokeism Destroys Everything (*The Saad Truth*, 1754),
     https://youtu.be/EIS6hbPryqY.

42. Josephine McKenna (March 24, 2016). "We are brothers": Pope Fran-
     cis washes feet of migrants. *USA Today*, https://www.usatoday.com
     /story/news/world/2016/03/24/we-brothers-pope-francis-washes-feet
     -migrants/82214856/.

43. Justin McLellan (August 30, 2024). Migrant morality: Pope doubles down on
     message of acceptance. *United States Conference of Catholic Bishops*, https://
     www.usccb.org/news/2024/migrant-morality-pope-doubles-down-message
     -acceptance.

44. Jonathan Y. Tan (2019, abstract). Pope Francis's preferential option for migrants, refugees, and asylum seekers. *International Bulletin of Mission Research*, 43(1), 58–66.

45. Zamira Rahim (September 14, 2018). Dalai Lama says "Europe belongs to the Europeans" and suggests refugees return to native countries. *Independent*, https://www.independent.co.uk/news/world/europe/dalai-lama-europe-refugee-crisis-immigration-eu-racism-tibet-buddhist-a8537221.html.

46. Stoyan Zaimov (October 7, 2015). World's first openly lesbian bishop to remove crosses, build Islamic prayer room in Swedish Seamen's Church. *Christian Post*, https://www.christianpost.com/news/worlds-first-openly-lesbian-bishop-to-remove-crosses-build-islamic-prayer-room-in-swedish-seamens-church.html.

47. Ciera Horton (July 25, 2016). United Methodists elect first openly gay bishop. *Baptist Press*, https://www.baptistpress.com/resource-library/news/united-methodists-elect-first-openly-gay-bishop/.

48. Interview posted on his X account (@chaotichermes) on September 22, 2025, https://x.com/chaotichermes/status/1970246556956680631.

49. Malika Rafiq (2021). Violence verbale envers la femme Marocaine: Proverbes injurieux envers la femme Marocaine [Verbal violence against Moroccan women: Proverbs offensive to Moroccan women]. *Faits de langue et société*, 7, 83–94.

50. Gad Saad (May 3, 2016). My Chat with Nicolai Sennels, Danish Psychologist (*The Saad Truth*, 166), https://www.youtube.com/watch?v=mFIfEHeHqwc.

51. Jesus Mesa (October 10, 2024). Denmark pays for prosthetic leg of Nigerian pirate who attacked its navy. *Newsweek*, https://www.newsweek.com/denmark-pays-prosthetic-leg-nigerian-pirate-who-attacked-its-navy-1967139. I originally learned of this case via Jonathan Pallesen on X, https://x.com/jonatanpallesen/status/1844119985481982023.

52. Marta I. Sanchez, Fleur Ponton, Andreas Schmidt-Rhaesa, David P. Hughes, Dorothee Misse, and Frederic Thomas (2008). Two steps to suicide in crickets harbouring hairworms. *Animal Behaviour*, 76(5), 1621–1624.

53. Douglas Sandoval (October 27, 2023). Being Jewish does not absolve you from praising Hamas, or attacking Israeli victims. *The Algemeiner*, https://www.algemeiner.com/2023/10/27/being-jewish-does-not-absolve-you-from-praising-hamas-or-attacking-israeli-victims/.

54. Madmanfilms (March 11, 2024). Jonathan Glazer's acceptance speech after winning Best International Feature at the 2024 Oscars, https://www.youtube.com/shorts/YHkTZ-yeb44.

55. The National News (September 8, 2024). Jewish filmmaker calls out Isra-el's "genocide in Gaza" at Venice Film Festival, https://www.youtube.com /watch?v=MgP8uh42t9w.

56. Rami Amichay (November 16, 2023). "The peace movement was orphaned," says son of activist killed on Oct. 7. *Reuters*, https://www.reuters.com/world /the-peace-movement-was-orphaned-says-son-activist-killed-oct-7-2023-11-16/.

57. BBC News (April 15, 2011). Italian activist found dead in Gaza after abduction, https://www.bbc.com/news/world-middle-east-13088630.

58. Elizabeth Loftus and Katherine Ketcham (1994). *The Myth of Repressed Memory: False Memories and Allegations of Sexual Abuse*. New York; St. Martin's Press; Richard Ofshe and Ethan Watters (1994). *Making Monsters: False Memories, Psychotherapy, and Sexual Hysteria*. New York: Charles Scribner's.

59. Nick Haslam (September 23, 2023). Gabor Maté claims trauma contributes to everything: From cancer to ADHD. But what does the evidence say? *The Conversation*, https://theconversation.com/gabor-mate-claims-trauma-contribute s-to-everything-from-cancer-to-adhd-but-what-does-the-evidence-say-207144; Stanton Peele and Alan Cudmore (December 5, 2011). The seductive, but dangerous, allure of Gabor Maté. *Psychology Today*, https://www.psychology today.com/us/blog/addiction-in-society/201112/the-seductive-dangerous-all ure-gabor-mat.

60. https://compassionateinquiry.com.

61. https://x.com/GadSaad/status/1887184679155200236.

Chapter 4: Blank Slate Felons

1. Friedrich Wilhelm Nietzsche (1917). *Beyond Good and Evil* (p. 113). New York: Modern Library Publishers. Accessed at: https://archive.org/details/beyond goodandevi00nietuoft.

2. Fox Butterfield (April 5, 2002). Teenagers sentenced for killing two professors, *New York Times*, https://www.nytimes.com/2002/04/05/us/teenagers-are -sentenced-for-killing-two-professors.html.

3. NBC News (September 15, 2003). Dartmouth murders, NBC News, https:// www.nbcnews.com/id/wbna3079852. As excerpted from Dick Lehr and Mitchell Zuckoff (2003). *Judgment Ridge*. New York: HarperCollins.

4. Tim Callery (April 18, 2024). Parole granted for man convicted in murders of Dartmouth professors in 2001. WMUR9 (ABC), https://www.wmur.com /article/half-susanne-zantop-james-parker-parole-granted/60536412#.

5. Office of the State's Attorney for Baltimore City (November 12, 2025). Cold case unit secures life without parole for repeat murderer, https://www.stat torney.org/media-center/press-releases/3177-cold-case-unit-secures-life-witho ut-parole-for-repeat-murderer.

6. Mike Pescaro (February 2, 2024). Lynn man convicted of sexually assaulting Boston woman after breaking into home. NBC Boston, https://www.nbc boston.com/news/local/lynn-man-convicted-of-sexually-assaulting-boston -woman-after-breaking-into-home/3267589/.

7. Roger Shattuck (1996). *Forbidden Knowledge: From Prometheus to Pornography* (p. 156). New York: St. Martin's Press.

8. Lauren G. Beatty and Tracy L. Snell (2021). Profile of prison inmates, 2016. US Department of Justice, https://bjs.ojp.gov/content/pub/pdf/ppi16.pdf.

9. Richard Pollina (September 30, 2025). Grieving father blasts pols for allowing daughter Logan Federico's career criminal killer to remain on the streets. *New York Post*, https://nypost.com/2025/09/30/us-news/grieving-father-of-lo gan-federico-blasts-pols-for-lax-crime-policies-that-allowed-daughters-career -criminal-killer-to-remain-on-the-streets/.

10. That's Life (August 12, 2020). She forgave her mum's killer then he murdered her too! https://www.thatslife.com.au/true-crime/she-forgave-her-mums-kill er-then-he-murdered-her-too/.

11. https://www.biblegateway.com/passage/?search=Luke%206&version=NIV.

12. Matt Delaney (February 12, 2023). California baker who died in robbery wouldn't want robbers to go to jail, family says, *Washington Times*, https:// www.washingtontimes.com/news/2023/feb/12/california-baker-who-died -robbery-wouldnt-want-rob/.

13. Clarissa-Jan Lim (September 11, 2024). Trump used an 11-year-old's death to foment anti-immigrant hate. The boy's father wants an apology. MSNBC, https://www.msnbc.com/top-stories/latest/aiden-clark-father-trump-vance -springfield-ohio-rcna170615.

14. Chris Nesi (March 2, 2025). Boston Mayor Michelle Wu, other "woke" city officials offer condolences to kin of armed maniac shot by off-duty cop at Chick-fil-A. *New York Post*, https://nypost.com/2025/03/02/us-news/boston-m ayor-michelle-wu-woke-city-officials-offer-condolences-to-kin-of-armed-mani ac-shot-by-off-duty-cop-at-chick-fil-a/.

15. Terry Newman (May 9, 2025). RCMP puts land, African Nova Scotian acknowledgements before missing kids. *National Post*, https://nationalpost

.com/opinion/terry-newman-rcmp-puts-land-african-nova-scotian-acknowle
dgements-before-missing-kids.

16. https://x.com/GadSaad/status/1839685753103630496.

17. Maryanne Fisher and Anthony Cox (2010). Man change thyself: Hero versus
    heroine development in Harlequin romance novels. *Journal of Social, Evolu-
    tionary, and Cultural Psychology, 4*(4) 305–316.

18. https://www.goodreads.com/list/show/25465.All_Time_Dominant_Al
    pha_Romance_Heroes.

19. Gad Saad (March 8, 2018). Is toxic masculinity a valid concept? On the
    dangers of pathologizing manhood. *Psychology Today,* https://www.psychol
    ogytoday.com/ca/blog/homo-consumericus/201803/is-toxic-masculinity
    -valid-concept.

20. Susan Kelly and Robin I. M. Dunbar (2001). Who dares, wins: Heroism versus
    altruism in women's mate choice. *Human Nature, 12*(2), 89–105; Hannes Rusch,
    Joost M. Leunissen, and Mark Van Vugt (2015). Historical and experimental
    evidence of sexual selection for war heroism. *Evolution and Human Behavior,
    36*(5), 367–373.

21. Alice Gainer, Dick Brennan, and Tim McNicholas (December 10, 2024). Dan-
    iel Penny found not guilty in NYC subway chokehold death of Jordan Neely.
    CBS News, https://www.cbsnews.com/newyork/news/daniel-penny-verdict
    -nyc-subway-chokehold-jordan-neely/.

22. Chantal Da Silva (June 29, 2023). Charges dropped against NYC man accused
    in fatal subway stabbing. NBC News, https://www.nbcnews.com/news
    /us-news/charges-dropped-jordan-williams-nyc-man-accused-fatal-subway
    -stabbing-rcna91780.

23. Pelin Gul and Tom R. Kupfer (2019). Benevolent sexism and mate preferences:
    Why do women prefer benevolent men despite recognizing that they can be
    undermining? *Personality and Social Psychology Bulletin, 45*(1), 146–161.

24. Will Ferrell Welcomes Honorees Adele, Kerry Washington, and More |
    Women in Entertainment 2023, *Hollywood Reporter,* https://www.youtube
    .com/watch?v=FStb_FhPPVY; https://www.foxnews.com/media/actor-will
    -ferrell-asks-time-women-run-planet-male-leaders-doing-good.

25. Sarah Ritchie and Nick Murray (December 11, 2024). Elon Musk calls
    Trudeau an "insufferable tool" for comments on Kamala Harris's defeat. *Na-
    tional Post,* https://nationalpost.com/news/canada/elon-musk-justin-trudeau
    -insufferable-tool.

26. Luter Ray Abel (August 24, 2021). Trudeau's patronizing brand of feminism. *National Review,* https://www.nationalreview.com/corner/trudeaus-patronizi ng-brand-of-feminism/.

27. Gad Saad (September 27, 2021). My Chat with Megyn Kelly (*The Saad Truth,* 1301), https://www.youtube.com/watch?v=Hs33J3XNJDc [24:01–26:38]. Edited for clarity.

28. Juliet Watson and Sarah Casey (2023). A male feminist walks into a bar: Male feminist capital and the "bloke turn" in feminism. *Feminist Media Studies,* 23(6), 2728–2744.

29. Allan Hall (July 5, 2016). Left-wing German politician who was raped by migrants admits she LIED to police about her attackers' nationality because she did not want to encourage racism. *Daily Mail,* https://www.dailymail.co .uk/news/article-3675154/Left-wing-German-politician-raped-migrants-adm its-LIED-police-attackers-nationality-did-not-want-encourage-racism.html; Archived Facebook letter written by Selin Gören (in German), https://archive .is/XZsev#selection-397.0-441.55.

30. Joe Roberts (September 6, 2017). Afghan national "raped EU official's daughter to satisfy sexual urges before killing her." *Metro,* https://metro.co .uk/2017/09/06/afghan-national-raped-eu-officials-daughter-to-satisfy-sexual -urges-before-killing-her-6906912/; Allan Hall (March 22, 2018). Adult Afghan asylum seeker who lied he was a child refugee before raping and murder- ing EU official's daughter is jailed for life in Germany. *Daily Mail,* https:// www.dailymail.co.uk/news/article-5530867/Afghan-murdered-EU-officials -daughter-jailed-life-Germany.html.

31. Allan Hall (December 6, 2016). Family of EU official's teenage daughter who was raped and killed "by Afghan migrant" ask for well-wishers to donate money to refugee charity as teenage "killer" is revealed. *Daily Mail,* https:// www.dailymail.co.uk/news/article-4004480.

32. Frank Chung (December 7, 2023). Outrage as eight of nine men convicted of gang rape of 15-year-old in Germany receive no prison time, https://www .news.com.au/lifestyle/real-life/news-life/outrage-as-eight-of-nine-men-conv icted-of-park-gangrape-15yearold-in-germany-receive-no-prison-time/news-st ory/353bcbf9437ea62eea0ee3c6cc0c2cc7.

33. James Jackson (June 28, 2024). German woman given harsher sentence than rapist for calling him "pig." *The Telegraph,* https://www.telegraph.co.uk /world-news/2024/06/28/german-woman-given-harsher-sentence-than-rapist -for-calling/.

34. Soeren Kern (March 5, 2016). Germany: Migrant rape crisis worsens: Public

spaces are becoming perilous for women and children. *Gatestone Institute*, https://www.gatestoneinstitute.org/7557/germany-rape-migrants-crisis; "Cologne is every day": Europe's rape epidemic (March 12, 2016), https://www.news.com.au/finance/economy/world-economy/cologne-is-every-day-europes-rape-epidemic/news-story/e2e618e17ad4400b5ed65045e65e141d.

35. Corey Charlton (January 12, 2016). The Arabic gang-rape "Taharrush" phenomenon which sees women surrounded by groups of men in crowds and sexually assaulted . . . and has now spread to Europe. *Daily Mail*, https://www.dailymail.co.uk/news/article-3395390/The-Arabic-gang-rape-Taharrush-phenomenon-sees-women-surrounded-groups-men-crowds-sexually-assaulted-spread-Europe.html.

36. Ayaan Hirsi Ali (February 13, 2021). When Europe ignored the sex crimes of immigrants, all women suffered. *New York Post*, https://nypost.com/2021/02/13/when-europe-ignored-sex-crimes-of-immigrants-all-women-suffered/.

37. Anthony Blair (December 3, 2024). US woman, 20, faces 10 years in jail for "accidentally stabbing man to death after he groped her at train station." *U.S. Sun*, https://www.the-sun.com/news/13016849/american-woman-stabs-man-germany-kaiserslautern-eritrean/.

38. Dana Kennedy (November 27, 2021). Canadian school cancels ISIS survivor Nadia Murad over Islamophobia fears. *New York Post*, https://nypost.com/2021/11/27/toronto-school-cancels-isis-survivor-event-with-nadia-murad/.

39. https://x.com/normmacdonald/status/809637479674281984

40. Joseph Goldstein (September 20, 2015). U.S. soldiers told to ignore sexual abuse of boys by Afghan Allies. *New York Times*, https://www.nytimes.com/2015/09/21/world/asia/us-soldiers-told-to-ignore-afghan-allies-abuse-of-boys.html.

41. Flora Drury (January 7, 2016). The secret shame of Afghanistan's bacha bazi "dancing boys" who are made to dress like little girls, then abused by paedophiles, *Daily Mail*, https://www.dailymail.co.uk/news/article-3384027/Women-children-boys-pleasure-secret-shame-Afghanistan-s-bacha-bazi-dancing-boys-dress-like-little-girls-make-skirts-abused-paedophiles.html; Rustam Qobil (September 8, 2010). The sexually abused dancing boys of Afghanistan. BBC News, https://www.bbc.com/news/world-south-asia-11217772.

42. Paul Bentley (January 25, 2013). Muslim abuser who "didn't know" that sex with a girl of 13 was illegal is spared jail, *Daily Mail*, https://www.dailymail.co.uk/news/article-2268395/Adil-Rashid-Paedophile-claimed-Muslim-upbringing-meant-didnt-know-illegal-sex-girl-13.html.

43. Dan Woodland (November 29, 2024). Asylum seeker sex pest targeted two women on the train in "terrifying ordeal" before sexually assaulting one—but is SPARED jail after judge is told he "has no friends in the UK." *Daily Mail*, https://www.dailymail.co.uk/news/article-14140803/Asylum-seeker-sex-pest-targeted-two-women-train-terrifying-ordeal-sexually-assaulting-one-SPARED-jail-judge-told-no-friends-UK.html.

44. Stewart Carr (March 18, 2023). Iranian man who raped his lodger in London "can't be deported in case he is persecuted in his homeland for being a convicted rapist." *Daily Mail*, https://www.dailymail.co.uk/news/article-11877091/Convicted-rapist-fighting-deportation-allowed-stay-Britain-crime-judge-rules.html.

45. Lettice Bromovsky (March 25, 2025). Paedophile migrant who attacked a teenage girl is allowed to stay in the UK "because he's an alcoholic." *Daily Mail*, https://www.dailymail.co.uk/news/article-14536929/Paedophile-migrant-attacked-teenage-girl-allowed-stay-UK.html.

46. Charles Hymas (February 14, 2025). Zimbabwean paedophile allowed to stay in UK because he would face "hostility" back home. *The Telegraph*, https://www.telegraph.co.uk/news/2025/02/14/zimbabwean-paedophile-allowed-to-stay-in-uk/.

47. Taryn Pedler (March 25, 2025). Austrian migrant gang-rape horror: Girl, 12, "passed around like a 'trophy' by more than a dozen boys" during horrifying repeated sex attacks in Vienna. *Daily Mail*, https://www.dailymail.co.uk/news/article-14534349/Austrian-migrant-gang-rape-horror-Girl-12-passed-like-trophy-dozen-boys-horrifying-repeated-sex-attacks-Vienna.html.

48. Lizzie Dearden (October 24, 2016). Man who raped 10-year-old boy at swimming pool in Austria has sentence overturned by Supreme Court. *Independent*, https://www.independent.co.uk/news/world/europe/iraqi-refugee-raped-10yearold-boy-swimming-pool-vienna-austria-sentence-conviction-overturned-supreme-court-a7377491.html; Adam Withnall (December 14, 2016). Man who raped child in swimming pool because it was "a sexual emergency" has jail sentence increased on appeal. *Independent*, https://www.independent.co.uk/news/world/europe/austria-swimming-pool-rape-theresienbad-vienna-iraqi-refugee-a7473441.html.

49. Chris Tomlinson (May 24, 2017). "Sexual emergency" migrant who raped 10-year-old boy has sentence reduced. *Breitbart*, https://www.breitbart.com/europe/2017/05/24/migrant-raped-10-year-old-boy-sentence-drastically-reduced/.

50. Reuters in Bornheim (January 15, 2016). German town bans male refugees from swimming pool. *The Guardian*, https://www.theguardian.com/world/2016/jan/15/german-town-bans-male-refugees-from-swimming-pool.

51. Gad Saad (August 24, 2025). Red-Haired White Women Are Assaulting One-Legged Swimmers of Color (*The Saad Truth*, 1881), https://youtu.be /naZRbgOdI5E. See also https://www.spiegel.de/panorama/stadt-bueren -verteidigt-plakat-mit-grapschender-frau-kampagne-gegen-uebergriffe-im-sch wimmbad-a-5a9fe6d4-42b7-46de-8a30-a17b47f57d2a.

52. Chris Tomlinson (September 13, 2018). Dutch court gave shorter sentence to migrant who raped disabled woman to spare him deportation. *Breitbart*, https://www.breitbart.com/europe/2018/09/23/dutch-court-admits-giving-li ght-sentence-migrant-avoid-deportation/.

53. https://thepeoplesledger.com/finnish-city-plagued-with-rape-crimes-by- migrants-tells-women-to-say-dont-touch-my-no-no-square/. This link is no longer accessible, but the initiative is described in Finnish here: https://yle .fi/a/3-11237843. I satirized this utter insanity on my YouTube channel: Gad Saad (December 27, 2024). Finland Has Solved the Migrant Rape Crisis— the No-No Square Dance (*The Saad Truth*, 1790), https://www.youtube.com /watch?v=Gr3sTMpZxn0&t=3s.

54. Denise Wall (May 3, 2018). Supreme court denies appeal in sexual abuse of 10-year-old. *Yle*, https://yle.fi/a/3-10188676; Chris Baynes (January 17, 2019). Finland to change law to recognize sex without consent as rape. *Independent*, https://www.independent.co.uk/news/world/europe/finland-rape-law-con sent-child-sex-abuse-antti-hakkanen-a8733146.html; Chris Baynes (May 24, 2018). Sweden passes new law recognizing sex without explicit consent as rape. *Independent*, https://www.independent.co.uk/news/world/europe/rape -law-sweden-sex-without-consent-metoo-a8367996.html.

55. TT/The Local (June 29, 2016). Swedish police to hand out anti-groping arm- bands. The Local, https://www.thelocal.se/20160629/swedish-police-to-hand -out-anti-groping-armbands.

56. Stefan Hedlund (February 9, 2024). Sweden looks into the abyss. GIS, https:// www.gisreportsonline.com/r/sweden-immigrants-crisis/#.

57. Amanda Kijera (April 23, 2010). We are not your weapons—We are women. *American Renaissance*, https://www.amren.com/news/2010/04/we_are_not _your/.

58. Melanie Newman, Julie Bindel, and Hayley Dixon (June 9, 2021). Oxfam training guide blames "privileged white women" over root causes of sexual violence. *The Telegraph*, https://www.telegraph.co.uk/news/2021/06/09 /oxfam-training-guide-blames-privileged-white-women-root-causes/.

59. Chris Menahan (June 23, 2021). Doctoral candidate who sought to prove justice system was "racist against blacks" stabbed to death by black male

in Chicago. *InformationLiberation*, https://www.informationliberation
.com/?id=62329.

60. Anne-Marie Curatolo (July 18, 2013). Jacques Lachance appointed director
of Security, https://www.concordia.ca/cunews/main/stories/2013/07/18
/jacques-lachance-appointed-director-of-security.html.

Chapter 5: Settled Science, Taboo Trade-Offs

1. Thomas Henry Huxley (September 15, 1870). *Nature*, vol. 2 (p. 402), https://
books.google.ca/books?id=8YUCAAAAIAAJ.

2. Alan Page Fiske and Philip E. Tetlock (1997). Taboo trade-offs: Reactions to
transactions that transgress the spheres of justice. *Political Psychology*, 18(2),
255–297.

3. See Daniel Kahneman (2011). *Thinking, Fast and Slow*. New York: Farrar,
Straus and Giroux, and references therein.

4. Evanthia Dimara, Steven Franconeri, Catherine Plaisant, Anastasia Bezeria-
nos, and Pierre Dragicevic (2018). A task-based taxonomy of cognitive biases
for information visualization. *IEEE Transactions on Visualization and Computer
Graphics*, 26(2), 1413–1432; The Decision Lab. Cognitive biases, https://thede
cisionlab.com/biases (accessed on November 20, 2025).

5. Amos Tversky and Daniel Kahneman (1981). The framing of decisions and
the psychology of choice. *Science*, 211(4481), 453–458.

6. Gad Saad and Tripat Gill (2014). The framing effect when evaluating prospective mates: An adaptationist perspective. *Evolution and Human Behavior*, 35(3),
184–192.

7. Alan Page Fiske and Philip E. Tetlock (1997). Taboo trade-offs: Reactions to
transactions that transgress the spheres of justice. *Political Psychology*, 18(2),
255–297; Philip E. Tetlock (2003). Thinking the unthinkable: Sacred values
and taboo cognitions. *Trends in Cognitive Sciences*, 7(7), 320–324; Allegra Ma-
guire, Emil Persson, and Gustav Tinghög (2023). Opportunity cost neglect: A
meta-analysis. *Journal of the Economic Science Association*, 9(2), 176–192.

8. Karl R. Popper (1959). *The Logic of Scientific Discovery* (p. 53). London: Hutchi-
son. Accessed at: https://archive.org/details/logicofscientifi00popp/page/52
/mode/2up.

9. Gad Saad (November 1, 2023). Happiness, Marriage, Careers, & Evolution—
With Psychiatrist Dr. Alex Curmi (*The Saad Truth*, 1623), https://youtu.be
/Ipmx36xdLow.

10. Vipin K. Gupta, Chhavi Saini, Meher Oberoi, Gagan Kalra, and Md Imran Nasir (2020). Semmelweis reflex: An age-old prejudice. *World Neurosurgery*, *136*, e119–e125; K. Codell Carter and Barbara R. Carter (1994). *Childbed Fever: A Scientific Biography of Ignaz Semmelweis*. Westport, CT: Greenwood Press.

11. Irvine Loudon (2013). Ignaz Phillip Semmelweis' studies of death in childbirth. *Journal of the Royal Society of Medicine*, *106*(11), 461–463.

12. Theodore G. Obenchain (2016). *Genius Belabored: Childbed Fever and the Tragic Life of Ignaz Semmelweis* (p. 3). Tuscaloosa: University of Alabama Press.

13. *New York Times* (June 7, 1981). Graduates hear Vonnegut on when it's honorable to be a "wise guy." https://archive.nytimes.com/www.nytimes.com/books/97/09/28/lifetimes/vonnegut-commencement.html. Many thanks to my friend Randy O. Wayne, a plant biologist at Cornell University, for having alerted me to this commencement speech.

14. Juan Miguel Campanario (2009). Rejecting and resisting Nobel class discoveries: Accounts by Nobel Laureates. *Scientometrics*, *81*(2), 549–565; Fiona MacDonald (August 19, 2016). 8 scientific papers that were rejected before going on to win a Nobel Prize. *ScienceAlert*, https://www.sciencealert.com/these-8-papers-were-rejected-before-going-on-to-win-the-nobel-prize.

15. Allen B. Weisse (2012). Self-experimentation and its role in medical research. *Texas Heart Institute Journal*, *39*(1), 51–54.

16. Barry J. Marshall (December 8, 2005). Helicobacter connections. Nobel Lecture, https://www.nobelprize.org/uploads/2018/06/marshall-lecture.pdf.

17. Veronica H. Paulus and Akshaya Ravi (October 10, 2024). The Nobel laureate Harvard didn't want. *Harvard Crimson,* https://www.thecrimson.com/article/2024/10/10/nobel-laureate-denied-harvard-tenure/.

18. Stefan Riedel (2005). Edward Jenner and the history of smallpox and vaccination. *Baylor University Medical Center Proceedings*, *18*(1), 21–25.

19. Charles N. J. McGhee, Jie Zhang, and Dipika V. Patel (2020). A perspective of contemporary cataract surgery: The most common surgical procedure in the world. *Journal of the Royal Society of New Zealand*, *50*(2), 245–262.

20. David J. Apple (2006). *Sir Harold Ridley and His Fight for Sight: He Changed the World So That We May Better See It*. Thorofare, NJ: Slack Incorporated.

21. Ullica Segerstrale (2013). *Nature's Oracle: The Life and Work of W. D. Hamilton*. Oxford, UK: Oxford University Press.

22. University of Houston Energy Fellows (December 14, 2016). Fact checking the claim of 97% consensus on anthropogenic climate change. *Forbes*, https://

www.forbes.com/sites/uhenergy/2016/12/14/fact-checking-the-97-consensus
-on-anthropogenic-climate-change/.

23. Terrence D. Hill, Ginny Garcia-Alexander, Andrew P. Davis, Eric T. Bjork-
     lund, Luis A. Vila-Henninger, and William C. Cockerham (2022). Political
     ideology and pandemic lifestyles: The indirect effects of empathy, authori-
     tarianism, and threat. *Discover Social Science and Health*, 2(1), 14, https://doi
     .org/10.1007/s44155-022-00014-0.

24. La Presse Canadienne (January 2, 2022). Quebec backtracks, plans to allow
     dog-walking after curfew. *The Gazette*, https://montrealgazette.com/news
     /local-news/walking-your-dog-is-no-longer-an-exception-to-quebecs-curfew.

25. Luke Kemp (April 28, 2021). The "Stomp Reflex": When governments abuse
     emergency powers. BBC, https://www.bbc.com/future/article/20210427-the
     -stomp-reflex-when-governments-abuse-emergency-powers.

26. Lee Clarke and Caron Chess (2008). Elites and panic: More to fear than fear
     itself. *Social Forces*, 87(2), 993–1014.

27. Mallory Simon (June 5, 2020). Over 1,000 health professionals sign a letter
     saying, Don't shut down protests using coronavirus concerns as an excuse.
     CNN, https://www.cnn.com/2020/06/05/health/health-care-open-letter
     -protests-coronavirus-trnd.

28. https://x.com/GadSaad/status/1327414661260701696.

29. Gad Saad (November 18, 2022). My Chat with Dr. Jay Bhattacharya—COVID,
     Healthcare, and Academic Freedom (*The Saad Truth*, 1484), https://youtu
     .be/Aol8CZ0AO7g; Gad Saad (December 15, 2022). My Chat with Dr. Scott
     Atlas, Advisor on Pres. Donald Trump's COVID Task Force (*The Saad Truth*,
     1494), https://youtu.be/079O4aQ3ZKE; Gad Saad (February 28, 2023). My
     Chat with Psychiatrist Dr. Aaron Kheriaty, Author of *The New Abnormal* (*The
     Saad Truth*, 1521), https://youtu.be/8P0JzvLGkaE; Gad Saad (March 22, 2024).
     My Chat with Fired Harvard Epidemiologist Dr. Martin Kulldorff (*The Saad
     Truth*, 1663), https://youtu.be/W-1rxAtrMxU.

30. Angelo Maria Pezzullo, Cathrine Axfors, Despina G. Contopoulos-Ioannidis,
     Alexandre Apostolatos, and John PA Ioannidis (2023). Age-stratified infec-
     tion fatality rate of COVID-19 in the non-elderly population. *Environmental
     Research*, 216, 114655.

31. Gad Saad (January 4, 2019). My Chat with Matt Ridley, Bestselling Author &
     Member of UK's House of Lords (*The Saad Truth*, 817), https://youtu.be/EbLi
     JbSTIcQ; Gad Saad (May 26, 2020). My Chat with Bestselling Author Matt
     Ridley (*The Saad Truth*, 1062), https://youtu.be/kEPz2YjRewM.

32. Matt Ridley and Alina Chan (2021). *Viral: The Search for the Origin of COVID-19*. London: HarperCollins.

33. Brandy Zadrozny (April 29,2020). YouTube, Facebook split on removal of doctors' viral coronavirus videos. NBC News, https://www.nbcnews.com /tech/tech-news/youtube-facebook-split-removal-doctors-viral-coronavirus -videos-n1195276.

34. Gad Saad (March 27, 2025). Dr. Matt Ridley—*Birds, Sex & Beauty*—*Charles Darwin's Strangest Idea* (*The Saad Truth*, 1829), https://youtu.be/qYh JSTmS60c.

35. Gad Saad (April 19, 2020). Life is a series of trade-offs. *Psychology Today*, https://www.psychologytoday.com/ca/blog/homo-consumericus/202004 /life-is-a-series-of-trade-offs.

36. Thomas Sowell (1995). *The Vision of the Anointed: Self-Congratulation as a Basis for Social Policy* (p. 142). New York: Basic Books.

37. Peter Singer (1981). *The Expanding Circle: Ethics and Sociobiology*. Oxford, UK: Clarendon Press.

38. Aurélien Miralles, Michel Raymond, and Guillaume Lecointre (2019). Empathy and compassion toward other species decrease with evolutionary divergence time. *Scientific Reports*, *9*(1), 19555.

39. Steven Arnocky and Mirella Stroink (2010). Gender differences in environ-mentalism: The mediating role of emotional empathy. *Current Research in Social Psychology*, *16*(9), 1–14.

40. Right Voice Refined (June 18, 2024). WEF Leader Ida Auken: "Smartphones Enable Car Sharing Revolution." https://www.youtube.com/watch?v=Icb Fq7IoT-o. I have edited the transcript for clarity (e.g., removed unnecessary utterances and added punctuation).

41. https://x.com/GadSaad/status/1809613304731427010.

42. https://medium.com/world-economic-forum/welcome-to-2030-i-own -nothing-have-no-privacy-and-life-has-never-been-better-ee2eed62f710.

43. Beryl Wajsman (February 13, 2025). $800 million for bike paths! The new mayor better change priorities . . . *The Suburban*, https://www.thesuburban .com/opinion/editorials/800-million-for-bike-paths-the-new-mayor-better -change-priorities/article_7c554dea-e82b-11ef-a213-9f7a6a77a5ca.html.

44. Gad Saad (November 30, 2024). How Montreal became the antisemitism cap-ital of North America. *New York Post*, https://nypost.com/2024/11/30/opinion /how-montreal-became-the-antisemitism-capital-of-north-america/.

45. Charles King (2016). Empathic activism: Only the radical power of empathy can save the world. In Pam Morrison, Quanta Gauld, and Veronica Wain (Eds.), *Promises, Pedagogy and Pitfalls: Empathy's Potential for Healing and Harm* (pp. 135–146), Leiden, Netherlands: Brill; Panu Pihkala (2022). Toward a taxonomy of climate emotions. *Frontiers in Climate, 3*, 738154; Stefan Brönnimann and Jeannine Wintzer (2019). Climate data empathy. *Wiley Interdisciplinary Reviews: Climate Change, 10*(2), e559; Jaime Berenguer (2007). The effect of empathy in proenvironmental attitudes and behaviors. *Environment and Behavior, 39*(2), 269–283; Natalia V. Czap, Hans J. Czap, Gary D. Lynne, and Mark E. Burbach (2015). Walk in my shoes: Nudging for empathy conservation. *Ecological Economics, 118*, 147–158.

46. Jeremy Williams (January 26, 2022). Why climate change is inherently racist. BBC, https://www.bbc.com/future/article/20220125-why-climate-change-is-inherently-racist.

47. Samuel Mann, Tara McKay, and Gilbert Gonzales (2024). Climate change-related disasters & the health of LGBTQ+ populations. *Journal of Climate Change and Health, 18*, 100304.

48. Leo Galuh (April 3, 2024). How climate change is hitting vulnerable Indonesian trans sex workers. *Independent*, https://www.independent.co.uk/climate-change/news/indonesian-transgender-climate-change-bandung-b2522422.html.

49. Maham Kaleem (March 15, 2023). Environmental action needs to combat Islamophobia. *David Suzuki Foundation*, https://davidsuzuki.org/expert-article/environmental-action-needs-to-combat-islamophobia/.

50. Paul R. Ehrlich (1968). *The Population Bomb*. New York: Ballantine Books.

51. https://languages.mit.edu/events/is-islamophobia-accelerating-global-warming/.

52. Deroy Murdock (June 17, 2016). See Something, Say *Nothing* policy kills thousands, *National Review*, https://www.nationalreview.com/2016/06/orlando-shooting-political-correctness-islamophobia-see-something-say-nothing/. Listen to Michael Tuohey in his own words, https://x.com/GadSaad/status/1833946006792405450.

53. Steven Erlanger (April 7, 2016). Blaming policy, not Islam, for Belgium's radicalized youth. *New York Times*, https://www.nytimes.com/2016/04/08/world/europe/belgium-brussels-islam-radicalization.html.

54. Lily Kinyon, Nives Dolšak, and Aseem Prakash (2023). When, where, and which climate activists have vandalized museums. *npj Climate Action, 2*(1), 27; Vittoria Benzine (October 31, 2022). Here is every artwork attacked by cli-

mate activists this year, from the "Mona Lisa" to "Girl with a Pearl Earring." *Artnet News*, https://news.artnet.com/art-world/here-is-every-artwork-attacked-by-climate-activists-this-year-from-the-mona-lisa-to-girl-with-a-pearl-earring-2200804.

55. Myron Ebell and Steven J. Milloy (September 18, 2019). Wrong again: 50 years of failed eco-pocalyptic predictions. *Competitive Enterprise Institute*, https://cei.org/blog/wrong-again-50-years-of-failed-eco-pocalyptic-predictions/; Mark J. Perry (April 21, 2022). 18 spectacularly wrong predictions were made around the time of the first Earth Day in 1970, expect more this year. *American Enterprise Institute*, https://www.aei.org/carpe-diem/18-spectacularly-wrong-predictions-were-made-around-the-time-of-the-first-earth-day-in-1970-expect-more-this-year/.

56. Noah Rothman (February 5, 2024). The latest things climate-change fanatics insist you make do with less of. *National Review*, https://www.nationalreview.com/corner/the-latest-things-climate-change-fanatics-insist-you-make-do-with-less-of/. On a related note, see also Noah Rothman (2022). *The Rise of the New Puritans: Fighting Back Against Progressives' War on Fun*. New York: Broadside Books.

57. World Weather Attribution (January 28, 2025). Climate change increased the likelihood of wildfire disaster in highly exposed Los Angeles area, https://www.worldweatherattribution.org/climate-change-increased-the-likelihood-of-wildfire-disaster-in-highly-exposed-los-angeles-area/.

58. Anthony Blair, Priscilla DeGregory, and Alex Oliveira (October 9, 2025). Alleged LA Palisades firebug Jonathan Rinderknecht threatened to burn down sister's house before arrest: feds. *New York Post*, https://nypost.com/2025/10/09/us-news/alleged-la-palisades-firebug-jonathan-rinderknecht-threatened-burn-down-sisters-house-before-arrest/.

59. Robin Morgan (Ed.). (1970). *Sisterhood Is Powerful: An Anthology of Writings from the Women's Liberation Movement* (p. 537). New York: Vintage Books. Accessed at: https://archive.org/details/sisterhoodispowe00vint/page/536/mode/2up.

60. Linda Gordon (1971). Functions of the family. In Leslie B. Tanner (Ed.), *Voices from Women's Liberation* (pp. 181–188). New York: New American Library, Inc. Accessed at: https://archive.org/details/voicesfromwomens00tann/page/n5/mode/2up.

61. Kathi Weeks (2023). Abolition of the family: The most infamous feminist proposal. *Feminist Theory*, 24(3), 433–453.

62. Gad Saad (May 31, 2010). Two paths to immortality, neither of which requires religion: Ways to be immortal without the help of God. *Psychology Today*,

https://www.psychologytoday.com/ca/blog/homo-consumericus/201005
/two-paths-to-immortality-neither-of-which-requires-religion.

63. https://birthstrikemovement.org.

64. Grégoire Zimmermann, Joëlle Darwiche, Nadine Messerli-Bürgy, Stijn Van
    Petegem, Bénédicte Mouton, Gaëlle Venard, and Jean-Philippe Antonietti
    (2024). "Bringing children in a burning world?" The role of climate anxiety
    and threat perceptions in childbearing motivations of emerging adults in
    Switzerland. *Emerging Adulthood*, *12*(5), 925–938; Sabrina Helm, Joya A. Kem-
    per, and Samantha K. White (2021). No future, no kids—no kids, no future?
    An exploration of motivations to remain childfree in times of climate change.
    Population and Environment, *43*, 108–129; Matthew Schneider-Mayerson and
    Kit Ling Leong (2020). Eco-reproductive concerns in the age of climate
    change. *Climatic Change*, *163*(2), 1007–1023.

65. Jade S. Sasser (2024). *Climate Anxiety and the Kid Question: Deciding
    Whether to Have Children in an Uncertain Future*. Berkeley: University of
    California Press.

66. Jade S. Sasser (September 11, 2024). "It's almost shameful to want to have
    children." *Los Angeles Times*, https://www.latimes.com/environment
    /story/2024-09-11/climate-anxiety-and-the-kid-question.

67. Olivia Land (December 19, 2023). Humans may be fueling global warming
    by breathing: New study. *New York Post*, https://nypost.com/2023/12/19/news
    /humans-may-be-fueling-global-warming-by-breathing-new-study/.

68. Richard Topolski, J. Nicole Weaver, Zachary Martin, and Jason McCoy (2013).
    Choosing between the emotional dog and the rational pal: A moral dilemma
    with a tail. *Anthrozoös*, *26*(2), 253–263.

69. Jack Levin, Arnold Arluke, and Leslie Irvine (2017). Are people more dis-
    turbed by dog or human suffering? Influence of victim's species and age.
    Society & Animals, *25*(1), 1–16.

70. Philip W. Bateman and Lauren N. Gilson (2025). Bad dog? The environmental
    effects of owned dogs. *Pacific Conservation Biology*, *31*(3), PC24071. doi:10.1071/
    PC24071; Donnachadh McCarthy (May 5, 2021). By owning a pet, you are
    doing more damage to the environment than you might realise. *Independent*,
    https://www.independent.co.uk/climate-change/opinion/pets-uk-ownership
    -cats-dogs-carbon-environmental-impact-b1249610.html.

71. https://montreal.ca/en/topics/spayingneutering-pets.

72. Matthew Sedacca and Alex Oliveira (November 12, 2024). P'Nut the Squir-
    rel was "marked for death" and decapitation from the start—as rabies test

results reveal tragic twist. *New York Post*, https://nypost.com/2024/11/12
/us-news/pnut-the-squirrel-was-marked-for-death-and-decapitation-from-the
-start-as-rabies-test-comes-back-negative-in-tragic-twist/.

73. *Proceedings of the Standing Senate Committee on Legal and Constitutional Affairs*,
28 (May 10, 2017), https://sencanada.ca/en/Content/Sen/Committee/421
/LCJC/28EV-53308-E.

74. United Nations General Assembly (Seventy-Ninth Session, August 27, 2024).
Violence against women and girls, its causes and consequences, https://
documents.un.org/doc/undoc/gen/n24/249/94/pdf/n2424994.pdf; Caroline
Downey (October 23, 2024). Female athletes lost almost 900 medals to trans-
identifying men worldwide, U.N. report finds. *National Review*, https://www
.nationalreview.com/news/female-athletes-lost-almost-900-medals-to-trans
-identifying-men-worldwide-u-n-report-finds/.

75. Chris Nesi (October 23, 2024). Woke doc refused to publish $10 million trans
kids study that showed puberty blockers didn't help mental health. *New York
Post*, https://nypost.com/2024/10/23/us-news/doctor-refused-to-publish-trans
-kids-study-that-showed-puberty-blockers-didnt-help-mental-health/.

76. Bethan Sexton (December 26, 2024). Judge tells court to respect pronouns
of rapist who now wants to be known as a woman. *Daily Mail*, https://www
.dailymail.co.uk/news/article-14228245/Judge-tells-court-respect-pronouns-tr
ansgender-rapist-treamine-carroll.html.

77. Brad Hunter (February 1, 2023). Study finds nearly 45% of trans-women
inmates convicted of sex crimes, *Toronto Sun*, https://torontosun.com/news
/national/study-finds-nearly-45-of-trans-women-inmates-convicted-of-sex
-crimes.

78. Caroline Downey (October 26, 2021). Judge rules Loudoun County teen sexually assaulted female student in girls' bathroom. Yahoo! News, https://www
.yahoo.com/news/judge-rules-loudoun-county-teen-131413442.html.

79. Ian Gallagher and Glen Owen (April 5, 2025). "I am expected to tolerate
racism, deny biological reality and suppress my deeply held Christian beliefs":
Nurse who called transgender paedophile "Mr" is suspended after investigation. *Daily Mail*, https://www.dailymail.co.uk/news/article-14575579/Nurse
-called-transgender-paedophile-Mr-suspended.html.

80. Gad Saad (November 15, 2022). Physicist Sean Carroll Confirms That Biological Sex Is a Spectrum & Not Binary (*The Saad Truth*, 1481), https://youtu.be
/iZq-5aiZwvA.

81. Gad Saad (March 3, 2019). Finger Diversity and Fluidity—Let's Stop Focusing
on the Number 10 (*The Saad Truth*, 861), https://youtu.be/F84QRYwQWQg.

82. Gad Saad (August 1, 2023). Neil deGrasse Tyson & the Gender Spectrum—My Male-to-Female Transformation (*The Saad Truth*, 1591), https://youtu.be/f39nBhLZEiU.

83. Toshiko Kaneda and Carl Haub (November 15, 2022). How many people have ever lived on earth? PRB, https://www.prb.org/articles/how-many-people-have-ever-lived-on-earth/.

84. The Editors (July 3, 2025). A blow to trans insanity, a victory for common sense. *National Review*, https://www.nationalreview.com/2025/07/a-blow-to-trans-insanity-a-victory-for-common-sense/.

85. Jim Geraghty (September 3, 2025). Malcom Gladwell reaches his tipping point on trans athletes. *National Review*, https://www.nationalreview.com/the-morning-jolt/malcolm-gladwell-reaches-his-tipping-point-on-trans-athletes/.

Chapter 6: Selling Indulgences

1. While the source of this quote is disputed, its general meaning can be traced back to both Aristotle and Plato. Aristotle: "it is when equals possess or are allotted unequal shares, or persons not equal equal shares, that quarrels and complaints arise." (Nichomachean Ethics, Book 5, chapter 3, section 6), https://www.perseus.tufts.edu/hopper/text?doc=Perseus%3Atext%3A1999.01.0054%3Abook%3D5%3Achapter%3Dpos%3D270%3Asection%3D6. Plato: "for when equality is given to unequal things, the resultant will be unequal, unless due measure is applied" (Plato's Laws 6, 757a), https://www.perseus.tufts.edu/hopper/text?doc=Perseus%3Atext%3A1999.01.0166%3Abook%3D6%3Apage%3D757.

2. Gottfried G. Krodel (1963). *Luther's Works, vol. 48: Letters I* (p. 46). Philadelphia: Fortress Press / St. Louis: Concordia Publishing House. Accessed at: https://archive.org/details/in.ernet.dli.2015.178444.

3. https://www.oed.com/search/dictionary/?scope=Entries&q=american+dream.

4. https://www.france24.com/en/20200901-cause-of-all-ills-lebanon-s-complex-power-sharing-system.

5. https://www.foxnews.com/video/6360423204112 [0:00–0:33].

6. Katherine Timpf (May 6, 2015). Professor: If you read to your kids, you're "unfairly disadvantaging" others. *National Review*, https://www.nationalreview.com/2015/05/professor-if-you-read-your-kids-youre-unfairly-disadvantaging-others-katherine-timpf/.

7. The White House (February 14, 2024), https://bidenwhitehouse.archives
   .gov/briefing-room/statements-releases/2024/02/14/fact-sheet-biden-harris-a
   dministration-releases-annual-agency-equity-action-plans-to-further-advance
   -racial-equity-and-support-for-underserved-communities-through-the-federal
   -government/.

8. Hope Yen (June 30, 2022). Buttigieg launches $1B pilot to build racial equity
   in roads. Associated Press, https://apnews.com/article/race-and-ethnicity
   -racial-injustice-transportation-pete-buttigieg-48e09f253781c89359d875f19
   fc70f9d; Caitlin Doornbos (April 20, 2023). Dum idea: Buttigieg wants to
   spend $20 million on female crash dummies. *New York Post*, https://nypost
   .com/2023/04/20/buttigieg-wants-to-spend-20-million-on-female-crash
   -dummies/.

9. Caroline Downey (July 2, 2024). Non-binary ex-Biden official Sam Brinton
   gets plea deal with no jail time. *National Review*, https://www.nationalreview
   .com/news/non-binary-ex-biden-official-sam-brinton-gets-plea-deal-with-no
   -jail-time/.

10. Carolyn Pedwell (2012). Economies of empathy: Obama, neoliberalism, and
    social justice. *Environment and Planning D: Society and Space*, 30(2), 280–297;
    Eric Leake (2016). Empathizer-in-Chief: The promotion and performance of
    empathy in the speeches of Barack Obama. *Journal of Contemporary Rhetoric*,
    6(1/2), 1–14; Collen J. Shogan (2009). The contemporary presidency: The polit-
    ical utility of empathy in presidential leadership. *Presidential Studies Quarterly*,
    39(4), 859–877. See also http://cultureofempathy.com/obama/, which includes
    links to many of Obama's empathy-related speeches.

11. Sara H. Konrath, Edward H. O'Brien, and Courtney Hsing (2011). Changes
    in dispositional empathy in American college students over time: A meta-
    analysis. *Personality and Social Psychology Review*, 15(2), 180–198; Sara Konrath,
    Alison Jane Martingano, Mark Davis, and Fritz Breithaupt (2025). Empathy
    trends in American youth between 1979 and 2018: An update. *Social Psycholog-
    ical and Personality Science*, 16(3), 252–265.

12. Steven J. Lenzner (January 28, 2008). Empathy, Anyone? *Washington Exam-
    iner*, https://www.washingtonexaminer.com/magazine/1747432/empathy
    -anyone/.

13. Daniel A. Cox (June 8, 2021). The state of American friendship: Change,
    challenges, and loss. The Survey on American Life (American Enterprise
    Institute), https://www.americansurveycenter.org/research/the-state-of-am
    erican-friendship-change-challenges-and-loss/; Samuel J. Abrams (February
    23, 2022). Polarization in American family life is overblown. The Survey
    on American Life (American Enterprise Institute), https://www.americans

urveycenter.org/polarization-in-american-family-life-is-overblown/; Anna
Brown (April 24, 2020). Most Democrats who are looking for a relationship
would not consider dating a Trump voter. Pew Research Center, https://
www.pewresearch.org/short-reads/2020/04/24/most-democrats-who-are-loo
king-for-a-relationship-would-not-consider-dating-a-trump-voter/.

14. Lisa Farwell and Bernard Weiner (2000). Bleeding hearts and the heartless:
Popular perceptions of liberal and conservative ideologies. *Personality and
Social Psychology Bulletin*, *26*(7), 845–852; Stephen G. Morris (2020). Empathy
and the liberal-conservative political divide in the US. *Journal of Social and
Political Psychology*, *8*(1), 8–24; Yossi Hasson, Maya Tamir, Kea S. Brahms,
J. Christopher Cohrs, and Eran Halperin (2018). Are liberals and conserva-
tives equally motivated to feel empathy toward others? *Personality and Social
Psychology Bulletin*, *44*(10), 1449–1459; James P. Casey, Eric J. Vanman, and
Fiona Kate Barlow (2025). Empathic conservatives and moralizing liberals:
Political intergroup empathy varies by political ideology and is explained by
moral judgment. *Personality and Social Psychology Bulletin*, *51*(5), 678–700; Eliz-
abeth N. Simas, Scott Clifford, and Justin H. Kirkland (2020). How empathic
concern fuels political polarization. *American Political Science Review 114*(1),
258–269; Adam Waytz, Ravi Iyer, Liane Young, and Jesse Graham (2016).
Ideological differences in the expanse of empathy. In Piercarlo Valdesolo and
Jesse Graham (Eds.), *Social Psychology of Political Polarization* (pp. 61–77). New
York: Routledge.

15. Gad Saad (November 15, 2023). Concordia University is unsafe for Jewish
students and professors like me. *National Post*, https://nationalpost.com
/opinion/gad-saad-concordia-university-is-unsafe-for-jewish-students-and
-professors-like-me.

16. Andy Riga (May 27, 2024). Antisemitism is a "significant problem" on
campus, McGill and Concordia admit. *Montreal Gazette*, https://montre
algazette.com/news/local-news/mcgill-concordia-antisemitism-israel
-palestinian-protesters.

17. James D. Paul and Robert Maranto (2021). Other than merit: The prevalence
of diversity, equity, and inclusion statements in university hiring. American
Enterprise Institute, https://www.aei.org/wp-content/uploads/2021/11
/Other-than-merit-The-prevalence-of-diversity-equity-and-inclusion
-statements-in-university-hiring.pdf.

18. David Hunt, Collin May, Ven Venkatachalam, and Alex Emes (January 29,
2025). DEI and academic hiring in public universities: An index of university discrimination in Canada. The Aristotle Foundation for Public Policy,
https://aristotlefoundation.org/study/dei-and-academic-hiring-in-public-univ
ersities-an-index-of-university-discrimination-in-canada/.

19. Jennifer Kabbany (January 9, 2024). UMich now has more than 500 jobs dedicated to DEI, payroll costs exceed $30 million. The College Fix, https://www.thecollegefix.com/umich-now-has-more-than-500-jobs-dedicated-to-dei-payroll-costs-exceed-30-million/.

20. John Sailer (January 9, 2023). How DEI is supplanting truth as the mission of American universities. *The Free Press*, https://www.thefp.com/p/how-dei-is-supplanting-truth-as-the.

21. I first reported some of these examples here: Gad Saad (2025). Universities as dispensers of parasitic ideas. In Lawrence Krauss (Ed.), *The War on Science: Thirty-Nine Renowned Scientists and Scholars Speak Out About Current Threats to Free Speech, Open Inquiry, and the Scientific Process* (pp. 69–77). Brentwood, TN: Post Hill Press.

22. As originally found on https://decolonizinglight.com. The site has since been deleted but the quotes in question can be obtained via a web archival search and secondary sources. See https://web.archive.org/web/20200620140458/http://decolonizinglight.com/ and John Rigolizzo (December 17, 2022). "Decolonizing Light": Canadian university project aims to redefine "Physics as a Social Field." *Daily Wire*, https://www.dailywire.com/news/decolonizing-light-canadian-university-project-aims-to-redefine-physics-as-a-social-field.

23. https://chanda.science.

24. Chanda Prescod-Weinstein (April 25, 2015). Decolonising science reading list. Medium, https://medium.com/@chanda/decolonising-science-reading-list-339fb773d51f#.egg56n259.

25. https://germantownjewishcentre.org/chanda-prescod-weinstein/.

26. https://ucalgary.ca/live-uc-ucalgary-site/sites/default/files/teams/136/Journey%20to%20reconciliation-MAHart%20-%20Dec%2015-2020.pdf.

27. Daniel Bartlett (September 8, 2023). Concordia launches a plan to decolonize and Indigenize its curriculum and pedagogy. *Concordia News*, https://www.concordia.ca/news/stories/2023/09/08/concordia-launches-a-plan-to-decolonize-and-indigenize-its-curriculum-and-pedagogy.html.

28. https://queercode.org.

29. Dylan Paré (August 31, 2021). A critical review and new directions for queering computing and computing education. *Oxford Research Encyclopedia of Education*, https://doi.org/10.1093/acrefore/9780190264093.013.1524.

30. https://uwaterloo.ca/news/waterloo-rises-again-qs-world-subject-rankings and https://www.waterlooedc.ca/blog/university-of-waterloo-macleans-rankings-2020.

31. https://cs.uwaterloo.ca/nserc-crc-tier1. The site is no longer accessible to the public, but it is archived here: https://archive.is/2024.03.29-201800/https://cs.uwaterloo.ca/nserc-crc-tier1.

32. https://research.ubc.ca/sites/research.ubc.ca/files/vpri/CRC-Tier1-Oral _Cancer_Research.pdf.

33. Jamie Sarkonak (December 30, 2024). Ottawa-funded social justice research isn't science. *National Post*, https://nationalpost.com/opinion/ottawa-funded -social-justice-research-isnt-science; Gad Saad (October 1, 2025). The cult of diversity, inclusion, and equity destroys science. *National Post*, https://na tionalpost.com/opinion/gad-saad-the-cult-of-diversity-inclusion-and-equity -destroys-science.

34. Bradford Richardson (January 15, 2018). Reshmi Dutt-Ballerstadt, English professor, says "meritocracy" is white supremacist. *Washington Times*, https:// www.washingtontimes.com/news/2018/jan/15/reshmi-dutt-ballerstadt-english -professor-says-mer/.

35. Jeff Fuhrer (2023). *The Myth That Made Us: How False Beliefs About Racism and Meritocracy Broke Our Economy (and How to Fix It)*. Cambridge, MA: MIT Press.

36. Michael J. Sandel (2020). *The Tyranny of Merit: What's Become of the Common Good?* New York: Farrar, Straus and Giroux.

37. Naa Oyo A. Kwate and Ilan H. Meyer (2010). The myth of meritocracy and African American health. *American Journal of Public Health*, *100*(10), 1831–1834.

38. College Fix Staff (December 23, 2024). 103 things higher ed declared racist in 2024. The College Fix, https://www.thecollegefix.com/103-things-higher -ed-declared-racist-in-2024/; Matt Lamb (May 15, 2024). "Romance" is white supremacy, Black Studies professor says. The College Fix, https://www .thecollegefix.com/romance-is-white-supremacy-black-studies-professor -says/.

39. Chinyere Odim and Prudence Carter (2023). "Acting white" and opposi-tional culture in education. In Gene Jarrett (Ed.), *Oxford Bibliographies in African American Studies*. New York: Oxford University Press. doi:10.1093 /obo/9780190280024-0123.

40. Shaun Harper (July 9, 2023). Eliminating standardized tests to achieve racial equity in post-affirmative action college admissions. *Forbes*, https:// www.forbes.com/sites/shaunharper/2023/07/09/eliminating-standardized -tests-to-achieve-racial-equity-in-post-affirmative-action-college-admissio ns/; Betsy McCaughey (March 10, 2022). Racial-equity warriors are hurt-ing the disadvantaged by dumbing down schools, *New York Post*, https:// nypost.com/2022/03/10/racial-equity-warriors-are-actually-hurting-the

-disadvantaged/; Margaret Peppiatt (November 9, 2021). To combat racism, professor urges peers to embrace labor-based grading, The College Fix, https://www.thecollegefix.com/to-combat-racism-professor-urges-peers-to -embrace-labor-based-grading/; Matt Lamb (September 18, 2024). "Traditional grading" favors white people: Pitt instructor, The College Fix, https://www.thecollegefix.com/traditional-grading-favors-white-people-pitt -instructor/.

41. Associated Press (September 29, 2024). Penn Law suspends professor for one year over comments on race. NBC News, https://www.nbcnews.com/news /us-news/penn-law-suspends-professor-one-year-comments-race-rcna173206.

42. Megan Zerez (September 19, 2024). Professor who made controversial remarks on Gaza war returns to teaching amid outcry. *The Ithaca Voice*, https:// ithacavoice.org/2024/09/professor-who-made-controversial-remarks-on-gaza -war-returns-to-teaching-amid-outcry/.

43. Jennifer Mobilia (September 30, 2025). Ian Roberts accused of lying about earning doctoral degree. Yahoo! News, https://www.yahoo.com/news/arti cles/ian-roberts-accused-lying-earning-030444323.html.

44. US Immigration and Customs Enforcement (September 26, 2025). ICE arrests criminal alien serving as Des Moines Public Schools superintendent; prior weapons charges and in possession of loaded gun at time of arrest, https:// www.ice.gov/news/releases/ice-arrests-criminal-alien-serving-des-moines-pu blic-schools-superintendent-prior.

45. Samantha Hernandez and Kate Kealey (September 27, 2025). Des Moines school board votes to put Superintendent Ian Roberts on leave after ICE arrest. *Des Moines Register*, https://www.desmoinesregister.com/story/news /education/2025/09/27/dmps-board-meeting-superintendent-ian-roberts -arrested-ice/86377063007/.

46. Max Sherry (January 30, 2023). Lionel Messi and Argentina slammed for "lack of black representation" during World Cup victory. SPORTbible, https:// www.sportbible.com/football/argentina-lack-of-black-representation-at-world -cup-in-qatar-439847-20230130.

47. https://x.com/GadSaad/status/1744047767628955961.

48. Solomon E. Asch (1956). Studies of independence and conformity: I. A minority of one against a unanimous majority. *Psychological Monographs: General and Applied 70*(9), 1–70; Stanley Milgram (1963). Behavioral study of obedience. *Journal of Abnormal and Social Psychology, 67*(4), 371–378; Craig Haney, Curtis Banks, and Philip Zimbardo (1973). Interpersonal dynamics in a simulated prison. *International Journal of Criminology and Penology, 1*, 69–97.

49. Marcella H. Boynton, David B. Portnoy, and Blair T. Johnson (2013). Exploring the ethics and psychological impact of deception in psychological research. *IRB, 35*(2), 7–13.

50. CanMEDS Project Foundational Report Executive Summary (October 2023, p. 11), https://widgixca-library.s3.amazonaws.com/library/50001532 /2023CanMEDSFoundationalReportENFinal.pdf.

51. CanMEDS Project Foundational Report Executive Summary (October 2023, pp. 11–12), https://widgixca-library.s3.amazonaws.com/library/50001532 /2023CanMEDSFoundationalReportENFinal.pdf.

52. Michael Higgins (November 27, 2023). "Anti-racist" doctors would put social justice above medical expertise. *National Post*, https://nationalpost.com /opinion/michael-higgins-anti-racist-doctors-would-put-social-justice-above -medical-expertise; Umberin Najeeb and Arno K. Kumagai (2024). Uprooting the CanMEDS flower? Equity, social justice, and the Medical Expert role. *Canadian Medical Education Journal, 15*(3), 104–106.

53. Oath at University of Minnesota Medical School's White Coat Ceremony, August 19, 2022 (October 13, 2022). *FIRE*, https://www.youtube .com/watch?v=g_OVOUzU8YA.

54. https://web.archive.org/web/20170627232127/https://www.faa.gov/jobs /diversity_inclusion/.

55. Emma Colton (January 14, 2024). FAA's diversity push includes focus on hiring people with "severe intellectual" and "psychiatric" disabilities. *New York Post*, https://nypost.com/2024/01/14/news/faas-diversity-push-includes -hiring-people-with-intellectual-and-psychiatric-disabilities/.

56. Riley Hoffman, Leah Sarnoff, Mary Kekatos, and William Mansell (March 7, 2025). LA fires aftermath: How people are rebuilding after losing almost everything. ABC News, https://abcnews.go.com/US/la-wildfires-aftermath -insurance-housing-rebuild-update/story?id=119209482.

57. Monica Sager (January 10, 2025). LAFD deputy chief faces backlash for past remarks on fire victims. *Newsweek*, https://www.newsweek.com/lafd-deputy -chief-faces-backlash-past-remarks-fire-victims-2013351.

58. Sung-Man Shin, Clifton Chow, Teresita Camacho-Gonsalves, Rachel J. Levy, I. Elaine Allen, and H. Stephen Leff (2005). A meta-analytic review of racial-ethnic matching for African American and Caucasian American clients and clinicians. *Journal of Counseling Psychology, 52*(1), 45–56; Sonia V. Otte (2022). Improved patient experience and outcomes: Is patient–provider concordance the key? *Journal of Patient Experience, 9*, 1–7.

59. Gad Saad (March 29, 2021). The evolving role of corporate responsibility over the past century. *Arabian Business*, https://www.arabianbusiness.com /spotlight/461046-the-evolving-role-of-corporate-responsibility-over-the-past -century.

60. Stanley M. Davis (1987). *Future Perfect*. Reading, MA: Addison-Wesley.

61. For a discussion of various facets of woke capitalism, please see Stephen R. Soukup (2021). *The Dictatorship of Woke Capital: How Political Correctness Captured Big Business*. New York: Encounter Books; Nicolai J. Foss and Peter G. Klein (2023). Why do companies go woke? *Academy of Management Perspectives*, *37*(4), 351–367; Nicolai Foss and Peter G. Klein (2024). Strategy under woke capitalism. In Ashton L. Hawk, Marcus M. Larsen, Michael J. Leiblein, and Jeffrey J. Reuer (Eds.), *Strategy in a Turbulent Era* (pp. 186–205). Northampton, MA: Edward Elgar Publishing; David L. Bahnsen (2022). Woke corporations: Cowardice and crusaders for the worst. *Texas Review of Law & Politics*, *27*(3), 699–714.

62. Belinda Parmar (November 27, 2015). The most (and least) empathetic companies. *Harvard Business Review*, https://hbr.org/2015/11/2015-empathy-index. See also https://theempathybusiness.com/.

63. Jaguar | Copy Nothing (November 19, 2024), https://www.youtube.com /watch?v=rLtFIrqhfng.

64. Conor Murray (November 22, 2024). Jaguar rebrand sparks confusion, angers anti-"woke" critics. *Forbes*, https://www.forbes.com/sites/conormur ray/2024/11/20/jaguar-rebrand-sparks-confusion-angers-anti-woke-critics-inc luding-elon-musk-and-andrew-tate/.

Chapter 7: Govern Me Harder, Daddy!

1. C. S. Lewis (1970). *God in the Dock: Essays on Theology and Ethics* (p. 292). Grand Rapids, MI: William B. Eerdmans Publishing Company. Accessed at: https:// archive.org/details/godindockessayso0000lewi/page/292/mode/2up.

2. N. V. Varghese (2018). Criticality, empathy and welfare in educational discourses. *Contemporary Education Dialogue*, *15*(2), 122–142.

3. Masumi Kameda (2024). Mass empathy in New Deal and Stalinist Propaganda: The path to victimhood culture. *Interface-Journal of European Languages and Literatures*, *23*, 17–44.

4. Outong Chen, Fang Guan, Yu Du, Yijun Su, Hui Yang, and Jun Chen (2021). Belief in Communism and Theory of Mind. *Frontiers in Psychology*, *12*, https:// doi.org/10.3389/fpsyg.2021.697251.

5. M. Alex Wagaman and Elizabeth A. Segal (2014). The relationship between empathy and attitudes toward government intervention. *Journal of Sociology & Social Welfare*, 41(4), 91–112.

6. Stanley Feldman, Leonie Huddy, Julie Wronski, and Patrick Lown (2020). The interplay of empathy and individualism in support for social welfare policies. *Political Psychology*, 41(2), 343–362.

7. Margaret M. Braungart (1984). Aging and politics. *Journal of Political & Military Sociology*, 79–98.

8. Joseph S. Alpert (2016). If you are not a liberal when you are Young, you have no heart, and if you are not a conservative when Old, you have no brain. *American Journal of Medicine*, 129(7), 647–648; Johnathan C. Peterson, Kevin B. Smith, and John R. Hibbing (2020). Do people really become more conservative as they age? *Journal of Politics*, 82(2), 600–611; Ilse Cornelis, Alain Van Hiel, Arne Roets, and Malgorzata Kossowska (2009). Age differences in conservatism: Evidence on the mediating effects of personality and cognitive style. *Journal of Personality*, 77(1), 51–88; Sam Peltzman (2019). Political ideology over the life course. Available at SSRN 3501174, https://ssrn.com/abstract=3501174; Benny Geys, Tom-Reiel Heggedal, and Rune J. Sørensen (2022). Age and vote choice: Is there a conservative shift among older voters? *Electoral Studies*, 78, 102485; James Tilley and Geoffrey Evans (2014). Ageing and generational effects on vote choice: Combining cross-sectional and panel data to estimate APC effects. *Electoral Studies*, 33, 19–27.

9. Pew Research Center (September 2022). Modest declines in positive views of "Socialism" and "Capitalism" in U.S., https://www.pewresearch.org/politics/2022/09/19/modest-declines-in-positive-views-of-socialism-and-capitalism-in-u-s/; Victims of Communism Memorial Foundation (October 2020). U.S. attitudes toward socialism, communism, and collectivism, https://victimsofcommunism.org/wp-content/uploads/2020/10/10.19.20-VOC-YouGov-Survey-on-U.S.-Attitudes-Toward-Socialism-Communism-and-Collectivism.pdf; Jason Clemens and Steven Globerman (2023). Perspectives on Capitalism and Socialism: Polling Results from Canada, the United States, Australia, and the United Kingdom. Fraser Institute, https://www.fraserinstitute.org/sites/default/files/perspectives-on-capitalism-and-socialism-polling.pdf.

10. Daniel Grühn, Kristine Rebucal, Manfred Diehl, Mark Lumley, and Gisela Labouvie-Vief (2008). Empathy across the adult lifespan: Longitudinal and experience-sampling findings. *Emotion*, 8(6), 753–765.

11. Axios (June 9, 2019). "Axios on HBO" poll: 55% of women prefer socialism,

https://www.axios.com/2019/06/09/axios-hbo-poll-55-percent-women-prefer
-socialism.

12. Murilo Johas Menezes (August 8, 2019). Can we create an empathic alternative to the capitalist system? World Economic Forum, https://www.weforum
.org/agenda/2019/08/empathy-can-create-a-new-economic-system/.

13. Paul H. Rubin (2003). Folk economics. *Southern Economic Journal*, *70*(1),
157–171; Pascal Boyer and Michael Bang Petersen (2018). Folk-economic beliefs: An evolutionary cognitive model. *Behavioral and Brain Sciences*, *41*, e158,
doi:10.1017/S0140525X17001960.

14. Paul H. Rubin (December 4, 2017). This explains man's fatal attraction to
communism. Foundation for Economic Education, https://fee.org/articles
/this-explains-mans-fatal-attraction-to-communism/.

15. Regent University (October 28, 2020). The psychological absurdity of communism, https://ccta.regent.edu/the-psychological-absurdity-of-communism/#.

16. Noah Rothman (April 14, 2016). The character of a socialist. *Commentary*,
https://www.commentary.org/noah-rothman/the-character-of-a-socialist/.

17. George B. Lockwood (1905). *The New Harmony Movement* (p. 185). New York:
D. Appleton and Company. Accessed at: https://libsysdigi.library.illinois
.edu/oca/Books2008-06/newharmonymoveme00lock/newharmonymove
me00lock.pdf.

18. Paul H. Rubin (2000). Hierarchy. *Human Nature*, *11*(3), 259–279; Chris von
Rueden (2020). Making and unmaking egalitarianism in small-scale human
societies. *Current Opinion in Psychology*, *33*, 167–171; Eric Alden Smith and
Brian F. Codding (2021). Ecological variation and institutionalized inequality
in hunter-gatherer societies. *Proceedings of the National Academy of Sciences*,
118(13), e2016134118; Eric Alden Smith, Jennifer E. Smith, and Brian F. Cod-
ding (2023). Toward an evolutionary ecology of (in)equality. *Philosophical
Transactions of the Royal Society B*, *378*(1883), 20220287; Sergey Gavrilets (2012).
On the evolutionary origins of the egalitarian syndrome. *Proceedings of the
National Academy of Sciences*, *109*(35), 14069–14074.

19. Gary Bernhard and Kalman Glantz (January 15, 2020). Why socialism fails.
Psychology Today, https://www.psychologytoday.com/us/blog/evolution-in
-daily-life/202001/why-socialism-fails.

20. Lawrence W. Reed (February 8, 2020). Margaret Thatcher on socialism: 20 of
her best quotes. Foundation for Economic Education, https://fee.org/articles
/margaret-thatcher-on-socialism-20-of-her-best-quotes/.

21. https://www.oxfordreference.com/display/10.1093/acref/97801918
    26719.001.0001/q-oro-ed4-00010826.

22. Eric Hammer and Daniel B. Klein (June 26, 2024). The welfare state is
    devoid of generosity. Adam Smith Works Series: Just Sentiments, https://
    www.adamsmithworks.org/documents/hammer-klein-welfare-state-devoid
    -ofgenerosity.

23. Charlotte Sleigh (2002). Brave new worlds: Trophallaxis and the origin of
    society in the early twentieth century. *Journal of the History of the Behavioral
    Sciences*, *38*(2), 133–156.

24. Julian Huxley (1949). *Ants* (p. 3). London: Dennis Dobson. Accessed at:
    https://archive.org/details/in.ernet.dli.2015.460830/page/n7/mode/2up.

25. Claudia Dreifus (June 15, 2009). A conversation with Bert Hölldobler: Insects
    succeeding through cooperation. *New York Times*, https://www.nytimes
    .com/2009/06/16/science/16conv.html.

26. Heng-Fu Zou (April 2023). "Karl Marx was right, but he picked the wrong
    species" (p. 6). Working paper, https://down.aefweb.net/WorkingPapers
    /w660.pdf.

27. The biologist Peter A. Corning has argued that human beings are naturally
    suited to live in so-called fair societies that are neither socialist nor capitalist.
    In a trivial sense, this is true in that there are elements of our human nature
    that render us to be both cooperative and competitive; Peter A. Corning
    (2003). "Fair Shares": Beyond capitalism and socialism, or the biological basis
    of social justice. *Politics and the Life Sciences*, *22*(2), 12–32; Peter Corning (2011).
    The Fair Society: The Science of Human Nature and the Pursuit of Social Justice.
    Chicago: University of Chicago Press.

28. Murray N. Rothbard (2016/1982). *The Ethics of Liberty* (p. 162). New York: New
    York University Press.

29. Abi Wilkinson (July 24, 2017). Why not fund the welfare state with a 100%
    inheritance tax? *The Guardian*, https://www.theguardian.com/commentis
    free/2017/jul/24/utopian-thinking-fund-welfare-state-inheritance-tax.

30. Roberta Calvet Christian and James Alm (2014). Empathy, sympathy, and tax
    compliance. *Journal of Economic Psychology*, *40*, 62–82.

31. For a historical perspective of Canada's personal income tax, see William Wat-
    son and Jason Clemens (Eds.). (2017). The history and development of Canada's
    personal income tax. Fraser Institute, https://www.fraserinstitute.org/sites
    /default/files/history-and-development-of-canadas-personal-income-tax.pdf.

32. Robert Bellafiore (November 13, 2018). Summary of the latest federal income tax data, 2018 update. Tax Foundation, https://taxfoundation.org/summary -latest-federal-income-tax-data-2018-update/.

33. Demian Brady (April 15, 2024). Tax complexity 2024: It takes Americans billions of hours to do their taxes. National Taxpayers Union Foundation, https://www.ntu.org/foundation/detail/tax-complexity-2024-it-takes-americ ans-billions-of-hours-to-do-their-taxes.

34. Frederick Douglass Project Writings: West India Emancipation, University of Rochester, https://rbscp.lib.rochester.edu/4398.

35. https://www.archives.gov/founding-docs/declaration-transcript.

36. https://foreignaffairs.house.gov/press-release/icymi-chairman-mast -discusses-foreign-aid-review-dei-on-face-the-nation/.

37. https://x.com/DOGE/status/1890849405932077378.

38. Rand Paul (December 23, 2024). The Festivus Report 2024, https://www.hsgac.senate.gov/wp-content/uploads/FESTIVUS -REPORT-2024.pdf.

39. Citizens Against Government Waste (2024). 2024 Congressional Pig Book Summary, https://www.cagw.org/2024-congressional-pig-book/.

40. https://www.zerohedge.com/technology/elon-musk-building-backbone-ame ricas-high-tech-2030s-economy-and-numbers-prove-it.

41. Larry King, host (December 1, 2002), "Interview with Bono," *Larry King Weekend*, CNN, https://transcripts.cnn.com/show/lklw/date/2002-12-01 /segment/00.

42. ABC News (August 10, 2013). A sweet solution to the sticky wage disparity problem, https://abcnews.go.com/Business/companies-follow-ben-jerrys -lead-wages/story?id=19920634.

43. Josh Bivens and Jori Kandra (October 4, 2022). CEO pay has skyrocketed 1,460% since 1978. Economic Policy Institute, https://www.epi.org/publica tion/ceo-pay-in-2021/.

44. Ronald Reagan (August 12, 1986), https://www.reaganlibrary.gov/archives /speech/presidents-news-conference-23.

45. Albert Camus (1995/1960). *Resistance, Rebellion, and Death* (p. 101). New York: Random House, https://archive.org/details/resistancerebell00camu_0 /page/100/mode/2up.

46. Gad Saad (June 14, 2012). Don't romanticize the Canadian healthcare system. *Psychology Today*, https://www.psychologytoday.com/intl/blog/homo -consumericus/201206/don-t-romanticize-the-canadian-healthcare-system.

47. Ted Rechtshaffen (February 7, 2019). Trudeau is right: 40% of Canadians don't pay income taxes, which means someone else is picking up the bill. *Financial Post*, https://financialpost.com/personal-finance/taxes/trudeau-is-right-40-of -canadians-dont-pay-income-taxes-which-means-someone-else-is-picking-up -the-bill.

48. NBC News (June 27, 2019). Health care for undocumented immigrants: Where the candidates stand, https://www.nbcnews.com/video/health-care -for-undocumented-immigrants-where-the-candidates-stand-62832710000.

49. Chris Lambie (December 13, 2024). Montreal man, 39, dies from aneurysm after giving up on a six-hour wait at ER. *National Post*, https://nationalpost .com/news/canada/montreal-man-dies-er-hospital-wait.

50. Stéphanie Girard and Francesca Roy (May 16, 2025). Quebec's French lan- guage requirements for commerce and business: Reform of the Charter of the French language. Smart & Biggar, https://www.smartbiggar.ca/insights/pub lication/quebecs-french-language-requirements-for-commerce-and-business -reform-of-the-charter-of-the-french-language.

51. Graeme Hamilton (May 4, 2016). Quebec cracks down on English brand names, forces prominent French signage to be included. *National Post*, https:// nationalpost.com/news/canada/quebec-cracks-down-on-english-brand -names-forces-prominent-french-signage-to-be-included.

52. Marc Cassivi (August 1, 2023). Pousse, mais pousse égal. *La Presse*, https:// www.lapresse.ca/arts/chroniques/2023-08-01/pousse-mais-pousse-egal.php.

53. Gad Saad (May 1, 2024). Don't insult our accents! And other lessons from the Quebec cancel mob. *National Post*, https://nationalpost.com/opinion/dont-ins ult-our-accents-and-other-lessons-from-the-quebec-cancel-mob.

54. Edward A. Gutiérrez (September 12, 2025). Publius Flavius Vegetius Renatus, Epitome of Military Science (c. AD 380s). Hoover Institution, https://www .hoover.org/research/publius-flavius-vegetius-renatus-epitome-military -science-c-ad-380s.

55. This stems from an African proverb, which Theodore Roosevelt referenced in a letter that he wrote to Henry Sprague in 1900, in several subsequent speeches, and referenced in his autobiography.

56. Robert Ardrey (1966). *The Territorial Imperative: A Personal Inquiry into the*

Animal Origins of Property and Nations. New York: Atheneum; Konrad Lorenz (1966). *On Aggression*. New York: Harcourt, Brace & World.

57. https://www.congress.gov/87/statute/STATUTE-76/STATUTE-76-Pg748.pdf.

58. Giselle Ruhiyyih Ewing (May 13, 2023). Biden calls white supremacy "most dangerous terrorist threat" in speech at Howard. *Politico*, https://www.politico.com/news/2023/05/13/biden-howard-university-white-supremacy-terrorism-00096811; Danielle Kurtzleben (June 23, 2021). Top general defends studying critical race theory in the military. NPR, https://www.npr.org/2021/06/23/1009592838/top-general-defends-studying-critical-race-theory-in-the-military.

59. Pete Hegseth (2024). *The War on Warriors: Behind the Betrayal of the Men Who Keep Us Free*. New York: Broadside Books. See also Amber Smith (2024). *Unfit to Fight: How Woke Policies Are Destroying Our Military*. Washington, DC: Regnery; Michel Maisonneuve (2024). *In Defence of Canada: Reflections of a Patriot*. Toronto: Sutherland House Books; John Robson (November 16, 2022). The retired general who spoke truth about Canadian wokeness. *National Post*, https://nationalpost.com/opinion/he-retired-general-who-spoke-truth-about-military-wokeness.

60. Brittany Vonow (December 13, 2017). British Army drew up £500K proposal to scrap "Be the Best" motto because it was "non-inclusive." *The Sun*, https://www.thesun.co.uk/news/5205232/british-army-proposal-scrap-be-the-best-motto/.

61. Sebastian Mohr, Birgitte Refslund Sørensen, and Matti Weisdorf (2021). The ethnography of things military—empathy and critique in military anthropology. *Ethnos*, 86(4), 600–615.

62. Tunnel to Towers Foundation, https://t2t.org/.

Chapter 8: Inoculation Against Suicidal Empathy

1. George Roche (1993). The road to freedom. *Imprimis*, 22(7), https://imprimis.hillsdale.edu/the-road-to-freedom/.

2. https://www.metmuseum.org/art/collection/search/338473.

3. Walter Mischel (2014). *The Marshmallow Test: Mastering Self-Control*. New York: Little, Brown; Renée M. Tobin and William G. Graziano (2010). Delay of gratification: A review of fifty years of regulation research. In Rick H. Hoyle (Ed.), *Handbook of Personality and Self-Regulation* (pp. 47–63). Hoboken, NJ: Wiley-Blackwell.

4. Irwin W. Silverman (2003). Gender differences in delay of gratification: A meta-analysis. *Sex Roles*, *49*(9/10), 451–463; Jessica Weafer and Harriet de Wit (2014). Sex differences in impulsive action and impulsive choice. *Addictive Behaviors*, *39*(11), 1573–1579.

5. Peter Dizikes (February 22, 2011). When the Butterfly Effect took flight. *MIT Technology Review*, https://www.technologyreview.com/2011/02/22/196987 /when-the-butterfly-effect-took-flight/. For an application of this concept in economics, see Paul Ormerod (1999). *Butterfly Economics: A New General Theory of Social and Economic Behavior*. New York: Pantheon Books.

6. Mariel K. Goddu and Alison Gopnik (2024). The development of human causal learning and reasoning. *Nature Reviews Psychology*, *3*(5), 319–339; Deanna Kuhn (2012). The development of causal reasoning. *Wiley Interdisciplinary Reviews: Cognitive Science*, *3*(3), 327–335.

7. Gad Saad (August 22, 2025). Spreading reason & common sense in Iceland (*The Saad Truth*, 1879), https://www.youtube.com/watch?v=aAVflncjwKY [1:52:55–1:55:04].

8. Gad Saad (June 3, 2023). Lex Fridman's Stance on Positivity, Kindness, and Love (*The Saad Truth*, 1576), https://youtu.be/Ncn3JbpA9Cs.

9. Samuel P. Huntington (1993). The clash of civilizations? *Foreign Affairs*, *72*(3), 22–49. Additionally, in chapter 7 of *The Parasitic Mind*, I offer several distinct lines of evidence (e.g., canonical texts, historical data, terrorism databases, FBI most wanted list) that demonstrate unequivocally the violent nature of Islamic doctrines.

10. William Poundstone (1993). *Prisoner's Dilemma: John von Neumann, Game Theory, and the Puzzle of the Bomb* (p. 118). London: Oxford University Press.

11. Robert Axelrod (1984). *The Evolution of Cooperation*. New York: Basic Books.

12. Arunas L. Radzvilavicius, Alexander J. Stewart, and Joshua B. Plotkin (2019). Evolution of empathetic moral evaluation. *eLife*, *8*, e44269, https:// doi.org/10.7554/eLife.44269; Daniel C. Batson, Judy G. Batson, R. Matthew Todd, Beverly H. Brummett, Laura L. Shaw, and Carlo M. R. Aldeguer (1995). Empathy and the collective good: Caring for one of the others in a social dilemma. *Journal of Personality and Social Psychology*, *68*(4), 619–631; Nancy Eisenberg and Paul A. Miller (1987). The relation of empathy to prosocial and related behaviors. *Psychological Bulletin*, *101*(1), 91–119; Yingying Yin and Yong Wang (2023). Is empathy associated with more prosocial behaviour? A meta-analysis. *Asian Journal of Social Psychology*, *26*(1), 3–22.

13. Gilbert Roberts (1998). Competitive altruism: From reciprocity to the handicap principle. *Proceedings of the Royal Society of London. Series B: Biological*

Sciences, 265(1394), 427–431; Amotz Zahavi (1995). Altruism as a handicap: The limitations of kin selection and reciprocity. *Journal of Avian Biology, 26*(1), 1–3.

14. The Council on Foreign Relations (April 28, 2023). A brief history of U.S. foreign aid, https://education.cfr.org/learn/reading/brief-history-us-foreign-aid.

15. Government of Canada. Project profile—Accelerated sanitation in northern Ghana, https://w05.international.gc.ca/projectbrowser-banqueprojets /project-projet/details/d000076001#.

16. Colin Perkel (July 31, 2018). Diplomats fretted about Canadian funding for Ghana outdoor defecation campaign. *National Post*, https://nationalpost.com /pmn/news-pmn/canada-news-pmn/diplomats-fretted-about-canadian -funding-for-ghana-outdoor-defecation-campaign.

17. William D. Hamilton (1964). The genetical evolution of social behavior. *Journal of Theoretical Biology, 7*, 1–52; Robert Trivers (1971). The evolution of reciprocal altruism. *Quarterly Review of Biology, 46*, 35–57.

18. Gad Saad and Tripat Gill (2003). An evolutionary psychology perspective on gift giving among young adults. *Psychology & Marketing, 20*(9), 765–784.

19. April Bleske-Rechek, Lyndsay A. Nelson, Jonathan P. Baker, Mark W. Remiker, and Sarah J. Brandt (2010). Evolution and the trolley problem: People save five over one unless the one is young, genetically related, or a romantic partner. *Journal of Social, Evolutionary, and Cultural Psychology, 4*(3), 115–127.

20. Sigal Tifferet, Gad Saad, Mali Meiri, and Nir Ido (2018). Gift giving at Israeli weddings as a function of genetic relatedness and kinship certainty. *Journal of Consumer Psychology, 28*(1), 157–165.

21. Gregory John Depow, Zoë Francis, and Michael Inzlicht (2021). The experience of empathy in everyday life. *Psychological Science, 32*(8), 1198–1213.

22. David Brooks (September 30, 2011). The limits of empathy. *New York Times*.

23. https://x.com/GadSaad/status/1784770878409949659.

Acknowledgments

1. https://x.com/GadSaad/status/1770076895935152307.

INDEX

ABOUT THE AUTHOR

GAD SAAD, PHD, is a professor and an evolutionary behavioral scientist. He has authored numerous scientific papers and pioneered the use of evolutionary psychology in marketing and consumer behavior. In addition to his scientific work, he is a leading public intellectual who often writes and speaks about idea pathogens that are destroying logic, science, reason, and common sense. He is the host of *The Saad Truth* podcast, and his book *The Parasitic Mind: How Infectious Ideas Are Killing Common Sense* became an international bestseller.